McGRAW-HILL

Handbook of English

Dianne Sawada 11A
Downsview Collegia

104 Wyndale Dr.

Ch-7-8565

McGRAW-HILL
Handbook of English

Harry Shaw

Humanities Editor, Harper & Brothers
Formerly Director, Workshops in Composition
New York University

Virginia Shaffer

Head of English Department
Forest Park High School, Baltimore, Maryland
Instructor in Writing, McCoy College
of The Johns Hopkins University

McGRAW-HILL BOOK COMPANY, INC.

NEW YORK   TORONTO   LONDON

McGRAW-HILL HANDBOOK OF ENGLISH

VII

Library of Congress catalog card number: 52–8324

Contents

Grammar

Usage

Capitalization

Punctuation

The Word

The Sentence

The Paragraph

The Whole Theme

The Research Paper

The Précis and the Paraphrase

Letters

Preface

It is important that all of us understand the structure of our language, the meaning of words, and methods of finding accurate information. Only through the development of skill in such matters can we be competent citizens, effective producers, and wise consumers. The *McGraw-Hill Handbook of English* is a ready reference for people who wish to express themselves clearly in writing, to read with understanding because the structure of sentences and paragraphs is clear to them, and to get information about subjects which concern them.

In this book the approach is entirely functional. Immediate application is made of the principles taught, and the student is referred to sections of the book that will help him make automatic the use of these principles in his writing and speaking.

Practice Material. Teachers and pupils using the book will find their tasks greatly simplified because there is an abundance of drill material. This material is presented in a variety of forms. Sometimes the drill material has been put in the form of a paragraph on safe driving, travel, or an amusing incident from the life of a literary figure, so that the student may learn good citizenship or broaden his cultural outlook as he studies his grammar. At other times, the drill is in the form of sentences taken directly from student papers. These sentences not only show natural errors but are based on writing about live subjects such as diesel engines, music, nature, dates, games, business. For use in correcting errors, drill taken from student papers seems preferable to paragraphs composed for this purpose by authors. The latter often struggle so hard to introduce the errors for correction that the writing becomes artificial. Seven thousand student themes were the basis of the drills in this book.

Special effort has been made to provide for different levels of instruction. After each major principle has been explained in very simple terms, the drill is arranged in sections. The first section begins with quite easy sentences and then moves on to the type of sentence used by average students. The second section of drill on the same principle has more mature sentences on more adult subjects. These can be used for superior students or for review with students who have mastered the easier section. The teacher who wishes to have his class divided into homogeneous groups can easily make the group assignments because the sentences are arranged in groups of graded difficulty.

Motivation. The main divisions of the book are preceded by simple motivating statements that will help the student to understand the purpose of the material contained in the section.

Tests. Diagnostic and achievement tests are included for major principles developed in the book.

Placement. The materials of the book have been successfully used over a range of grade levels. The book will be valuable also in many types of class since material from technical and business papers, as well as academic selections, appears. Adult education classes will find the book particularly useful. Because the background of students in these classes varies greatly, each student must be able to work on his own problems. The clear, simple explanations of the rules in this book and the frequent cross references to related materials will enable adult students to make individual use of the book. Finally, secretaries and other business people will find the book valuable for quick reference.

Symbols. The end papers of the book give numbers which instructors can conveniently use to indicate errors. Each student can then work on his special problem.

Acknowledgments. For assistance in preparing the manuscript, the authors are indebted to a number of people. Miss Elizabeth Connelly, Head of the English Department at the Patterson Park High School in Baltimore, and Mrs. Thea Hodes, teacher of superior children at School No. 49 in Baltimore, read parts of the manuscript and offered valuable advice on the adjustment of the material to suit the needs of students of varying intelligence levels. Mrs. Philip Edwards, Director of Young People's Work at the Enoch Pratt Free Library, and her assistants gave invaluable help in locating illustrative paragraphs in books popular with young people. Miss Bernice Wiese, Supervisor of School Libraries in Baltimore, examined the section on the use of the library and tried some of the material with students of several grade levels. To all these people and to the students at the Forest Park High School and at McCoy College of The Johns Hopkins University, who have made helpful suggestions while using the materials in this book, the authors are grateful.

HARRY SHAW *and* VIRGINIA SHAFFER

McGRAW-HILL

Handbook of English

Grammar

Grammar is not a static thing. It changes and grows as men put new life into it, and it has different levels for different occasions. In the casual English of informal conversation, many people today are using "It's me," or "Drive slow"; but these forms would not, of course, appear in formal writing.

Grammar is for use. The definitions and explanations given in this part of the book are valuable only when they help the student to write and speak more effectively. Because the types of words defined here function in many different kinds of sentences, it is important to remember that a given word is not always used as the same part of speech. It may be a noun in one sentence, a verb in another, an adjective in a third. How the word is used determines what part of speech it is.

> *Sailing* is my favorite sport. (Noun)
> We were *sailing* across the bay. (Verb)
> Far off we could see a small *sailing* vessel. (Adjective)

> This *book* is good reading. (Noun)
> We *book* plays, vaudeville acts, and lectures. (Verb)
> The *book* agent called on us yesterday. (Adjective)

In the pages that follow, the essential principles of grammar are reviewed. If there has been some tendency to permit variations of the forms commonly accepted as correct, these variations are presented.

A glossary of grammatical terms follows the chapter on "Grammar." If the chapter uses terms with which you are unfamiliar, turn to the glossary.

1. NOUNS

1a. Definition.

A *noun* is the name of a person, place, or thing.

> man, officer, Thomas Jefferson, park, street, desk, team, courage

1b. Kinds of nouns.

A *common noun* is the name of any one of a class of persons, places, or things. It is not written with a capital letter.

> horse, child, garden, alley, tub, book, engineer

A *proper noun* is the name of a particular person, place, or thing. It is written with a capital letter. (See Section 21g.)

> General Bradley, President Roosevelt, Patterson Park, Linden Avenue

An *abstract noun* is the name of something that cannot be perceived by the senses.

> honesty, intelligence, grace

A *collective noun* names a group of persons or objects.

> class, crowd, army, fleet, family

NOTE: Abstract nouns and collective nouns are usually common nouns.

EXERCISE 1

On a sheet of paper, write with a capital letter each of the nouns in this list that should be capitalized.

1. company	6. maryland	11. southern high school
2. high school	7. january	12. king
3. secretary	8. general electric company	13. automobile
4. tuesday	9. english	14. lincoln park
5. junior	10. harper & brothers	15. doctor

1c. Number.

Nouns may be *singular* or *plural.* If the noun means *one* person, place, or thing, it is *singular* in number. If it means more than one, it is plural in number. *Field* is singular; *fields* is plural.

EXERCISE 2

Study Section 39d. Then on a sheet of paper write the correct plural form of each of the following words:

1. tomato	6. woman	11. pony
2. lady	7. piano	12. valley
3. sister-in-law	8. sheep	13. alumnus
4. phenomenon	9. chief	14. canoe
5. James	10. wolf	15. knife

1d. Gender.

Nouns have four genders: *masculine* (*man, boy*), *feminine* (*woman, girl*), and *neuter* (*desk, road*). When a noun may be either masculine or feminine, it has *common gender* (*person, playmate, companion*).

EXERCISE 3

Write on your paper the feminine form of each of these nouns:

1. drake	6. alumnus	11. tiger
2. executor	7. lion	12. gander
3. master	8. duke	13. patron
4. emperor	9. poet	14. host
5. king	10. marquis	15. actor

1e. Case.

Nouns have three cases: *nominative, possessive, objective*. Nouns in the nominative and objective cases have the same form: *boy* (*nominative*), *boy* (*objective*). The possessive case requires an apostrophe and *s* (*boy's*). (See Section 26.)

1f. Uses of nouns in the nominative case.

The most important uses of nouns in the nominative case are the following:

1. *Subject of a verb.* (See Section 3.)

The *storm* caught the ship in mid-ocean.

Suddenly the *winds* roared in a great blast of fury.

Across the deck swept huge *waves*.

The *passengers* rushed to their cabins when the *waves*
rolled over the deck.

2. *Predicate noun*, also called *predicate complement,
predicate nominative,* or *subjective complement.* (See
Section 14.)

A *predicate* is a word or word group that tells something about the subject. The *simple predicate* is the verb.
The *complete predicate* is the verb and its modifiers. A
predicate noun is a noun used in the predicate to point
back to the subject. It follows the verb *be* (*am, is, are,
was, been, be, were*) or some other linking verb (*become,
seem*).

Jerry is the *boy* to play halfback.

The *Americans* are the *people* who have led the struggle
for liberty.

Those *girls* were the *winners* of the basketball tournament.

The *man* on the witness stand seemed a *person* of hon-
esty.

3. *Noun of direct address.* (See Section 23e.)

Bruce, will you ride to the canyon with me?

4. *Noun in an absolute expression.* (See Section 74e.)

Night having fallen, we camped near the trail.

5. *Appositive* with a noun in the nominative case. (See
Section 14.)

Melody, my *horse,* saw me from the corral.

1g. Uses of nouns in the objective case.

The most important uses of nouns in the objective case follow. (For further explanation, see Section 14. See also Section 4d for *adverbial objective*.)

1. *Direct object of a verb.*

> We won the *game*. (*Game* is the direct object of the verb *won*.)

2. *Indirect object of a verb* (object of *to* or *for* understood).

> Shall I give *Ted* a sweater at Christmas? (*Ted* is the indirect object of the verb. *Sweater* is the direct object.)

3. *Object of a preposition.*

> Mother brought some souvenirs from *Atlantic City*. (*Atlantic City* is the object of the preposition *from*.)

4. *Appositive* with a noun in the objective case. (See Section 23g.)

> We met Mr. Townley, the *sheriff*.

5. *Objective complement,* or *predicate objective*. (See Section 14g.)

> We thought you to be *John*.
> I consider her a good *player*.

6. *Subject of an infinitive.* (See Sections 3g and 14e.)

> I wanted *John* to go to the movies.
> Sally asked the *chairman* to take a walk with her.

7. *Object of an infinitive.* (See Sections 3g and 14f.)

> His desire to please the *voters* was great.
> The ship was anchored to save *fuel*.

8. *Object of a participle.* (See Sections 3g and 14f.)

> Waving his *hat*, Rusty galloped down Main Street.

9. *Object of a gerund.* (See Section 3g.)

> Catching a *mustang* is not an easy job.

10. *Adverbial objective* (noun used as adverb).

The ranch was sold last *year*.
We stayed *home* all day.

EXERCISE 4

Arrange the nouns in these sentences in two columns. Put those in the nominative case in one column and those in the objective case in another column. Beside each noun, write the reason why you have listed it as nominative or objective. The first two nouns have been listed as examples.

Nominative		*Objective*	
leopard	subject	zoo	object of preposition

Recently a leopard escaped from a zoo in Ohio. Some hunters had caught the animal on Christmas and shipped it to the United States for display in a new zoo where the animals were not confined in cages but were allowed to roam at will over a wide territory surrounded by deep moats. The animals could not escape because the moats were too broad for even the leopard to leap. Or so thought the keepers of the zoo. But this leopard was a wily beast. He apparently figured the distance carefully and with a great bound jumped across the moat. From one end of the country to another, the newspapers carried big headlines that told of the chase. Armed groups sought him in the park near the zoo and in the surrounding neighborhood. At first the superintendent of the zoo wanted the beast to be caught alive, but after a few hours, the danger seemed so great that hunters were told to shoot the animal at sight. Because the zoo keepers considered the leopard to be a very dangerous beast, they warned the people nearby to keep their children inside and to look for any evidence that would lead to the capture. For two days the whole country read the news avidly. Then the headlines announced that the zoo would try to trap the animal with food. By this time some people had begun to consider the zoo and the police to be very ineffectual. Then huge pieces of drugged meat were placed on the ground near a cage in which the leopard's mate was held, and the next morning the hungry animal was found hardly able to stand up because the drug was so strong. He was seized, and the country relaxed. By the following day the leopard had died—from shock.

2. PRONOUNS

2a. Definition.

A *pronoun* is a word used in place of a noun.

2b. Kinds of pronouns.

There are several kinds of pronouns: *personal, relative, demonstrative, interrogative, reflexive, intensive, indefinite,* and *reciprocal.*

1. A *personal pronoun* is a direct substitute for a noun. Like a noun, it has number, gender, and case. It also has *person.* Person is shown in pronouns by a change of form to indicate the person speaking (*first person*), the person spoken to (*second person*), or the person or thing spoken about (*third person*). See the following table of forms of personal pronouns:

SINGULAR

Nominative		*Possessive*	*Objective*
1st person:	I	my, mine	me
2nd person:	you	your, yours	you
3rd person:			
masculine	he	his	him
feminine	she	her, hers	her
neuter	it	its	it

PLURAL

1st person:	we	our, ours	us
2nd person:	you	your, yours	you
3rd person:			
all genders	they	their, theirs	them

Grammatical problems frequently arise from the fact that, unlike nouns, personal, relative, and interrogative pronouns have distinct case forms. These problems are discussed in Section 14.

2. A *relative pronoun* relates or connects a clause to its *antecedent*—the noun to which it refers. The most often

used relative pronouns are *who, which,* and *that. Who-ever, whichever,* and *whatever* are less frequently employed compound forms; *whosoever, whichsoever,* and *whatsoever* have almost entirely gone out of current use. *Who* and *whoever* are the only relative pronouns with complete case forms. Relative pronouns do not show changes in form for person, gender, or number. See the following table of case forms for *who* and *whoever:*

Nominative	Objective	Possessive
who	whom	whose
whoever	whomever	whosever

The choice of a relative pronoun is determined by its antecedent; the case form for *who* and *whoever* is determined by the way the pronoun is used in the relative clause. (See Section 14.) *Who* is used to refer only to persons; *which* is used to refer to things (inanimate objects and animals), and to persons considered as a group; *that* may be used to refer to either persons or things.

> The flier *who* served in World War II is now an airline official.
> Radar equipment *which* is to be used for small ships must be installed carefully.
> The crew *which* won the race was excused from classes.
> The hat *that* I bought last summer is now out of fashion.
> The man *that* I saw was named Mortimer Taylor.

3. A *demonstrative pronoun* points out and identifies. It has number but no gender or case. The demonstrative pronouns are *this, that, these, those.*

> *This* is the way to kick a spiral.
> *That* is my new television set.
> *These* are your books; *those* on the desk are mine.

4. An *interrogative pronoun* (*who, whom, whose, which, what,* occasionally *whoever, whichever, whatever*) introduces a question. The case forms for the interroga-

tive pronoun *who* are the same as those for the relative pronoun *who*.

> *Who* shall demand that a pardon be granted?
> *Which* is the route we should take from Hammond?
> *What* do you have in mind?
> *Whom* do you recognize?

5. A *reflexive pronoun* is used for reference to the subject of the sentence. It is composed of one of the personal pronouns plus *self* or *selves: myself, yourself, himself, herself, itself, ourselves, yourselves, themselves*. These pronouns are also called *compound personal pronouns*. In formal speech or writing, these pronouns are not used as subjects.

> Wrong: Helen, Sue, and *myself* went on a hike.
> Right: His laboratory assistant burned *himself*.
> Right: They appointed *themselves* as cheer leaders.

6. An *intensive pronoun* is used for emphasis. Intensive pronouns and reflexive pronouns have the same form.

> Right: The nurse *herself* was at fault.
> Right: We students *ourselves* are wholly responsible.

7. *Indefinite pronouns* are somewhat less exact in meaning than other pronouns. Among the more frequently used indefinite pronouns are *another, any, anyone, anything, everybody, everyone, everything, few, many, nobody, none, one, several, some, each*. The pronoun *one* and its compound forms, and compound forms built on the element *-body* take the possessive form (*anyone's, everybody's*). Indefinite pronouns involve grammatical problems which are discussed in Section 11d.

8. A *reciprocal pronoun* indicates an interchange of action suggested by the verb. This interchange may be seen in the following sentences involving the only two reciprocal pronouns in English:

> The two teams complimented *each other*.
> The members of the squad shouted at *one another*.

3. ASSERTING WORDS: VERBS AND VERBALS

3a. Definition.

A *verb* expresses action or state of being. *Linking*, or *copulative*, verbs show the relationship of the subject to the predicate noun. (See *Glossary*.)

> Morgan *kicked* the ball with all his strength.
> *Be* ready at eight o'clock.
> Howard *became* a statesman and *wrote* a number of books.

3b. Verb phrases.

Auxiliary, or helping, verbs, such as *may, can, must, would, should, do, did, shall, will,* and all forms of *be* and *have*, are often used with other verbs to give special meanings. Such combinations are called *verb phrases*.

> On one of the lawns in the outskirts of the village a woman *was cutting* the grass with a motorized lawn mower.
> But the man of the soil *had been pushed* more and more out of the American picture.
> A careful analysis of the oxygen *should have been made* at the time.

3c. Kinds of verbs.

Verbs are classified as *transitive* or *intransitive*.

A *transitive* verb is regularly accompanied by a direct object.

>   v.   o.
> The engineers *threw* a *bridge* across the river.
>   v.   o.
> The refugees *ate bits* of bread found on the road.
>   v.   o.
> An old woman *seized* a squawking *goose* and ran into the house.

An *intransitive verb* requires no object.

> Automobiles from Paris *crept* along the roads.
> People *ran* wildly in every direction.

Many verbs can be used in both a transitive and an intransitive sense.

> We *read* the news with great care. (Transitive)
> We *read* until late at night. (Intransitive)

3d. Voice.

Transitive verbs are further classified as to *voice—active* or *passive*.

A verb is in the active voice when the subject performs the action.

> We *built* a large house in the country.
> The engineers *have developed* new types of electrical refrigerators.
> The Marshall Plan *helps* the reconstruction of Europe.

A verb is in the passive voice when its subject receives the action. Notice that some form of the verb *be* (*am, is, are, was, were, been, be*) is used with another verb in the passive voice.

> A large house *was built* in the country.
> New types of electrical refrigerators *were developed* by the engineers.
> The reconstruction of Europe *was helped* by the Marshall Plan.

EXERCISE 5

Make a list of the verbs in the following paragraph and tell whether each is transitive or intransitive, active or passive:

When we reached Pampatar, we were entertained by a pearl merchant, who showed us the town and then took us to call on his family. While we talked to his mother and sister, the pearl merchant knocked a few coconuts from a tree in the patio, cracked their tops, and handed them to us. From these we drank the sweet milk as we discussed life in a small Venezuelan town. All of the women of Pampatar were happy when a boat stayed for a day at their town, for then they could visit the barber on the ship and have their hair waved. It was amusing to see the line of women leaving the barber shop. Black hair lay in rigid, even canals on every head.

3e. Mood.

The *mood of a verb* shows the mood or manner in which the speaker thinks of the action.

A verb in the *indicative mood* states a fact.

> The farmer *planted* his crop early.

A verb in the *imperative mood* expresses a command.

> *Clean* your room.
> *Open* your books to page 10.

A verb in the *subjunctive mood* indicates a condition contrary to fact or a wish. The subjunctive is discussed in Section 17c–g.

> If you *were* in Europe, you would find life very different.
> I wish I *were* in the South where it is always warm.

3f. Tense.

Tense indicates the *time* of the action or state expressed by a verb.

Every verb has three *principal parts* which are used as a basis for the formation of tenses. Many mistakes are made in usage because people do not understand how to form these tenses or how to use them. (See Sections 15–16.)

The *principal parts* of a verb are the *present, past, past participle*.

Present	*Past*	*Past Participle*
talk	talked	talked
skate	skated	skated
hurry	hurried	hurried
do	did	done
sing	sang	sung
draw	drew	drawn

If the second and third principal parts of a verb add *d* or *ed*, the verb is called a *regular verb*. Otherwise it is an *irregular verb,* and its parts should be memorized. Notice the irregular verbs in the preceding list.

EXERCISE 6

Write the principal parts of each of the following verbs. Then write sentences using each of these verbs in the past tense. (For a discussion of tenses and their use, see Section 16.)

go	drown	lead	come
drink	speak	shrink	sneak
give	tear	show	dive
hide	do	swing	draw
ring	write	freeze	eat
choose	swim	sting	fall
twist	steal	forget	throw
begin	attack	bite	sing
blow	break	beat	wear

The following is a conjugation of the verb *to drive.* The principal parts are: present, *drive;* past, *drove;* past participle, *driven.*

INDICATIVE MOOD
PRESENT TENSE

	Active Voice		Passive Voice	
Person	Singular	Plural	Singular	Plural
First	I drive	we drive	I am driven	we are driven
Second	you drive	you drive	you are driven	you are driven
Third	he drives	they drive	he is driven	they are driven

Emphatic Present

First	I do drive	we do drive
Second	you do drive	you do drive
Third	he does drive	they do drive

Progressive Present | | Progressive Present

First	I am driving	we are driving	I am being driven	we are being driven
Second	you are driving	you are driving	you are being driven	you are being driven
Third	he is driving	they are driving	he is being driven	they are being driven

PAST TENSE

Person	Active Voice		Passive Voice	
	Singular	*Plural*	*Singular*	*Plural*
First	I drove	we drove	I was driven	we were driven
Second	you drove	you drove	you were driven	you were driven
Third	he drove	they drove	he was driven	they were driven

Emphatic Past

First	I did drive	we did drive
Second	you did drive	you did drive
Third	he did drive	they did drive

Progressive Past	*Progressive Past*
I was driving	I was being driven

FUTURE TENSE*

Person	Active Voice		Passive Voice
	Singular	*Plural*	
First	I shall (will) drive	we shall (will) drive	I shall (will) be driven
Second	you will drive	you will drive	
Third	he will drive	they will drive	

Progressive Future

I shall be driving

PRESENT PERFECT TENSE

Person	Active Voice		Passive Voice
	Singular	*Plural*	
First	I have driven	we have driven	I have been driven
Second	you have driven	you have driven	
Third	he has driven	they have driven	

Progressive Present Perfect

I have been driving

PAST PERFECT TENSE

Person	Active Voice		Passive Voice
	Singular	*Plural*	
First	I had driven	we had driven	I had been driven
Second	you had driven	you had driven	
Third	he had driven	they had driven	

Progressive Past Perfect

I had been driving

* Note that the future tense is formed by *will* or *shall* and the infinitive (without *to*).

FUTURE PERFECT TENSE

	Active Voice		Passive Voice
Person	*Singular*	*Plural*	
First	I shall (will) have driven	we shall (will) have driven	I shall (will) have been driven
Second	you will have driven	you will have driven	
Third	he will have driven	they will have driven	

Subjunctive Mood*

PRESENT TENSE

	Active Voice		Passive Voice
Person	*Singular*	*Plural*	(if) I be driven
First	(if) I drive	(if) we drive	
Second	(if) you drive	(if) you drive	
Third	(if) he drive	(if) they drive	

PAST TENSE

	Active Voice		Passive Voice
Person	*Singular*	*Plural*	
First	(if) I drove	(if) we drove	(if) I were driven
Second	(if) you drove	(if) you drove	
Third	(if) he drove	(if) they drove	

PRESENT PERFECT TENSE

	Active Voice		Passive Voice
Person	*Singular*	*Plural*	
First	(if) I have driven	(if) we have driven	(if) I have been driven
Second	(if) you have driven	(if) you have driven	
Third	(if) he have driven	(if) they have driven	

* In the place of a future subjunctive, the form *(if) I should drive,* is used. The subjunctive is rarely used except in the present and past tenses.

PAST PERFECT TENSE

	Active Voice		Passive Voice
Person	Singular	Plural	
First	(if) I had driven	(if) we had driven	(if) I had been driven
Second	(if) you had driven	(if) you had driven	
Third	(if) he had driven	(if) they had driven	

IMPERATIVE MOOD

	Active Voice	Passive Voice
Tense		
Present	(you) drive	(you) be driven

VERBALS

PARTICIPLES

	Active Voice	Passive Voice
Tense		
Present	driving	being driven
Past	driven	driven
Perfect	having driven	having been driven

GERUNDS

	Active Voice	Passive Voice
Tense		
Present	driving	being driven
Perfect	having driven	having been driven

INFINITIVES

	Active Voice	Passive Voice
Tense		
Present	to drive	to be driven
Perfect	to have driven	to have been driven

3g. Verbals.

Understanding the difference between verbs and verbals will help you to avoid one of the most serious errors in writing, the half sentence or fragment. A *verb* is used as the simple predicate of a sentence; with the subject, the verb may make a complete statement. A *verbal* cannot be used as a simple predicate of a sentence. (See Section 57.)

He *kicked* the ball. (Verb)
Kicking the ball (Verbal)
To kick the ball (Verbal)

There are three types of verbals: *participles, gerunds,*
and *infinitives.* (For help in using verbals, see Sections
67 and 14k.)

1. A *participle* is a word which has the function of both
verb and adjective. The present participle always ends in
ing (*speaking, singing*). The past participle is the third
principal part of the verb. The perfect participle consists
of *having* or *having been* plus the past participle (*having
spoken, having been driven*).

Notice the past participles in the following list of principal parts:

		Past Participle
walk	walked	walked
smile	smiled	smiled
draw	drew	drawn
see	saw	seen
sing	sang	sung

Notice that some of the past participles end in *ed* and
some in *n;* others change their form completely (*sung*).
The participle can take an object and be modified by an
adverb. It is often used in a group of words called a *participial phrase.* (See Section 6b.)

The ball *kicked* by the player went into the stand. (Participle used as an adjective)

The crowd *cheering* the *team* could be heard a mile away.
(1 participle used as an adjective in a participial
phrase; 2 object of participle)

We followed the crowd, *cheering lustily.* (1 participle
used as an adjective in a participial phrase; 2 adverb
modifying participle)

2. An *infinitive* is the form of the verb usually preceded
by *to.*

to walk   to observe   to have enjoyed

An infinitive may be used as a noun, an adjective, or an adverb.

> *To travel* is my greatest pleasure. (Infinitive used as noun)
> We have four days *to spend* in Billings. (Infinitive used as adjective)
> Bruce was glad *to have come*. (Infinitive used as adverb)

Sometimes the word *to* is omitted from the infinitive.

> Let me *go* with you.
> Will you help me *pack?*

The infinitive may take an object and be modified by an adverb or an adverbial phrase.

> To reach the *mountain* we walked twenty miles. (Object of infinitive)
> We tried to walk *faster*. (Adverb modifying infinitive)
> The snow began to drift *along the slope*. (Adverbial phrase modifying infinitive)

3. A *gerund* is a verbal noun. Gerunds have the same form as present or perfect participles, but are used as nouns instead of adjectives. A gerund may take an object and be modified by an adverb or an adjective.

> *Discovering* the *plans* of the enemy was the job of the intelligence service. (1 gerund; 2 object of gerund)
>
> *Working intelligently* is no easy task. (1 gerund; 2 adverb modifier)
>
> Our music teacher dislikes *loud singing*. (1 gerund; 2 adjective modifier)

EXERCISE 7

From the following paragraph, list in one column all verbs that are used as simple predicates; in another column, list all verbals. The listing has been made for the first two sentences.

Verbs	*Verbals*
had	to go
liked	sailing
had named	

Shelley, the English poet, had a tragic death. He liked to go out on the Mediterranean Sea in a light sailing vessel which he had named *Ariel*. But because he was very unskillful as a sailor, some of his friends worried about him constantly. Shelley, however, loved the beauty of the sea and the graceful fashion in which the boat slipped over the waves. One day, after visiting some friends, he set out for his home in Lerici in spite of a warning of a storm. Wishing to protect Shelley, a friend who was a good sailor wanted to accompany the writer in a larger boat named *Bolivar;* but he had not obtained port clearance papers, and the port authorities kept him from leaving. Shelley and his friend Williams were in a hurry; so they set out, leaving Trelawny fuming at the shore. The sailors on Trelawny's boat, greatly concerned about Shelley, watched the black clouds gathering. When the storm finally broke, Trelawny, worried about his friend, tried to get news of him. Meantime, Shelley's wife waited at Lerici, feeling sure that Shelley could not have been so foolish as to set out in the storm. Finally, she decided to go to Leghorn to see what had happened to him. Reaching the city, she begged for news and was told that Shelley had indeed set out just before the storm. Panic-stricken, Mary made inquiries in every direction, but getting news of her husband was difficult. At last she and Trelawny learned that parts of a wreck had been cast upon the shore at Via Reggio, and Trelawny went to examine them. Convinced that part of the wreck was from Shelley's boat, Trelawny still did not give up hope; but several days later the body of Shelley was washed upon the shore. He was only thirty years old when he died.

4. MODIFYING WORDS: ADJECTIVES AND ADVERBS

4a. Definition of adjective.

An *adjective* modifies a noun or a pronoun.

4b. Uses of adjectives.

Adjectives may be used in the following ways:

To describe: a *black* dress; an *easy* lesson; an *American* soldier; the *cheering* crowd: the winners, *tired* and *hungry*

To point out: *this* bus, *that* sweater
To tell number or numerical order: *five* boys, *second* day
To show possession: *your* trip, *Harold's* car, *whose* hat
To show quantity: *some* money, *few* tickets

The articles *a, an,* and *the* are adjectives. *An* is used before words beginning with a vowel sound (including silent *h*) but not before long *u*. *A* is used before consonant sounds, and before long *u*.

an apple, an hour, an opportunity, a hero, a European, a university

An adjective is called a *predicate adjective* or *predicate complement* when it is related to the subject by a linking verb (*be, feel, become, taste, seem, appear, look, sound,* for example).

The water felt *warm*.
The corn is *green*.

For proper use of adjectives and adverbs, see Section 18.

EXERCISE 8

In one column, list each adjective in this paragraph. In another column, list the noun that each adjective modifies.

Across a sea that was now turquoise, now emerald, we could watch the Venezuelan coastline with the purple Andes in the background. Flying fish stood a moment on their tails, flew a little distance, and dived back into the sea. The air was still. The fresh odor of the sea mingled with the heavy smell of sweat from the stevedores' bodies. In a few moments a dozen small boats had reached the side of our ship, and their brown-skinned occupants were slipping into the clear water to find the money that the passengers had thrown down for them.

4c. Definition of adverb.

An *adverb* modifies a verb, an adjective, or another adverb.

4d. Uses of adverbs.

An adverb tells *how, when, where, why, to what extent.*

> We saw a parade *recently.* (When)
> We *certainly* did enjoy the music played by the bands. (To what extent)
> *Here* we saw soldiers from many countries. (Where)
> The taxis drove *madly* through the streets of Paris. (How)

If we tell how madly the taxis drove, we have an adverb modifying another adverb.

> *quite*
> The taxis drove *very* madly through the streets.
> *too*

The following examples show adverbs used to modify adjectives:

> When the day was over, our chauffeur was *very* tired. (*Very* modifies the adjective *tired.*)
> He was *almost* sick with fatigue. (*Almost* modifies the adjective *sick.*)

Occasionally a noun is used as an adverb. (This use of a noun is called the *adverbial objective.*)

> After the game we went *home.*

Several adverbs—especially *only, hardly, even,* and *merely*—distort meaning unless the writer is careful to put them next to the words they modify. Notice the changes in meaning and emphasis in the following sentences; notice the ambiguity in some:

> Only carelessness wrecked our plan.
> Carelessness only wrecked our plan.
> Carelessness wrecked only our plan.
> Carelessness wrecked our only plan.
> Carelessness wrecked our plan only.

Neither adjectives nor adverbs should be used profusely. Overuse of either robs sentences of conciseness and force. Both adjectives and adverbs can help to make writing specific and vivid, but writing that is heavily larded with them is weak, flabby. Particular errors in the use of adjectives and adverbs are discussed in Sections 18 and 65.

EXERCISE 9

In one column on your paper, list each word (including verbals) used as an adverb in the following paragraph. In a second column, list the word that each adverb modifies.

Have you read *The Ancient Mariner?* Many very interesting stories are told about the author of the poem, Samuel Coleridge. Among them are some particularly good tales of the poet's skill as a talker. The best story of his love for talking is very amusing indeed. One day Coleridge met Lamb walking rapidly to work and stopped to talk to him. Lamb, who wanted to reach his job on time, tried to escape; but Coleridge quickly grabbed the button of his listener's coat and insisted upon finishing his story. For a few minutes Lamb waited patiently, but Coleridge seemed likely to talk for a long time. Presently Lamb took a knife from his pocket and carefully cut off the button that Coleridge was holding. At five o'clock that evening Lamb, returning from work, saw Coleridge still holding the button and still talking vigorously.

5. JOINING WORDS: PREPOSITIONS AND CONJUNCTIONS

5a. Definition of preposition.

A *preposition* is a linking word used to show the relationship of a noun or pronoun to some other word in the sentence. It is usually followed by an object. (See Section 14c.)

5b. List of prepositions.

Here is a list of common prepositions:

about	along	behind	beyond
above	among	below	by
across	around	beneath	concerning
after	at	beside	down
against	before	between	during

except	like	on	toward
for	near	over	under
from	of	through	upon
in	off	to	with

Some prepositions are composed of more than one word:

according to	back of	in addition to
ahead of	because of	in place of
as far as	contrary to	in spite of
instead of	by means of	in front of

The meaning of a sentence is sometimes confused if prepositions are not used correctly in combination with other words. (See Section 43.)

Between is used when two are considered.
Among is used when more than two are considered.

> I must choose *between* dancing and tennis.
> The money was divided *among* six heirs.

NOTE: In casual speech, *between* is sometimes used when more than two are considered.

Beside means *next to.*
Besides means *in addition to.*

> The most popular boy in school sits *beside* me in French.
> What are you studying *besides* English and math?

c. Definition of conjunction.

A *conjunction* is a linking word used to connect words or groups of words in a sentence.

d. Kinds of conjunctions.

Coördinating conjunctions join words or groups of words of equal rank; for example, *and, but, for, or nor.*
Certain coördinating conjunctions used in pairs are called *correlative conjunctions.* Most frequently used of these are *either . . . or; neither . . . nor; both . . . and; whether . . . or.*

Subordinating conjunctions join dependent clauses to main clauses; for example, *if, as, since, because, although, while, so that, when.* (See Section 7.)

Conjunctive adverbs are adverbs used as connectives. Examples are *however, moreover, nevertheless, therefore.*

In good writing, conjunctions must be chosen with care in order that they may show the exact relationship between ideas. Often a careless writer will use *and* where the relationship of clauses needs to be more accurately expressed, probably by use of subordination. Compare emphasis and meaning in these sentences:

> The search for the chemical formula has been rewarding and further investigation will make the rewards even greater.
>
> Although the search for the chemical formula has been rewarding, further investigation will make the reward even greater.

Common errors in the use of conjunctions are discussed in Sections 19a–c, 23a–c, and 63.

The conjunction is the seventh kind of word, or part of speech, that you have studied so far. There are eight parts of speech altogether. The seven parts of speech that you have studied are nouns, pronouns, verbs, adjectives, adverbs, prepositions, and conjunctions. The eighth part of speech is the *interjection,* which is simply an exclamatory word with little relation to the rest of the sentence. It is the least important of the eight parts of speech.

> *Oh,* must you go? (*Oh* is an interjection.)
>
> Here, *alas,* our good fortune came to an abrupt end. (*Alas* is an interjection.)

6. PHRASES

6a. Definition.

A phrase is a group of related words which does not contain a subject and predicate. It is important to know how to use phrases because their position in a sentence often determines the meaning. (See Section 65b.)

There has been much discussion of the new slum-clearing project in school.

The position of the phrase *in school* makes this sentence indicate that slum-clearing took place in school. Actually, the sentence should read:

There has been in school much discussion of the slum-clearing project.

Understanding the use of phrases also helps one to learn to punctuate correctly and so clarify the meaning of a sentence. (See Section 23.)

6b. Kinds of phrases.

Phrases often contain a *preposition*, a *participle*, a *gerund*, an *infinitive*, or a *verb*. (See Section 3g.)

Prepositional phrases:	to the dance, by my club, between the boys, of the tickets, at the end of the road
Participial phrases:	running a mile quickly, playing basketball, scratching his head, overcome by gas, exhausted after the journey
Gerund phrases:	visiting the animals, selling tickets, kicking the ball
Infinitive phrases:	to play the game well, to sing a song, to walk a mile, to see the circus, to shout loudly
Verb phrases:	have written, would have dived, am beginning

Notice that a phrase may contain another phrase. In the prepositional phrase *at the end of the road*, the object of the preposition *at* is modified by another prepositional phrase. Also, in the participial phrase *exhausted by the journey*, the participle is modified by a prepositional phrase.

Notice, too, that phrases containing present participles and those containing gerunds look alike. The use of such a phrase in a sentence determines whether it is a participial or a gerund phrase. (See Section 3g.)

Phrases (except verb phrases) are used as *nouns, adjectives,* or *adverbs.* Prepositional phrases are usually used as adjectives or adverbs; participial phrases, as adjectives; gerund phrases, as nouns; infinitive phrases, as nouns, adjectives, or adverbs. In some types of writing, it is desirable to expand a word into a phrase; in other types it is better to contract the phrase into a word. A knowledge of phrases helps to give a variety to sentence structure.

Noun phrases:

> *To manufacture automobiles* was a great undertaking (Infinitive phrase as subject)
> *Cranking the old 1910 model* often caused loss of temper (Gerund phrase as subject)
> Many manufacturers tried *to develop mass production* (Infinitive phrase as object of *tried*)
> The next step was *to invent a self-starter for the automobile.* (Infinitive phrase as predicate nominative. Notice that the infinitive phrase contains a prepositional phrase, *for the automobile.* This prepositional phrase is used as an adjective and modifies *self-starter.*)
> The plan *to develop a self-starter* caused tremendous expansion in the industry. (Infinitive phrase as appositive)

EXERCISE 10

On your paper, write the noun phrases that you find in the following sentences. In parentheses beside each phrase, write the kind of phrase (infinitive or gerund and its function in the sentence (subject, object of verb and so on).

> 1. Hearing soft music makes me sleepy.
> 2. Planting a garden is good fun.
> 3. He hates studying his lessons.
> 4. We decided to pay his way.
> 5. I want to play a harp.

6. Making a just peace is not an easy task.
7. Collecting stamps gave Morris many pleasant experiences.
8. I always enjoyed feeding the animals at the circus.
9. Leaving her family in a foreign country made Alice worry a great deal.
10. Shirley's decision to marry David upset her family very much.
11. Harold's greatest ambition was to make the football team.
12. To build a prosperous business had been his aim since childhood.
13. The French want to annex the Ruhr section.
14. The custom here is to go to bed early.
15. Jerry's plan to start a chicken farm surprised everybody.
16. Later, the Japanese started to make their own propaganda moving pictures.
17. Running a large farm taught him to accept life philosophically.
18. The big problem now is to keep totalitarian governments powerless.
19. The soldiers began to open their "K" rations.
20. He wanted to join the club, but to get in was very difficult.
21. She soon learned to keep house, to knit, and to sew.
22. To dig an oil well of 4000 feet is a job that will take a long time.
23. Arthur's chief desire was to be a successful farmer.
24. Some nations try to prevent psychological aggression.
25. Going to concerts in Boston gave Howard a new interest in music.

Adjective Phrases:

Adjective phrases, like adjectives, modify nouns or pronouns.

The bodies *of early automobiles* were high and open. (Prepositional phrase used as adjective modifying subject)

Women *wearing long dusters and goggles* sometimes drove the cars. (Participial phrase used as adjective modifying subject)

We had few opportunities then *to buy a car*. (Infinitive phrase used as adjective modifying object of verb)

One day we saw an early model *stalled on the road*. (Participial phrase used as adjective modifying object of verb. Notice that the participial phrase includes a prepositional phrase, *on the road*. The prepositional phrase is used as an adverb and modifies *stalled*.)

EXERCISE 11

On your paper, write the adjective phrases in the following sentences. Classify each phrase and tell what it modifies. Do not list separately prepositional phrases used as parts of other phrases.

1. A peasant singing a gay song trudged past us.
2. "Adonais" is a tribute to the memory of John Keats.
3. Sue bought a new dress to wear to the party.
4. Ichabod saw a strange object coming toward him.
5. There was ample time to finish the work.
6. The snowshoe rabbit has very large feet covered with soft white fur.
7. I should like a position in the saxophone section of the band.
8. Exhausted by the day's labor, he slept soundly.
9. Having beaten Southern High, we hoped to win the city championship.
10. There was a knock on the door, and a man of huge proportions entered.
11. You must break the lock on the cabinet and get the materials needed for the play.
12. The magazine made an effort to improve the morals of the community.
13. Caird, endorsed by the political machine and sponsored by liberal groups, saw his picture everywhere.
14. The election of a new legislative body has produced a shift in the balance of parties.
15. A man wearing a long, loose overcoat and carrying a cane entered the room.

16. Rex Hunter, making his start with the Royals, pitched his first game today.
17. The theater houses the Royal Players, sponsored and supported by the government.
18. We saw a number of students taking the examination for a civil service job.
19. Discussion of the controversial public-housing issue excited a committee of aldermen today.
20. People trying to get new automobile licenses formed a long line in front of the office of the Automobile Commissioner.

Adverbial phrases:

Yesterday a woman fell *on our sidewalk*. (Prepositional phrase modifying verb *fell*.)

She fell hard enough *to sprain her ankle*. (Infinitive phrase modifying adverb *enough*.)

She was easy *to lift*. (Infinitive phrase modifying adjective *easy*.)

Restrictive and nonrestrictive phrases:

If a phrase is essential in order to explain or identify the word to which it refers, the phrase is called *restrictive*. If the phrase is not absolutely necessary, it is called *non-restrictive*. Nonrestrictive phrases are always set off by commas from the remainder of the sentence.

The citizens' committee gains *in political stature*.

In this example the adverbial phrase is restrictive because it tells the particular way in which the committee gains.

The citizens' committee, *gaining in political stature*, began to demand reforms within the city government.

Here the adjective phrase is nonrestrictive because it is not essential to the writer's purpose in telling what the committee began to demand. See Section 23h for further discussion and examples of punctuation for restrictive and nonrestrictive phrases.

EXERCISE 12

On a sheet of paper, write the adverbial phrases in the following sentences. Classify each phrase and tell what it modifies. Do not list separately prepositional phrases used as parts of other phrases.

1. He flew to South America in a Douglas plane.
2. Suddenly, out of the darkness came an octopus.
3. During my spring vacation I took a trip with five friends.
4. George left home to seek his fortune.
5. I passed my driver's test and aided my father by delivering orders.
6. For the last two months, I have used a budget to keep my money in order.
7. Mr. Upton was walking down the street with a neighbor when the accident occurred.
8. The soldiers advanced in mass formation, while the guerrillas fired from behind trees.
9. On the eve of the wedding the bridal company was entertained by Mrs. Barton Remsen.
10. In Ecuador, dogs wander through the churches and sleep on the floor on hot afternoons.
11. The natives wear hibiscus blossoms in their hair and colored leaves in their arm bands.
12. The report is too complicated to be handled by the secretary.
13. By using screens, one can protect the plants from the cold.
14. Around the house we planted a hedge high enough to keep the world outside.
15. Schools have recently introduced courses in driver education to teach boys and girls how to drive.
16. In these days, it is very important to learn driving techniques because traffic is complicated by speed.
17. Statistics show that many accidents are caused by teen-age youths who take risks to show off before their friends.
18. At five o'clock this afternoon there was an accident near the Washington Boulevard.

19. It was caused by a boy of nineteen who wanted to show some friends how fast his car could go.
20. His car was smashed to pieces, and several people were seriously injured by the collision.

6c. Achievement test on phrases.

On your paper write all the phrases except verb phrases from the following sentences, and classify each as to kind. Tell how each phrase is used: that is, tell what part of speech it is and what it does in the sentence. Do not list separately prepositional or verbal phrases used as parts of other phrases.

1. Knitting stockings for the Red Cross consumed a great deal of her time.
2. Discharged by the army, he decided to go back to college.
3. Airmen have found the eagle flying 9,750 feet above the earth.
4. Plastics are becoming very popular in factories producing household objects.
5. Men working on the project will be research workers of wide experience.
6. The first step in the investigation is to isolate the cold virus.
7. The company has tried to improve conditions, but it has been blind to obvious problems.
8. He practiced law for three years and then joined the editorial staff of a large newspaper.
9. The man's main objective is to write stories of simple people.
10. Young people driving cars must learn to respect the law.
11. Finally, exhausted from fighting, he was sent to California for a rest.
12. Besides running a candy business here, Ted Saunders has started two stores in a nearby town.
13. The company employed a group of men whose job was to look for flaws in the garments finished by weavers.

14. At that time, no school in America would admit a woman to study medicine.
15. On the second floor of the building is an auditorium seating three hundred people.
16. The house, decorated with flags and bunting, was ready for the carnival.
17. Attracted by the noise, Sue left her room and hurried into the street.
18. Annually an American mother is chosen by the Mothers' Day Foundation to set an example for other mothers in the United States.
19. The native village has bamboo houses along irregular streets, the smell of oil everywhere, derricks enveloped in a haze of smoke, and the never-ceasing throb of engines.
20. Aiming at a medium income group, the manufacturers plan prefabricated houses to cost $4,000 to $10,000.
21. To build these houses is a problem in mass production.
22. Planned on a single pattern, the houses are provided with some variety through wings, porches, and garages.
23. The builders work hard to get the house under a roof in one day, but accomplishing the task is not always possible.
24. Selling these houses often requires high-powered salesmanship, but the salesmen try to meet all objections to standardization.
25. Special lessons in selling techniques are given to all employees of the company.

7. CLAUSES

7a. Definition.

A *clause* is a group of words which has both subject and predicate. Knowing how to use clauses will help you to write clear sentences. (See Section 23 for punctuation of clauses.) It will also aid in the development of mature sentences in which clauses are combined to show an exact relationship.

7b. Kinds of clauses.

An independent (main, principal) clause makes a complete statement and may stand alone; that is, it makes reasonable sense if the remainder of the sentence is omitted.

> I listened to a radio program.
> Although I should have been studying last night, *I listened to a radio program.*

Sometimes there may be more than one independent clause in a sentence.

> *John studied,* but *I listened to a radio program.*

A *dependent,* or *subordinate,* clause cannot stand alone. It depends upon the rest of the sentence for its meaning; it is subordinate. A dependent clause usually begins with a relative pronoun (such as *who, which, that*) or a *subordinating conjunction* (such as *if, as, since, because, although, while, when, where, until*).

Dependent clauses:

> although it is raining   if I learn to drive
> when I saw him   who would go with us

Like phrases, clauses are important in writing sentences. A style that is composed only of subject, verb, object, and a few word modifiers becomes very dull. A knowledge of clauses will help you to write sentences in which proper relationships are expressed.

Dependent clauses may be used as adjectives, adverbs, or nouns. According to its use as one of these parts of speech, a dependent clause is called an *adjective clause,* an *adverbial clause,* or a *noun clause.*

1. *Adjective clauses* are usually introduced by a relative pronoun (*who, which, that*) or by a subordinating conjunction (*when, where, why*). Sometimes, however, the relative pronoun is understood. A clause introduced by a relative pronoun is also called a *relative clause.* (See Section 23h.)

The roadster *which you wanted* has been sold. (Adjective clause modifying *roadster*)

I told him the reason *why I was not coming.* (Adjective clause modifying *reason*)

The man *whom you recommended* has done an excellent job. (Adjective clause modifying *man*)

He is a boy *I never admired.* (Adjective clause modifying *boy;* relative pronoun *whom* omitted)

EXERCISE 13

From the following sentences list the adjective clauses and tell what word each adjective clause modifies. Some sentences may contain no adjective clauses.

1. The check which you sent on Saturday has not arrived.
2. Most of the listeners to soap operas are housewives, who take a great interest in serial stories.
3. The fire started in the hotel coffee shop, which was closed.
4. Flames were discovered coming from the elevator shaft.
5. Today I interviewed a young woman who wishes to become a lawyer.
6. He just came back from Indiana, where he spent his Easter holiday.
7. Henry became acquainted with the soldiers who were stationed at a nearby camp.
8. Of all the good times that I had during vacation, I enjoyed our hay ride and barn dance the most.
9. In front of the stage was a pit where men stood to see the play.
10. The modern novel presents a picture of almost every aspect of human life.
11. Jane Austen wrote novels of manners, of which *Pride and Prejudice* is the most famous.
12. Mrs. Henry McClintock discussed the data which she had presented at the last meeting.
13. They must find a house in which they can live on a greatly reduced income.

14. There was a group of outlaws who endangered the lives of the people in the community.
15. A relative invited the boy to his home, where the youth found many enjoyable books.
16. This has been a period in which conversation has received little attention.
17. The road is a part of a main highway and leads eventually to the sea.
18. The time when she was to leave came quickly, and she took a boat for the country that she had never seen.
19. The moving picture advances rapidly, with little time that is not filled with mystery and intrigue.
20. The speaker urged parents to encourage a child who is skillful with his hands to become a satisfied craftsman instead of a second-rate white-collar worker.
21. The story tells of a family that inherited a house with sinister memories and of a spell which haunted all people connected with the place.
22. Dr. Newburg reported briefly concerning the jail committee which was appointed by the mayor on February 14.
23. The younger members of a Chinese family must pay every respect and show every courtesy to the older members.
24. A man who is an expert driver seldom finds it necessary to slam on his brakes, because he is alert to all driving conditions.
25. The country road where we took our driving lessons has become a broad highway filled with cars.

2. *Adverbial clauses* may express nine relationships.

Time (*when, before, while, since*):

When a boy drives a car, he must learn certain rules of the road. (Clause modifies verb *must learn.*)
He will watch pedestrians carefully *while he is driving.* (Clause modifies verb *will watch.*)

Place (*where, wherever*):

After finding the book *where I had left it,* I hurried back to the house. (Clause modifies the gerund *finding.*)

I am willing to go *wherever we can find good fishing.* (Clause modifies the infinitive *to go.*)

Manner (as, as if):

He kicked the ball *as if it were an apple.* (Clause modifies the verb *kicked.*)

Condition (if, so, unless, provided that):

If you have the blouse in blue, I will buy it. (Clause modifies the verb *will buy.*)

Cause (because, as, since):

The train, three hours late *because the engine had broken down,* was crowded with troops. (Clause modifies the adjective *late.*)

Purpose (in order that, so that):

We worked hard all day *so that the house would be pretty for the party.* (Clause modifies verb *worked.*)

Result (that, so that, so . . . that):

The pile of driftwood mounted, *so that soon we were able to start a blazing beach fire.* (Clause modifies verb *mounted.*)

We were *so* hungry *that we ate the stale crackers.* (Clause modifies adjective *hungry.*)

Degree or *Comparison (than, as much as, as . . . as, just as):*

John climbed farther *than you did.* (Clause modifies adverb *farther.*)

Concession (though, although):

Although the Socialists lost seats in the election, they received a large popular vote. (Clause modifies verb *received.*)

EXERCISE 14

Write the adverbial clauses found in the following sentences and tell what each adverbial clause modifies. Some sentences may contain no adverbial clauses.

1. As they reached a shady spot in the road, the cars stopped.
2. Before he was sent overseas, he was able to finish the sophomore year in college.
3. We reached camp just as the sun was setting.
4. When school was dismissed for the summer vacation, I immediately got a job in an office.
5. If you do not want any of the colors mentioned, we shall be glad to take your order for another shade.
6. One day while he was taking undersea pictures off the coast of Lower California, he encountered a huge porpoise.
7. Although he has always been pleasant to me, I do not like him.
8. During the last few days, it has rained so hard that the wheat has been ruined.
9. They were a well-to-do family until a crash in the stock market ruined them.
10. If you wish additional information concerning my character or ability, you may get in touch with Mr. Horace Brown.
11. The mayor has been so successful that he has been elected six times.
12. We worked for ten hours in order that the job might be completed.
13. After he was graduated from high school, he entered the University of Maryland.
14. Although he did not score, he made the best play of the game.
15. Speaking with quiet confidence, the statesman urged his country to coöperate with the rest of the world.
16. In the period from 1200 to 1600, famines were common in Europe because it was difficult to transport food.
17. When the crops failed, people died because they could not get food from other countries.
18. We have wasted our resources as if we thought the supply was limitless.
19. If we are not careful in the future, we may again be without materials necessary for comfortable living.
20. In order that we may preserve some of our wild life,

the government has set aside national parks and bird refuges.

21. However, these efforts are small, so that very little is accomplished.
22. Men are more eager for money than they are for protection of the country.
23. Since we must help feed the rest of the world, we should be more careful than we have been in the past.
24. The country has been so mechanized that Americans must think also of a possible petroleum shortage.
25. When we are no longer willing to waste our resources to make money quickly, we shall have learned an important lesson.

3. *Noun clauses* perform the functions of nouns. A noun clause is usually introduced by *that, who, which, where, when, why.* It is used as:

1. *Subject:*	*Who is guilty* does not concern me.
2. *Object of verb:*	I hope *that you will be able to go to college.*
3. *Object of preposition:*	We judge a man by *what he does.*
4. *Appositive:*	He reached the conclusion *that it was wise to stay out of Newberry.* (See Section 9, item 7.)
5. *Predicate noun:*	One serious problem is *that there is no running water.* (See Section 1f.)

CAUTION: Occasionally the relative pronoun or subordinate conjunction *that* is omitted.

I told him I would go. (*I would go* is the dependent clause.)
I told him that I would go.

EXERCISE 15

On your paper write all the noun clauses that you find in the following sentences and tell how each noun clause is used. Some of the sentences contain no noun clauses.

1. I promise that I will help you.
2. I hope that I can go to the party.
3. He asked how he could get to North Avenue.
4. I do not know what I should tell Edith about the party.
5. One result of my work in literature is that I have developed better taste in reading.
6. A recent experiment showed that music will decrease the time required for a job.
7. Success depends, in a measure, upon what characteristics we inherit from our parents.
8. The fact that it looks like rain has no effect on my decision to leave today.
9. That we shall win the pennant this year is a foregone conclusion.
10. The article says that youth should be taught to be responsible.
11. Who will inherit the money does not interest me.
12. The fact that he had learned scouting saved his life in the jungle.
13. We are judged by what we say.
14. The President's advisers feel that a cooling-off period in strike situations is highly desirable.
15. Why you like him is certainly a mystery.
16. He was born just a short distance from where he now lives.
17. A boy brought the message that an urgent call had come.
18. The conclusion is that international responsibility for internal affairs is cheaper than another war.
19. He said he would try to get to the party.
20. In 1798, a scientist named Malthus warned the world that the population would outgrow the food supply.
21. Nobody paid any attention to what he said.
22. Everybody thought that the abundant supply of food would last forever.
23. Now we again receive warnings that our food supply is not adequate.
24. What we can do to save our remaining resources is an important problem.

25. That we are wasting our land by bad farming methods is clear to everybody.

7c. Achievement test on clauses.

On your paper, write each dependent clause in the following sentences. Label it *noun, adjective,* or *adverb.*

1. He is one of the most skillful locksmiths that I have ever seen.
2. They moved to a farm in Iowa, where they spent fifteen years.
3. The book would be of great interest to a person who intends to become a journalist.
4. The businessmen knew what was coming.
5. Although she looked like a bright child, she found great difficulty in learning to read.
6. The truth of the matter is that he is very lazy.
7. I worked hard all morning so that I might go to the circus in the afternoon.
8. We spent the week end at one of those charming inns where George Washington slept.
9. When more than one hundred pounds of cargo are loaded on the llama's back, the animal simply lies down and refuses to move.
10. She had to get up very early in the morning because she often had to cook for as many as eighteen people.
11. That few citizens approve of every idea of their executives is likely to be the case.
12. Training schools for nurses brought into being the efficient, immaculate nurse that we take for granted today.
13. The conditions that one found in early hospitals would not be tolerated for a minute in these days.
14. When she was nineteen, she decided to go to Europe, where she planned to study medicine.
15. Although she looked delicate and frail, she was not made of the stuff which shrinks from a disagreeable task.
16. A new plastic material which is used in surgical dressings now pleases the patients very much because it does not stick to the wound.

17. Another change which has taken place in me is that I enjoy classical music.
18. Although the field of costume design is crowded, many new opportunities are expected to develop.
19. I was thinking that we could have a fine time if we were both accepted at the same college.
20. In the eighteenth century, smallpox was so common that scarcely anyone escaped from the malady.
21. I hope that Sally will be surprised because her mother is working very hard to make the party a success.
22. He reached the conclusion that it would be wise to go to college before going to law school.
23. Phyllis Grain found that she had married not only a spoiled husband, but all his relatives.
24. This is one of the most exciting stories I have ever read.
25. Many people who have frequent automobile accidents are emotionally childish and their driving licenses should be withdrawn.

8. SENTENCES

8a. Definition.

A *sentence* is a group of words containing a complete thought.

It must have a *subject* and a *predicate*. The subject is the name of the person or thing about which the verb makes a statement. The predicate is what is said of the subject; it must contain a verb which completes an independent statement. Such a verb is called a *finite* verb. Remember: participles, infinitives, and gerunds are not finite verbs.

8b. Kinds of sentences.

Sentences may be classified according to grammatical structure as *simple, compound, complex,* or *compound-complex.*

One of the greatest problems of inexperienced writers is learning to use the type of sentence which suits the idea to be presented. They must try, also, not to use the same kind of sentence too often. (See Section 74.)

A *simple sentence* expresses one complete thought. It may have a single subject or a compound subject; it may have a single verb or a compound verb, but all of the subjects must perform the action in all of the verbs.

> Ralph plays in the school orchestra. (One subject, *Ralph;* one verb, *plays*)
>
> Ralph and Sally play in the school orchestra and sing in the Glee Club. (Compound subject, *Ralph, Sally;* compound verb, *play, sing*)

Phrases do not affect the kind of sentence. A sentence may have many phrases and still be a simple sentence.

> They sold their wedding presents in order to get enough money to travel to Europe. (One subject, *they;* one verb, *sold;* simple sentence)

A *compound sentence* contains two or more independent clauses. It is really two simple sentences combined by an appropriate connecting link. This connecting link may be a coördinating conjunction (*and, but, for, or, nor*) preceded by a comma. It may also be a *conjunctive adverb* (*however, moreover, nevertheless, therefore, thus, then, so, yet, otherwise*) preceded by a semicolon. Or the connecting link may be omitted and a semicolon may be used. The compound sentence is useful when you wish to express two thoughts of equal value.

> Harold went to college for only a year, but his sister is a graduate of Goucher. (Two complete thoughts joined by *but* and a comma)
>
> I signed an application blank from our state university; however, I am not sure of going there. (Two complete thoughts joined by *however* and a semicolon)
>
> Sue is pretty; her sister is very homely. (Two complete thoughts separated by a semicolon)

A *complex sentence* contains one independent clause and one or more dependent clauses.

The sign of the complex sentence is the dependent or subordinate clause. (See Section 7b.) A complex sentence is used when the two ideas to be expressed are not equal in value. One of the parts depends on the other.

(dependent)   (independent)
When she was a little girl, she was very much interested in horses.

(independent)   (dependent)
A broken sign hung on the gate, which was partly open.

(dependent)   (independent)
When he was ready to make the trip, he had to wait on
(dependent)
Long Island because there was bad weather.

Careless writers sometimes make the mistake of using a subordinate clause as a sentence.

Although my violin is broken.
When the bell rang.

Clearly, these are not complete ideas. They are a part of a complex sentence. Be sure to write all the parts of a sentence before you use a period. (See Section 57.)

The *compound-complex sentence* has the characteristics of both the compound and the complex sentence. It has two independent clauses, as the compound sentence has, and at least one dependent clause, as the complex sentence has.

(dependent)   (independent)
When the legislature passed a sales tax, many people
(independent)
complained; but the governor agreed to use much of the money for improved schools.

Notice the punctuation of the preceding sentence. The two independent clauses are separated by a semicolon. (See Section 24c.) Knowing how to use these three kinds of sentences will help you to give variety, interest, and good form to your writing.

Sentences are also classified according to *meaning* and *purpose.*

A *declarative sentence* states a fact or makes an assertion.

> The plane has two motors.

An *interrogative sentence* asks a question.

> Do motion pictures teach crime?

An *imperative sentence* expresses an entreaty or command.

> Please come as soon as possible.
> Forward, march.

An *exclamatory sentence* expresses strong feeling.

> Oh, if he were only here!

EXERCISE 16

On your paper tell whether each of the following sentences is simple, compound, complex, or compound-complex and give the reason for your decision. For example, sentence 1 is complex because it contains one independent clause and one dependent clause.

1. He belongs to a club which is composed of famous men in sports.
2. After hearing his first concert, the child wanted to study music.
3. Thirty thousand people are killed annually in automobile accidents.
4. The Bastille was a strongly fortified structure used as a place of confinement for those who displeased the king or his court.
5. For six years his hobby has been chemistry, and he has even constructed his own laboratory.
6. By the end of the year, the building job was begun; but it did not progress rapidly.
7. The American soldier escaped with the assistance of a German youth, to whom he promised a large sum of money.
8. The author is very fond of moralizing and displays this interest in the book.

9. I have a very bad temper; and after an argument, I am inclined to sulk and be sarcastic.

10. Your party sounds like great fun, but I'm afraid that I shall not be able to come.

11. The tickets are to be printed with a perforated section that can be torn off.

12. At Des Moines, there was an officers' school for women; and WAC officers lived in rose-colored brick buildings.

13. The dance, accompanied by native drums, was a series of stamping steps in rhythmic patterns.

14. We drove up the mountain, shuddering at each narrow turn of the road.

15. Everyone said that it would be hard to get reservations at a hotel, but we didn't have any trouble.

16. Walking into his father's office, he calmly announced his intention to go to sea.

17. The National Institute of Health has planned a fight against the common cold.

18. After the graduation, she and her family went to Florida; they wanted to visit her brother, who is in business there.

19. Because of the strict censorship, my cousin could not say much about his activities; but he did tell me of the three missions which he made to China as a gunner on a B-24.

20. The death of Pericles symbolized the end of the greatest period in Athenian history.

21. Time after time, the person who discovers a fire rushes off in a frenzy of excitement, leaving the door wide open.

22. The people had vigor enough to make an attempt to free themselves.

23. He was graduated from Notre Dame with a law degree, but immediately went into journalism.

24. The luncheon club diet of chicken patties and canned green peas was too much for him; so he gave up his job as club reporter.

25. Highlight of the day's events will be seven races for speedboats and cruisers, for which the club will offer trophies worth one hundred dollars each.

EXERCISE 17

Follow the directions in Exercise 16.

1. The captain ordered his men to prepare to move back to the rest zone at sundown.
2. When the Marines landed in Okinawa, they were astonished to find swarms of spiders.
3. The resort was crowded with people, and the band kept up a ceaseless accompaniment.
4. The French children approached the American soldiers and held out their hands.
5. When Joan decided to accompany her aunt to Ocean City, she looked forward to a good time; but she was not counting on the really superb time that she had.
6. The book is written with a subtle suggestion of satire as if the author were trying to criticize in a mild manner the stuffiness of the period.
7. The client was ushered into the room to await an interview with the famous lawyer.
8. People who recognize the danger of potential epidemics recommend a world network of public health stations.
9. He is continually in trouble and has now spent a large part of his inheritance.
10. Although his composition was rejected for the Prix de Rome contest, this only served to make Ravel more popular; for everyone attributed the rejection to petty jealousies, intrigues, and politics.

EXERCISE 18

Use your knowledge of clauses and kinds of sentences to revise the following paragraph. On your paper, rewrite the paragraph. Remember that short, choppy, simple sentences do not make an interesting style; but when simple sentences are combined to make compound or complex sentences, you must be careful not to put too many ideas together merely because you want to vary your sentence structure. The ideas which appear in one sentence must be closely related, and the conjunctions used to join them must show what the relationship is. (See Sections 61, 62, and 63.)

Conservation of our resources is an important problem for the United States. Some farmers and timber land owners waste their land. They do not know how to use it wisely. Farmers plant the same crops year after year. The soil loses its richness. Wise farmers help their land. They plant special crops. These crops restore nitrogen to the soil. Range lands are another problem. They are often damaged by overgrazing. Then the animals do not get enough to eat. The owner must buy commercial feed. The overgrazed land is eroded by the wind. The topsoil is blown away. A third problem is insects. They eat the crops. They are hard to control. D.D.T. could be used to kill some of them. D.D.T. might kill valuable insects. Some of the valuable insects pollinate fruit trees.

EXERCISE 19

Follow the directions in Exercise 18.

Many high schools today are teaching boys and girls to be safe drivers. The instructors say a person must be an adult emotionally to drive well. Your little brother shows off for company. He is a baby. He wants to be seen. He hasn't learned to think. A person who thinks is growing up. He acts on reason. He does not act as a result of his feelings. A show-off in an automobile is a baby emotionally. He exceeds the speed limit. He takes ten people in a five-passenger car. He drives an old car. His car has bad brakes. He impatiently dashes past other cars on their right. He is like your little brother. He is showing off for a crowd. His showing off is more dangerous than that of your little brother. He may kill people. Little brother merely annoys people. Some boys are eighteen years old. They are still babies emotionally. They should not be permitted to drive cars.

9. GLOSSARY OF GRAMMATICAL TERMS

In a discussion of grammar and writing, many terms are used. Sometimes there are several terms which have the same meaning. If you have trouble with a term, consult the following pages.

1. ABSOLUTE EXPRESSION. An absolute expression is composed of a noun or pronoun and a participle.

> *The tire being flat,* we decided to pump it up.
> *Two hours having elapsed,* we again set out on our journey.
> The little boat hugged the shore, *its sails flapping in the wind.*

2. ACTIVE VOICE. (See Section 3d.)

3. ADJECTIVE. Defined and described in Section 4a–b. Errors in the use of adjectives are discussed and illustrated in Section 18.

4. ADVERB. (See Section 4c–d.)

5. ALLITERATION. Alliteration is the use of several words beginning with the same sound. It is usually not a good device to use in prose writing. At present it is used chiefly in advertising.

> Make Money with Munder
> Sales Service Simplified
> Tasty, Tempting, Tantalizing

6. ANTECEDENT. The substantive (noun or pronoun) to which a pronoun refers. (See Section 12.)

7. APPOSITIVE. A substantive added to another substantive to identify it or explain it. The appositive signifies the same thing as, and is said to be in apposition with, the substantive it explains.

> One important product, *rubber,* this country had to import. (*Rubber* is in apposition with *product.*)
> More hardy than wheat are these grains—*rye, oats,* and *barley.* (*Rye, oats,* and *barley* are in apposition with *grains.*)

An appositive agrees in number and case with the substantive to which it refers, and is set off by commas or dashes unless it is so closely related to the other substantive that the two words seem part of the same expression.

My friend *Andrew* built a sailboat. (The appositive is closely related to the noun to which it refers.)

8. AUXILIARY. A verb used to "help" another verb in the formation of tense and voice forms. *Be, can, do, have, may, must, ought, shall, will,* are examples.

He *has* gone away for a visit.
You *will* please turn out the light.
We *should have been* working with the stevedores on the dock.

9. CASE. (See Section le–g.)
10. CLAUSE. (See Section 7.)
11. COMPARISON. The change in the form of an adjective or adverb to indicate greater or smaller degrees of quantity, quality, or manner. The three degrees of comparison are positive, comparative, and superlative. (See Section 18e.)

small	smaller	smallest
little	less	least
wisely	more wisely	most wisely
quickly	less quickly	least quickly

The comparative degree is used to show relationship between two persons, objects, or ideas.

Fred is taller than I.
This box is less attractive than the other one.

The superlative degree is used to show relationships among three or more:

Alan is the tallest one in his family.
This sewing kit is the most attractive of the six available.

12. COMPLEMENT. A word or expression used to complete the idea indicated by another word or expression. A predicate complement may be a substantive or an adjective that completes the meaning of the copulative verb. It is also called the subjective complement, or predicate noun.

Mr. Crawford is a *salesman*. (Substantive used as predicate complement)

Jane is very *gay*. (Adjective used as predicate complement)

An objective complement is a noun or adjective that completes the meaning by telling something about the direct object. It is also called predicate objective.

They called the dog *Jerry*. (Noun)
We dyed the dress *blue*. (Adjective)

13. COMPLEX SENTENCE. (See Section 8b.)
14. COMPOUND SENTENCE. (See Section 8b.)
15. COMPOUND-COMPLEX SENTENCE. (See Section 8b.)
16. CONJUGATION. A list or table giving all the forms of a verb to show mood, tense, number, person, and voice. (See Section 3f.)
17. CONJUNCTION. (See Section 5.)
18. CONJUNCTIVE ADVERB. A word used sometimes as a conjunction and sometimes as an adverb. It often connects independent clauses. Some conjunctive adverbs are *however, moreover, nevertheless, consequently, therefore, thus, then, so, yet, otherwise*.
19. COPULA. Verbs such as *be, appear, seem, smell* are copulative (or linking) verbs, which express the relation betwen subject and complement.

The other man *was* his nephew.
That *seems* inexpensive.

20. DECLENSION. A list or table giving the different forms of a substantive to indicate case, number, person, and gender. When changes in a substantive are thus shown, the word is said to be *declined*. (*I, my, me*)
21. DIRECT ADDRESS. The substantive showing to whom speech is addressed (also called the vocative).

> *John,* where are you?
>
> When we finish rolling the court, *Fred,* we'll still have time for two sets of tennis.

22. ELLIPSIS. The omission of a word or words necessary to the grammatical completeness of a clause or sentence. In the sentences below, the words in parentheses might be omitted in speaking and writing; without such words the sentences are called *elliptical.*

> Some of the patriots carried guns; others, (carried) swords; still others, (carried) clubs and sticks.
>
> While (we were) drifting downstream, we grounded on a sand bar.
>
> He was eighteen years of age; his brother, (was) twelve (years of age).

23. EXPLETIVE. An expletive is a word used chiefly to introduce an idea. *It* and *there* are commonly used as expletives.

> *It* was Alice sitting there.
>
> *It* is a truism that men love freedom.
>
> *There* are four hundred people present.

24. FINITE VERB. A verb that is capable of making a complete and independent assertion.

> He *walked* to school.
>
> I *have finished* the job.

Verbals are not finite verbs.

25. GENDER. The classification of substantives according to sex. There are four genders: masculine, feminine, neuter, and common (either masculine or feminine): *boy, girl, it, individual.* In modern English, nearly all traces of grammatical gender have disappeared.

26. GERUND. A verbal noun. A gerund has the same form as the present or perfect participle. (See Section 3g.)

27. GRAMMAR. The science which deals with words and their relationships to each other. *Rhetoric* deals with the art of expressive speech and writing, with the laws of clear, effective writing; *grammar* is concerned with a consideration and account of the features of a language and with speech and writing according to various standards of usage.

28. IDIOM (idiomatic usage). The manner of expression characteristic of a language. (See Section 43.)

29. IMPERSONAL construction. The use of the pronoun *it* in a sentence like this:

> It is raining.

30. INFINITIVE. (See Section 3g.)

31. INFLECTION. A change in the form of a word to show a change in meaning.

32. INTERJECTION. A word that shows strong feeling.

> Heavens! You have broken the vase.

33. INTRANSITIVE VERB. A verb used in such a way that it does not require a direct object. (See Section 3c.)

> The poor man *trembled* as he *spoke*.

34. INVERTED ORDER. The arrangement of the words in a sentence so that the whole or a part of the predicate precedes the subject.

> In God we trust.
> Down from the hills came the guerrilla bands.

35. LINKING VERB. See *Copula* in this Glossary

36. MOOD. (See Section 3e.)

37. MODIFIER. A word that describes or limits another word. (See Section 4.)

38. NONRESTRICTIVE. A word or group of words not necessary to the thought. (See Section 23h.)

39. NOUN. (See Section 1.)

40. NUMBER. The change in the form of a substantive or verb to show whether one or more than one is indi-

cated. Using plural forms of pronouns or verbs is ordinarily more simple than forming noun plurals. (See Section 39d.) When in doubt concerning the singular or plural form of a noun, pronoun, or verb, consult your dictionary. The following examples may help to fix basic principles in mind.

> Singular: man, boy, lady, knife, he, is.
> Plural:　　men, boys, ladies, knives, they, are.

41. OBJECT. The substantive following a preposition, or the word, phrase, or clause indicating the thing or person affected by a transitive verb or verbal.

> He is in the *room*.
> The carpenters built a *house*.
> He said *that he would go*.

A *compound object* consists of two or more substantives used as object of a verb or a preposition.

> The Duanes built *the house and the barn*. (Compound object of verb)

42. PARALLELISM. The use of the same structural form for ideas of equal value. (See Section 70.)

43. PARENTHETICAL MATERIAL. Any expression which is not necessary for the grammatical completeness of the sentence in which it occurs. (See Section 23d.)

44. PARTICIPLE. (See Section 3g.)

45. PASSIVE VOICE. (See *Voice* below and Section 3d.)

46. PERSON. One of three relationships—that of speaker, that of person spoken to, and that of person or thing spoken about—in which a noun or pronoun may be used, with respect to the other words in a sentence. Nouns do not show person by changes in form. Personal pronouns indicate person by changes in form. Finite verbs undergo a few changes in form to show agreement with their subjects in person.

> I read, you read, he reads.

47. PHRASE. (See Section 6.)
48. PREDICATE. The part of a sentence which makes an assertion about the subject. A *simple predicate* is the verb (or verb phrase) alone; a *complete* predicate consists of the verb with any modifier, object, or other completing word which it may have.

> Mr. Tyler drove the ball nearly two hundred yards. (*Drove* is the simple predicate; *drove the ball nearly two hundred yards* is the complete predicate.)

49. PREPOSITION. (See Section 5a–b.)
50. PRINCIPAL PARTS. (See Sections 3f and 15.)
51. PRONOUN. (See Section 2.)
52. SENTENCE. (See Section 8.)
53. SUBJECT OF A SENTENCE. A substantive naming the person or thing about which an assertion is made. A *simple subject* is this substantive alone. A *complete subject* is a simple subject together with its modifiers. A compound subject consists of two or more substantives used as subjects of the same verb.

> The green *house* is for sale. (Simple)
> *The green house* is for sale. (Complete)
> *The green house and two acres of land* are for sale. (Compound)

54. SUBSTANTIVE. An inclusive term for a noun and all noun-equivalents. Pronouns, gerunds, noun phrases, and noun clauses are noun-equivalents. The following italicized expressions are used as substantives:

> The *dog* was three years old.
> *They* are coming tomorrow.
> *From New Orleans to Chicago* is a long distance.
> Are you positive *that he was here today?*

55. SYNTAX. Construction; the grammatical relations between words in sentences.

56. TENSE. See Section 3f.
57. TRANSITIVE VERB. A verb accompanied by a direct object which completes its meaning: The player *hit* the ball. My brother *studied* the assignment. (See Section 3d.)
58. VERB PHRASE. A verb together with an auxiliary: *shall take, shall have taken, will have been taken.* Distinguish between a verb phrase (as above) and a verbal. (See Section 3b.)
59. VERBAL. The verb form used as a noun, an adjective, or an adverb. (See Section 3g.)
60. VOICE. The change in the form of a verb to indicate whether the subject is the performer of the action (active voice) or is acted upon (passive voice).

Usage

The English that is used for serious essays, for magazine articles, or for research papers in history is more formal than the English used in ordinary conversation, in narrative compositions, or in friendly letters. Often colloquial English is used for the types of writing in the second group. It is important to understand the language and sentence structure appropriate to the occasion. Although much more use is made of informal than of formal English, there are occasions when educated people who have responsible positions must write business reports, articles for company journals, minutes of club meetings, and even articles for publication. To such people, a knowledge of formal English is imperative. The drill in this section includes experience with both formal and informal English because in daily living there is a need for both.

Do you say:

> "I didn't sleep good last night."
> "Jenny met Terry and I at the station."
> "One of the pages in my book are tore."
> "I was almost froze when I came home from the game."

All these sentences are incorrect. Take the Diagnostic Tests in Section 10 to see where you make mistakes. Then study the pages that will help you to correct your errors.

10. DIAGNOSTIC TESTS IN USAGE

10a. Diagnostic Test I (Sections 11–14).

Here is a chance for you to see how good your grammar is. All the sentences in the Diagnostic Test were written

56

in the compositions of students. Most of the sentences contain at least one error. On your paper, write the number of each sentence. Beside the number, write the correction or corrections and the reason for each correction. Do not rewrite the whole sentence unless it is impossible for you to show in a few words what the correction should be. If the sentence is correct, write C beside its number. When your paper has been checked and you know which principles are giving you trouble, turn to the sections that will explain your problem.

Examples:

1. Every one of the students have bought their class rings.
2. At one place which we visited were the famous Seminole Indian Village, the parrot farm, and the monkey jungle.

Correction

1. has   1. subject and verb agreement
    his   pronoun and antecedent agreement
2. C

1. The mailing lists contains the names of all the customers whom we think will be interested in the sale.
2. Every man, woman, and child were lost.
3. Lack of materials and modern equipment discourages nurses and doctors in many mental hospitals.
4. The bed of the river was shallow at some places and deep at others, which would make swimming dangerous.
5. It's hard to keep in touch with girls who you know at camp but who you do not see all winter.
6. A businessman must be careful not to offend anyone, particularly if their complaint is justified.
7. When people know little about gardening, there's many mistakes made in planting.
8. The available data indicates that the prevailing winds will be from the south.
9. I asked Father to let John and I go to New York.

10. The tunnels, Holland and Lincoln, extends under the Hudson River and connects Manhattan with New Jersey.

11. Roads are being constantly improved so that the chances of accidents due to a faulty highway are comparatively few.

12. Before one makes up their mind, they should consider all the factors involved.

13. I shall be very glad to come to your party because they are always such fun.

14. While the line was being arranged for the processional, I was wondering who I'd walk with.

15. I think it was her who broke my locker.

16. Why don't you and Marcia meet Dad and I in New York and go to Maine with us?

17. Each of us are expected to pay for the materials that we broke.

18. A discussion between you and I will have no results because neither of us are willing to compromise.

19. Either our buyer or one of our executives is going to London to obtain English tweeds for our fall stock.

20. Every one of the businesses were taxed heavily on their excess profits.

21. With my grandmother lives my two cousins, who are four years older than myself.

22. The chief topic of discussion are the problems caused by the overcrowding of the colleges.

23. Jerry, whom I noticed was quite good looking, was coming toward us.

24. If I had been her, I should not have approved of Bob going to Europe.

25. On the bed is a hat, two pairs of shoes, and a dress which is ready to be packed for the trip.

26. After some deliberation, the Board of Directors reorganized the business completely, which seemed to Ralph and I a good idea.

27. Please fill in the enclosed application blank and return same by Monday, June 10.

28. Employment problems is helped by modern machinery because people who buy them need somebody to work them.

29. It says in this book that it will increase sales if you improve the English of the salesmen.
30. Either you or I are sure to be the new president of the club.
31. The stenographer who you see in my office was employed by Mr. Shriver and he in my absence.
32. The inability of an individual to face the problems of marriage sometimes cause them to put off marriage until they are middle-aged.
33. I thought that Father was going to let Sally and I go to the movies tonight, which would have pleased us very much.
34. Measles are often serious. Me and my brother had them when we were children, and they nearly killed us.
35. In the backfield at least one of our men have the experience and speed that is necessary to carry the pigskin over the goal line.
36. Most Americans read the newspapers, and it is therefore an excellent means of disseminating propaganda.
37. The stewards of labor unions can write a report against the bosses which he feels is not following the contract.
38. The number of people who succeed in that line of work are very small.
39. The following description, together with the drawings, present a master plan for the development of an airport.
40. The direction of the runways have been decided after a consideration of the prevailing winds.
41. The gardener whom I hoped would do the work was sick today.
42. I'm sure it wasn't him whom you saw at the dance.
43. Mrs. Bingham is the only one of the women who have reached their quota.
44. Between you and I there will always be a friendly feeling.
45. The company thinks that whoever you choose as a representative will do a good job.
46. This is the boy whom you said you thought might do well in the job.

47. Freedom of the press and of public assembly do not necessarily mean that equal opportunity for the expression of all opinions are available.
48. Please give these books to whoever calls for them.
49. You have been here longer than her and ought to be more competent.
50. Are you one of those people who listens to a special radio program every day?

10b. Diagnostic Test II (Sections 15–19).

Follow the directions for Diagnostic Test I.

1. If the automobile test for a driver's license was a bit more difficult, teen-agers would be more better prepared to drive.
2. It's surprising how bravely some people can seem in real danger.
3. Really, if I were you, I'd get out of here in a hurry.
4. Most of the actors in the picture were unknown, but they performed like they were seasoned stars.
5. I could have shook her when she told that story.
6. Not paying much attention to where we were at, we missed our turn in the road.
7. When the boy attempted to pay his fare, he found that he left his wallet at home.
8. I suppose we all talk foolish when we are excited.
9. We should send for the doctor; Sue has felt badly all day.
10. Leaving Oklahoma City at eight in the morning, we arrived in Tulsa at noon.
11. Come quick; Mary has broke the window.
12. When I first seen you, I thought you were Dick.
13. Booth always does his work neater than Sarah.
14. Helen hasn't wore her new suit yet.
15. Moving to Delaware, we built a large stone house.
16. I am living on this same street for thirty years.
17. I wish I was able to work as rapid as you do.
18. I have had enough experience to sell most anything.
19. If he had not had the title searched, he would have lost his deposit on the house.
20. Get your *Home Magazine* by taking advantage of one of the most liberal offers ever made.

21. Graduating from high school in 1938, he took a job as an apprentice in a machine shop.
22. Finishing his work, he put his book away and turned on the radio.
23. The party would have been gayer if you were there.
24. One of the first lessons taught the salesmen is how to write legible.
25. I sure was glad that you got the engine started as quick as you did.
26. The J. V. team is doing pretty good this year.
27. There must be a new trial because this one has not been handled legal.
28. After laying asleep for an hour, Toby jumped up and began to bark.
29. The radio was so low that we had to set right beside it in order to hear it.
30. John has a tremendous appetite; last night he must have eat six ears of corn.
31. That dark face powder makes you look like you have jaundice.
32. I cannot study without you turn off the radio.
33. Suddenly, this here dark-complexioned man strikes the boy in the face.
34. The credit manager explained to Mrs. Pentz that he already wrote her two letters.
35. Since my twelfth birthday I was able to save an average of ten dollars a month.
36. At the end of the year he planned an escape. After all the details were thought out careful, he breaks out of prison and flees to the jungle.
37. He discovered that she was a girl from his own city, who eloped years ago with a guardsman in her father's regiment.
38. On the way home, we sang all the songs that we learned at camp.
39. Many times I have wished that I was able to visit the famous cities of Europe.
40. You should of saw Jake's face when the teacher sent him to the principal.
41. I will never forget our first night on the ocean.
42. I move that Robert sings a solo.

43. Beginning to build the house five months ago, w
finally completed the job today.
44. When she returned from her vacation, I asked Edit
what she did in Puerto Rico.
45. I should have liked to have gone to the play, but
sure was too sick to move.
46. I could have swore it was Hal I seen in the drugstore
47. The cobra is the most deadliest snake in the world.
48. To compete with the railroads, airlines have lowere
their rates considerable.
49. The radio commentator said that the ship had san
at 9:45.
50. The newspapers were enthusiastic about Gerty be
cause not many people have swam the English Chan
nel.

11. SUBJECT AND VERB AGREEMENT

11a. A verb must agree with its subject in person and number.

A *verb* is usually an action word like *run, go, sing.* (Se
Section 3.) It may, however, assert a condition or a state
The verbs *be* and *seem* assert a condition or a state. Be
cause action words stand out clearly in a sentence, it i
easy to begin the grammatical analysis of a sentence b
finding the verb. Then look for the person or thing tha
performs the action expressed by this verb. When yo
find it, you have the subject. A subject is always a word o
group of words used as a noun, or a pronoun.

Our *club* (subject) *gives* (verb) three dances each yea

In the preceding sentence, the subject and the verb ar
easy to find, but in some sentences the subject comes afte
the verb or is separated from the verb by other word
Before you try to make the verb agree with the subjec
be sure that you have the real subject. Then decid
whether it is singular or plural. Errors in verb forms fre
quently are made in the use of the present tense. In thi
tense, verbs in the third person singular end in *s;* verbs i

the third person plural do not usually end in *s*. (If you are uncertain about *person* and *number*, consult Section 1c and Section 2b.) Remember that as subjects, *I* and *we* are the forms for the first person; *you*, for the second person; *he, she, it*, and *they*, for the third person.

> The first dance helps us to pay for Christmas baskets for the poor. (The noun *dance* is third person singular. The verb *helps* is also third person singular.)
> The boys invite the pledges to the first football game. (*Boys* is third person plural. The verb *invite* is also third person plural.)
> I invite a different girl for each dance. (*I* is first person singular. The verb *invite* is also first person singular.)

NOTE: *Doesn't* is the correct contraction to use in the third person singular, present tense.

> Wrong: He *don't* play tennis.
> Right: He *doesn't* play tennis.

11b. *There* and *here* are not subjects.

After *there* and *here* you usually find the verb first and then the subject.

> Wrong: There *is* dances every Friday night at the community center.
> Right: There *are* dances every Friday night at the community center.
> Wrong: There *comes* the boys on the football team.
> Right: There *come* the boys on the football team.
> Wrong: Here *is* the tickets for the dance.
> Right: Here *are* the tickets for the dance.

11c. A prepositional phrase that follows the subject does not affect the number of the verb.

Do not make the verb agree with the object of a preposition.

> Wrong: One of the boys *preside* at the meeting.
> Right: One of the boys *presides* at the meeting.
> Wrong: The size of television pictures *are* at present quite limited.

Right: The size of the television pictures *is* at present quite limited.

Wrong: The owners of the campus store *jokes* with all the students.

Right: The owners of the campus store *joke* with all the students.

11d. Singular pronouns require singular verbs.

These pronouns are singular: *each, everyone, everybody, anyone, anybody, someone, somebody, no one, nobody, one, many a one, another, anything, either, neither.*

Wrong: Each of the boys *play* some game well.

Right: Each of the boys *plays* some game well.

Wrong: Everyone in the United States *are* concerned about the problems of peace.

Right: Everyone in the United States *is* concerned about the problems of peace.

Wrong: Neither of the senators *show* any uncertainty.

Right: Neither of the senators *shows* any uncertainty.

NOTE: The pronoun *none* may be used with either a singular or a plural verb, according to the sense of the sentence.

In informal or colloquial speech, the plural verb is often used with *everyone* or *each* if these words are followed by a phrase that seems to make their meaning plural, but careful speakers and writers follow the rule of agreement and use a singular verb with *everyone* or *each.*

Notice that *everyone* is written as one word. The expression *every one* (two words) is usually followed by an *of* phrase:

> *Everyone* is expected to come.
> *Every one* of us must bring a book.

11e. Words joined to a subject by *with, in addition to, as well as,* and *including* do not affect the verb.

> Our allies, as well as the enemy, *were* suffering.
> My whole equipment, including fishing rods, tackle, and knapsack, *was* lost on the trip.

11f. A compound subject joined by *and* requires a plural verb.

Mathematics and chemistry *are* my most difficult subjects.
Television and radio *have* revolutionized social habits.
On the landing field *stand* a B-36 and a small helicopter.

NOTE: When the two subjects form a single thought, a singular verb is used.

Bread and peanut butter *is* a nourishing food.
My comrade and friend *was* with me.

11g. If two or more subjects are joined by *and* and preceded by *every*, the verb is singular.

Every boy and girl in the auditorium *applauds* the principal when he appears on the stage.

11h. When two subjects are joined by *or*, *either . . . or*, *neither . . . nor*, the verb agrees with the subject nearer it.

Neither the student president nor his friends *want* to see Jack elected.
Either new athletic fields or a swimming pool *is* to be provided in the spring.
Either they or I *am* at fault.

11i. A collective noun usually takes a singular verb. If, however, the individuals of the group are considered, the verb is plural.

The team *fights* for victory.
Our class *sings* very well.
The family *disagree* on the question of my dates.

11j. For nouns plural in form but singular in meaning, use a singular verb.

Measles *is* sometimes serious.
Mathematics *is* a difficult subject.

NOTE: 1. Although authorities differ in their opinions about the number of some of these nouns, the following are usually considered to be singular: *physics, economics, news, politics, ethics, mumps, stamina.*

2. Subjects plural in form, which describe a quantity or number, require a singular verb when the subject is regarded as a unit.

> Ten miles *is* too far to walk.
> Two from five *leaves* three.
> Five dollars *is* the price.

3. A title of a book, play, film, painting, musical composition, or other such work is singular.

> *Pride and Prejudice* is my favorite novel.
> *The Frogs* is a play by Aristophanes.

11k. Fractions, and words such as *all*, *none*, *some*, will be singular if bulk or a total number or amount is implied, and plural if individuals are considered.

> Three-fourths of the roof *is* painted.
> Three-fourths of the members *are* here.
> All the girls *were* eager to have a beach party.
> All the food *was* gone.

11l. When the word *number* is preceded by the article *a*, it is plural. When it is preceded by *the*, it usually means a unit and is singular.

> A number of people *are* waiting outside.
> The number of people who have subscribed *is* eighty.

11m. If one subject is used affirmatively and the other negatively, the verb agrees with the subject that is used affirmatively.

> He, not I, *is* responsible.

11n. Be careful of the plurals of foreign nouns. (See Section 39d.) Some nouns retain the plural forms of the foreign language from which they have been taken.

Singular	*Plural*
datum	data
synopsis	synopses
alumnus	alumni

> The data are on your desk.
> Synopses of two stories were submitted.

11o. A verb does not agree with a predicate noun.

> The main thing to see is the beautiful gardens.

11p. A relative pronoun (*who, which,* or *that*) may be singular or plural, depending upon the word to which the pronoun refers.

> She is the only one of the students who has completed her work. (*Who* in this sentence refers to *one*. Therefore the verb *has* is singular.)
>
> He is one of the few players who have been on the team for three years. (*Who* refers to *players*. The verb *have* is therefore plural.)
>
> Of all the people in the class, Jane is the one who *deserves* most credit.
>
> Of all the people in the class, Jane and Helen are the ones who *deserve* most credit.

EXERCISE 1

Most of the following sentences contain errors in subject and verb agreement. Write on your paper the number of each sentence and the necessary correction or corrections. Write also an explanation of why you have made each correction. If no correction is necessary in a sentence, write C beside the sentence number.

1. Helen and her sister comes to school late every day.
2. Near the parking lot was several large department stores.
3. There is two or three boys trying out for each position on the team.
4. Recently there has been investigations of the injury caused to the brain by boxing.
5. Everyone in my classes are subscribing to the school paper.
6. The changes in the design of the house was made at the suggestion of the builder.
7. That don't make any difference.
8. Each of our customers receive a monthly statement.
9. The interior of the early theaters were not very attractive.
10. The revenue that is collected at the games support the teams.
11. Neither the professor nor his wife were at home.

12. The decision of the three officials were announced at noon.
13. During the last few years there has been many arguments over the place of sports in college life.
14. That cake's too sweet; it don't agree with me at all.
15. The brown puppy, as well as the black and the white ones, were sold to some tourists yesterday.
16. Mary's keen interest in life and people makes her parties a delightful experience.
17. Each of the class representatives have pledged support to the student president.
18. Coleridge's ideas of how a perfect society should be managed was very impractical.
19. Either Jane or I are going to suffer as a result of this.
20. The captain, together with all the boys on the team, were introduced from the platform.
21. Each of the amateur actors were beginning to feel stage fright.
22. The development of children depend in a large measure on family training.
23. The mother, as well as the children, have been quarantined.
24. Neither the man nor his lawyers are ready to agree to that proposal.
25. The number of people interested in geology is not very large.

EXERCISE 2

Follow the directions in Exercise 1.

1. The results obtained by our recent experiments with penicillin has been very gratifying.
2. First the sisters of the bride appears; then follows her aunt and uncle.
3. If one of these plans seem faulty, please discuss the issue with me.
4. Either our representatives or one of the officers of the company is going to Europe to settle the question.
5. *Gulliver's Travels* have been popular reading for many years.
6. The president of the company, in addition to several of the officers, were present at the meeting.

7. In the office of the president was a large mahogany desk, a swivel chair, and a few small straight chairs.

8. There's several questions that I want to ask you.

9. As the time of the celebrations approaches, each of the natives prepares for the dance.

10. If there is any complaints about the merchandise, please write us at once.

11. The letter, together with the advertising materials, was forwarded to him yesterday.

12. Everyone in the school have an opportunity to make some money on the side.

13. One of the men who has made great progress in the building of prefabricated houses is Foster Gunnison.

14. His development of porches, fireplaces, and garages provide variations of the standard prefabricated house.

15. The public thought that Leeuwenhoek and other scientists who believed his theory was crazy.

16. Please release him from the army; his mother and father needs him on the farm.

17. There was no running water and no sanitary arrangements anywhere in Warsaw.

18. Many people find that the comfort and security which comes with owning a home makes the cost seem reasonable.

19. The United States, together with Canada and some of the Latin-American countries, have the material resources for complete prosperity.

20. The structure of our politics and of our political traditions make any attempt at tariff reform very difficult.

EXERCISE 3

Follow the directions in Exercise 1.

1. Common sense, as well as economics, tell us that what a country sells to other countries must be balanced by what it buys from abroad.

2. The duties of the chief clerk includes authorization of overtime, arrangements for pay drafts, and handling the safe.

3. The material, mounted on large panels, explains the bases of the art of advertising; that is, how good design, coloring, and lettering attracts the customer.

4. We are pleased to say that all the necessary items, including clamps to pack the typewriter, has been shipped to you.

5. The data which we have gathered does not assist us in solving the problem.

6. In Fielding's work we often find little humorous touches that show the subtlety of his writing.

7. In the laboratory, the technician is able to perform various tests which, when combined with the proper clinical examination, diagnoses the case quickly and accurately.

8. The language, the approach, and the form of the sales letter is different for the various types of sale expected.

9. She wanted to send word that although her mother and father had been killed by the Nazis, she, with her husband and children, were alive.

10. A painting of the artist, as well as one of Borda and his priest brother, hangs on the wall at the rear of the church.

11. So far as finding the people who had been lost in the landslides were concerned, we had given up hope.

12. In 1910, there was constructed at Holtwood, Pennsylvania, a dam and a hydroelectric plant.

13. From the bottom of the Susquehanna River come deposits of fine particles of anthracite coal.

14. The full effect of the program will not be seen until a number of years has elapsed.

15. We live in one of those three-story houses that fronts on Moreland Drive and rents for $1800 a year.

16. Unified control of the three armed services are, according to the present plan, maintained under a single Secretary of Defense.

17. The rubber blades of the fan are not only a safety factor but adds to the quiet operation.

18. Mr. Eckels was one of the many people who was approached on the idea of buying a prefabricated house.

19. The rapid production methods and the mass construction used in building the prefabricated house keeps the price low.
20. Of all the women present, Mrs. Rutherford is the one who have done the best work.

12. PRONOUN AND ANTECEDENT AGREEMENT

12a. A pronoun should agree with its antecedent in gender, number, and person.

Our writing would be very dull if we repeated nouns again and again. Consequently, we use a pronoun instead of repeating the noun. But the meaning of the pronoun will not be clear unless it has the same gender, number, and person as the noun for which it stands. This noun is called the *antecedent*. (See Sections 1 and 2.)

> Orlon is an important synthetic material. It is said to be better than nylon. (*It* refers to *orlon,* the antecedent. Both *orlon* and *it* are neuter gender, singular number, third person.)

Pronouns do not necessarily agree with their antecedents in case.

12b. The words *each, either, neither, somebody, anybody, everybody,* and *nobody* are singular, and in formal English a pronoun referring to any one of these words should be singular (*he, his, him, she, her, it*).

In colloquial English the rule stated above has been relaxed somewhat. People who wish their language to sound informal and casual sometimes use *their* to refer to *everybody;* but this form should not appear in formal writing.

Colloquial: Everybody took *their* heavy coat to camp.
Formal: Everybody took *his* heavy coat to camp.
Colloquial: Each of the boxers was accompanied by *their* manager.
Formal: Each of the boxers was accompanied by *his* manager.

12c. *Who* refers to persons, *which* refers to things, and *that* refers to persons or things.

> The man *who* told me the story is your doctor.
> The book *which* you lent me contains some very exciting stories.
> The woman flier *that* took her plane on a round-the-world trip has been awarded a medal.

12d. *What* should not be used to refer to an expressed antecedent.

> Wrong: The book *what* you sent me as a graduation present arrived yesterday.
> Right: The book *that* you sent me arrived yesterday.
> Right: I heard *what* you said.

12e. A pronoun agrees with the nearer of two antecedents joined by *or* or *nor*.

> He loves everything or anybody *who* is connected with his work.
> In this cool room, neither the gardenia nor the roses will lose *their* freshness.

EXERCISE 4

Most of the following sentences contain errors in pronoun and antecedent agreement. Write on your paper the number of each sentence and the correction or corrections necessary. If a sentence contains colloquial expressions, change them to formal English. Write also an explanation of why you have made each change. If no correction is necessary in a sentence, write C beside the sentence number.

1. Everyone can spell if they try.
2. Every student must be in their place at 8:45.
3. Someone has forgotten their gloves.
4. The murder plays on television may not be true to life, but they are entertaining.
5. Anybody might be expected to lose their way on such a trip.

6. Everybody who goes to camp will enjoy their summer vacation.

7. We offer a money-back guarantee to each of our customers when he buys this new paint.

8. A business executive gets better work from their employees if they use a little kindness.

9. If next year's senior class has their way, the ruling will be changed.

10. There are many kinds of people who make pleasant guests.

11. When a company changes their system abruptly, they may cease to make money.

12. Everybody on the yacht awoke with slightly uncomfortable sensations in the pit of their stomachs.

13. The theater in Shakespeare's day was not so elaborate as they are today.

14. A student understands the national government better if they have a chance to participate in student government.

15. The football team has won every game they've played this year.

16. Every state, city, and town had a tremendous increase in their population.

17. We wondered how long it would take each of us to find our way around in a foreign country.

18. The diesel engine weighs much more than the gasoline engine, and therefore they are not used in automobiles.

19. The new television set was put into production early in October, and they are now being shipped to all parts of the country.

20. A thing which we all look forward to after a vacation is to tell your friends what a good time you had.

EXERCISE 5

Follow the directions in Exercise 4.

1. A person might become so much interested in radio serials that he would do anything to keep it on the air.

2. Sometimes when a person is restless, they turn on the radio and forget their restlessness.

3. In the early days, people believed in superstitions and thought that man had no business to poke their noses into scientific problems.

4. Fleas may cause cholera or bubonic plague if people are infested by them.

5. There were many boys besides me, and everyone was trying to get settled in their barracks.

6. The girls received as favors small keys of silver with the emblem of the club engraved on it.

7. The cars in the race are carefully checked to prevent anyone from slipping in a hot rod so that they can make new records.

8. The bill calls for the payment of ninety dollars a month to every veteran, regardless of their financial circumstances.

9. If a person works all the time and never plays, by the time they are in the prime of life, they are good for nothing.

10. Then the great ocean waves rolled on, continually washing the sand with its salty sprays.

11. Sometimes he turns on the porch light or the hall light and forgets to turn them off.

12. Any students who are interested should sign this sheet and indicate beside his name what courses he wishes to take.

13. In addition to qualifications for the job, one must also consider conditions under which you are willing to work.

14. To continue education under the G.I. Bill of Rights, one must have made satisfactory grades in all his courses.

15. Bacon introduced a new scientific approach to learning which would help everyone if they used it.

16. He broke down the hedges around his ground so that anybody who wanted fruit from the trees might gather whatever he liked.

17. Although I think that parties and dances are all right to a certain extent, I believe it is harmful when it is carried to excess.

18. When a person rides through our state, particularly in the industrial section, they are constantly going through ugly factory towns.
19. The television company wants to keep their color sets off the market for a time because they are not yet technically perfect.
20. A number of producers will piously pass resolutions proclaiming their interest in free enterprise, and then work hard to keep high tariff protection for its own product.

EXERCISE 6

Most of the following sentences contain errors in both verb and pronoun agreement. Write on your paper the number of each sentence and the necessary correction or corrections. Write also an explanation of why you have made each change. If no correction is necessary in a sentence, write C beside the sentence number.

1. Have either of the stenographers finished their work?
2. Each of the political machines are trying to put into office their chosen candidates.
3. Each of the boys have done what they were told to do.
4. When a child returns to school, one of the things in which he is interested at once is the sports.
5. Only one who has slept on such a bed know how hard they are.
6. Have either of you written your minutes?
7. Most of the time if a person riding in a train don't know the person sitting near him, they would not think of conversing.
8. The attendance and spirit at the games was never so great as it is now.
9. The data for your study has been compiled, and it will be submitted to you on Tuesday.
10. Every one of the students are required to pay their dues before May 1.
11. Each of the boys were eating their lunch when the coach entered the restaurant.

12. Each of the men after their appointment are given a course in business writing.
13. The maker of the prefabricated house says that the appearance of the house don't matter so long as they sell.
14. If any one of the employees is late, he must report at once to the supervisor.
15. Each of us, at one time or another, have expressed ourselves on the subject.

13. REFERENCE OF PRONOUNS

13a. A pronoun should refer unmistakably to a definite, expressed antecedent.

Sometimes the thought of a sentence is clear to the writer because he has the antecedent of his pronoun in his mind. The reader, however, cannot be expected to be a mind reader. He must be able to put his finger on the word to which the pronoun is meant to refer. Otherwise, he may misunderstand what he has read. Writing which is not perfectly clear to the reader is of little value. (See Sections 2 and 12.)

13b. The antecedent of each pronoun must be expressed, not merely implied.

Mrs. Seton told me the other day that she has taken a cottage at the seashore. He doesn't want to go, but she thinks the salt air will do him good.

Who is this *he?* No man has been mentioned. The antecedent is in the mind of the speaker.

Vague: I intend to be a lawyer because *it* is interesting work. (There is no antecedent for *it.*)
Improved: Because law is interesting work, I intend to be a lawyer.
Vague: I like to travel in Switzerland. *They* are always pleasant to visitors.
Improved: I like to travel in Switzerland. The Swiss are always pleasant to visitors.

3c. Avoid the indefinite use of *it* and *they*.

Indefinite: In this magazine article, it shows that war is horrible.

Better: This article shows that war is horrible.

Indefinite: They have good roads in Delaware.

Better: Delaware has good roads.

Vague: They say that Argentina is a wealthy nation.

Better: It is said that Argentina is a wealthy nation.

NOTE: *It* is sometimes used impersonally to introduce an idea. In these cases no antecedent is necessary.

It will be clear tomorrow.

It is necessary, it is true, it is certain, it is likely, it is imperative, are correct.

3d. Do not use impersonal *it* and the pronoun *it* in the same sentence.

Vague: We can send the refrigerator today, or we can keep it in the factory for a few days if *it* is necessary.

Better: We can send the refrigerator today, or we can keep *it* for a few days.

NOTE: In informal English, *it* sometimes refers to an idea instead of a single antecedent.

Informal: The boys were nervous, but they tried not to show it.

Formal: The boys were nervous, but they tried not to show their uneasiness.

3e. In formal writing avoid the use of *you* to mean people in general.

In colloquial or informal speech, expressions such as "You can see how important money is" or "Dancing makes you graceful" are permissible. Formal English requires the use of *one* or *anyone* in these statements.

Anyone can see how important money is.

Dancing makes one graceful.

13f. In formal writing avoid the use of *which*, *this*, *that* to refer to a whole clause.

> Informal: The company has had our entire building air conditioned, *which* makes working in ho weather very comfortable.
>
> Informal: We have rearranged the entire file, *which* wil make it easier to find things quickly.

In these sentences a whole statement is the anteceden of *which*. Such sentences can be improved in two ways.

1. Ahead of the word *which*, use *an act, a fact, a situa tion, a habit,* or *a procedure.* The noun preceding *which* will be its antecedent.

> Formal: The company has had our entire building air conditioned, a fact which makes working in ho weather comfortable.
>
> Formal: We have rearranged the entire file, a procedur which will make it easier to find things quickly.

2. Recast the sentence, omitting the word *which.*

> Improved: Because our building has been air-conditioned we can work in comfort during hot weather.
>
> Improved: Our new arrangement of the material in the fil makes it possible for us to find things quickly

NOTE: If the meaning is clear and the sentence would be come awkward or stilted if it were corrected, the informa construction may be used.

13g. Avoid ambiguous reference to either of two noun of the same gender.

> Vague: Howard told Arthur that he had been electec (Because *he* could mean either *Howard* or *A thur,* the sentence is not clear. It could be im proved by using *latter* or *former,* or by givin the exact words which Arthur said.)
>
> Improved: Howard told Arthur that the latter had bee elected.
>
> Improved: Howard said to Arthur, "You have been elected

Ambiguous reference can also be corrected by using a synonym for the antecedent or by changing the construction of the sentence.

Vague: He took the books from the boxes and placed *them* on the floor. (The books or the boxes?)

Improved: He took the books from the boxes and placed the volumes on the floor. (*Volumes* used as synonym for *books*.)

Improved: He removed the books and placed the boxes on the floor. (Construction changed.)

13h. Avoid the use of *same* as a pronoun. It should generally be used as an adjective (*same man, same house, same school*).

Wrong: Please fill out the blank and return same to us.

Right: Please fill out the blank and return it to us.

EXERCISE 7

Most of the following sentences contain errors in the use of pronouns and antecedents. Write on your paper the number of each sentence and the necessary correction or corrections. Write also an explanation of why you have made each correction. If no correction is necessary in a sentence, write C beside the sentence number.

1. In the Bible it tells us that there was a great flood.
2. When George met Frank, he was going to the football game.
3. In the story of *The Ancient Mariner,* Coleridge makes you feel that the supernatural is real.
4. He wrote about the common man, which in his day was a daring thing for a poet to do.
5. The teacher in charge of the corrective gymnasium work tries to correct your posture.
6. When the time came for me to go, I regretted it very much.
7. The people in this town don't do anything but play bridge.
8. In the guide book, it says that Florence has many famous art treasures.

9. When I visited Denver, I saw that they have very wide streets.
10. They have six theaters in our town.
11. The colonel is famous for telling humorous stories, and he gets it by remembering everything which he reads.
12. He called for aid from one of the men which stood on the shore.
13. Larry sent us some books which we enjoyed very much.
14. If the toaster won't work, we can't have it for lunch.
15. The lamp is very durable, which accounts for the low loss in breakage.
16. The building is poorly designed, which causes space to be wasted.
17. In this book it says that Jackson was a great general who never made a tactical mistake.
18. We had hot baths at the hotel, which for me was enough to make Dijon a landmark.
19. It has not been twenty years since the first house was built in this town, and it now contains 10,000 inhabitants.
20. The little girl asked her mother how old she was.

EXERCISE 8

Follow the directions in Exercise 7.

1. He was a businessman, and all his life he tried to make his son like it too.
2. Many students wanting to go to college have found it difficult to get in because they are so crowded.
3. My work in the senior year is very hard, but it is worth it to know that in June I shall graduate.
4. The poet Markham must have believed strongly in God because in his poems it mentions God frequently.
5. Our policy is to give service to members first, but to give it also to non-members when it is expedient.
6. Have your eyes examined; if you don't need them, the oculist will tell you.

7. The general thought well of him, which seemed to the young soldier quite a compliment.

8. John has lived many years in Tahiti, a circumstance which makes him a romantic figure to us.

9. Here, there are three food lines, which shortens the time spent in buying lunches.

10. When you walk through the halls, you can choose the person with whom you want to talk, which was not possible in our old school.

11. In mystery stories on the radio, criminals seem to be encouraged to continue their crimes, which is another reason why these programs should not be presented.

12. The grounds around the stadium are very small, and they have to walk miles from where they park.

13. The United States entered the war to make it safe for democracy.

14. Diggs and Haworth want the goods shipped by June 10, but we cannot do it.

15. If you are dissatisfied with the merchandise, return same at once.

16. The other day Daddy met his brother downtown driving his new car.

17. If Ed comes so early every morning, it makes the other employees seem lazy when they arrive at nine o'clock.

18. The staff officer's associates are usually well educated, honest, and industrious persons, which results in a smooth coöperation among them all.

19. Competitive gas companies are selling a large volume of gasoline, which indicates a large potential volume of sales for our service station if we build in this section.

20. When you reach the corner, read the signpost directions, which will keep you from turning off the road.

14. CASE OF PRONOUNS

There are three cases for nouns and pronouns: nominative, possessive, objective. Because nouns do not change their form to show the nominative or objective case, the rules given here are important chiefly for pronouns. (See section 2b.)

14a. The subject of a verb is in the nominative case. Th nominative forms are I, you, he, she, it, we, you, they.

Sarah and *I* have joined a club at school.
When Ned comes, *he* and *I* are going to build a boat.
We boys can do a better job without the girls.

14b. The pronoun following any part of the verb to (am, is, are, was, were, been, be) and referring to th subject is in the nominative case. It is called a predica nominative.

The officers of the class are Carol, Alfred, and *I*.
I am sure it was *he*.
Do you think it could have been *she* who sang on th radio last night?

NOTE: Colloquial English permits "It's me" or "It w him," but these forms should not appear in formal writin

14c. The object of a verb or a preposition is in the o jective case: me, you, him, her, it, us, them. (See Se tion 1g.)

Mother met Hilda and me at the station. (*Hilda* and *m* are objects of *met*.)
She had planned a big party for *us*. (*Us* is object of pre osition *for*.)
Between Hilda and me there has always been a re friendship. (*Hilda* and *me* are objects of prepositi *between*.)

NOTE: Common prepositions are *to, for, from, with, b between, near, beside, like,* and *but* when it means *excep* (See Section 5.)

Everybody came to the party but him. (Except him)

14d. The indirect object is in the objective case.

The indirect object is the object of *to* or *for* understoo

Uncle Fred sent *me* a bracelet from India. (*Bracelet* the direct object; *me* is the object of *to* understood
He offered *Mother* and *me* a trip to India to visit hi (Offered to Mother and me)

14e. The subject of an infinitive is in the objective case.

The infinitive is the form of the verb that usually has *to* in front of it—*to study, to write, to sing.* (See Section 3g.)

> I wanted *him* to run for class president. (The whole group of words is the object of *wanted; him* is the subject of *to run.*)
>
> Doris expected *me* to wait for her.
>
> Jack asked *me* to go to the dance.
>
> The music teacher let *Gordon and me* sing a duet. (A verb used after *let* is an infinitive although it is used without *to. Gordon and me* are subjects of the infinitive *to sing.*)
>
> My family will not let my *brother and me* go to cheap moving pictures.
>
> My father let *Jimmy and him* wash our car.

14f. The object of an infinitive or of any other verbal is in the objective case.

> The librarian wants to see *us.* (*Us* is the object of the infinitive *to see.*)
>
> Finding *you* here is a surprise. (*You* is the object of the gerund *finding.*)
>
> Having recognized *him* instantly, I hurried across the street. (*Him* is the object of the participle *having recognized.*)

14g. The objective complement of an infinitive is in the objective case.

> Aunt Jane took Lucy to be *me.*
>
> I thought you to be *him.* (If the subject of the infinitive is expressed, it is in the objective case. Then the objective case must follow *to be.* This construction is not frequently used and can be avoided if it is confusing.)

14h. An appositive must be in the same case as the word with which it is in apposition. (See Section 9.)

> The principal wants us all—Albert, Roland, and me—to run for the office. (*Albert, Roland, me,* are in apposition with *us* and must be in the same case.)

14i. The compound pronouns *myself, herself, himself, it-self, themselves, yourself, yourselves, ourselves* are used as intensive or reflexive pronouns.

Colloquial: Dave, Marian, and myself went on a picnic.

Formal: Dave, Marian, and I went on a picnic.

Colloquial: The party was for Dave, Marian, and myself.

Formal: The party was for Dave, Marian, and me.

Right: I'll make the sandwiches myself. (Intensive, for emphasis)

Right: The cat washed herself. (Reflexive. *Herself* refers to *cat*.)

NOTE: There are no words *hisself* or *theirselves*. The words to be used are *himself* and *themselves*.

14j. An elliptical clause with *than* or *as* requires the case called for by the complete clause.

In an elliptical clause in which the verb is omitted, the pronoun should be in the case which would be required if the clause were expressed in full.

Jack is taller than *I*. (Than I am.)

In this sentence the verb *am* is omitted but is understood. *I* is the subject of this omitted verb and therefore is in the nominative case.

Nobody cares more about you than *he*. (Than he does)

You are as good a student as *she*. (As she is)

Sometimes, as in the following example, the pronoun is used as the object of the understood verb.

I shall send him rather than *her*. (Than send her)

14k. The possessive case of a noun or pronoun should be used before a gerund. (See Section 3g.)

I do not approve of *his* playing football. (*Playing* is the gerund. It is the object of the preposition *of*.)

My teachers were not sure of my winning the prize. (*Winning* is the gerund.)

His singing could be improved. (*Singing* is the gerund.)

NOTE: Be sure to distinguish between gerund and participle. The latter is used as an adjective and does not have possessive case preceding it. We saw him standing on the corner. (*Standing* is a participle modifying *him*.)

CAUTION: *Them* is a pronoun and must not be used as an adjective.

Wrong: *Them* prizefighters put on a good show last night.
Right: *Those* prizefighters put on a good show last night.
Right: I enjoyed the good show put on by *them* last night.

EXERCISE 9

Most of the following sentences contain errors in the use of personal pronouns. Write on your paper the number of each sentence and beside it write the necessary correction or corrections. Write also an explanation of why you have made each correction. If no correction is necessary in a sentence, write C beside the sentence number.

1. One evening when Rosalie and me were home alone, we heard a strange noise.
2. We trembled for several minutes, but finally it was me who developed the courage to investigate.
3. I found that the children next door were trying to frighten Rosalie and I.
4. Although there was no danger, Mother didn't like to leave us girls alone after that experience.
5. Last week I saw Molly and he at the circus.
6. Sue, Phyllis, and myself were waiting for Zelda to come.
7. If anybody is late, it is always her.
8. There has always been trouble between Larry and he.
9. I think it was him who wrote the anonymous letter.
10. It could not have been him.
11. Even if Larry and him have trouble, I don't think boys like they ever feel depressed for very long.
12. Both Hugh and myself have been looking for a job.

13. Hugh found one sooner than me, but Joe and hi
were discharged a week later.

14. He didn't see them policemen until they were besid
our car.

15. Judy sent her first letter from Europe to Nelly and

16. Paula stopped to talk with Dad and I and to wish u
luck.

17. Since you invited Alice and I for a visit, her and
have made many plans.

18. At fifteen, Mary of Scotland married the dauphin c
France, who was a year younger than her.

19. Nobody besides myself has a copy of the article tha
my father wrote.

20. Yesterday Mr. Schmuck gave Aaron and I four passe
for *The Heiress*.

21. Aaron, Ben, and I decided to buy an additional sea
and invite Paula and Shirley.

22. Shirley disagreed with Ben and I in a discussio
about the story.

23. Finally it was her who gave in and let Ben and
have our way.

24. Do you remember me telling you about our Gle
Club?

25. It has given Happy and I many good times.

EXERCISE 10

Follow the directions in Exercise 9.

1. Yesterday my sister took pictures of my family an
myself.

2. The guard would not permit Alfred and he to ente
the building.

3. The Sherwoods want Judy and I to go with them t
Atlantic City.

4. The manager gave Miss Short and I complete direc
tions for the job.

5. There is no news of Major Tansig having taken th
city.

6. Nancy and me want to thank you for a wonderf
week end at the shore.

7. When the company gave Ed and her a bonus, they invested the money in good stocks.
8. It was hard for Beatrice and I to believe Dick's story.
9. Everybody went to the picnic but John and I.
10. I do not know anybody that I like better than him.
11. I am very glad it was she who won the contest.
12. We all expected the election returns to show the winner to be he.
13. I hope that the winner will be he.
14. When we arrived, everybody was talking about Janet and I.
15. We tried to prevent him enlisting in the army, but we had no success.
16. Let Ben and I work on the experiment because he and myself have done some similar experiments of our own.
17. How did the court prove it to be he that had helped the enemy?
18. Dad does not approve of Joe and I boxing.
19. A few days ago he told a group of we boys that forty-two boxers have died as a result of injuries.
20. "Every blow on the head," he told Joe and I, "causes damage to the brain."

41. The use of the case forms of the relative pronouns *who* and *whoever* (*who, whom, whose, whoever, whomever*) is determined by the way the pronoun is used in the relative clause which it introduces. (See Section 7b.)

1. In the following sentences, notice the use of the nominative case form *who:*

The sportsmen *who* sailed the boat over the rapids were Californians. (*Who* is the subject of the verb *sailed*.)

Our neighbor, *who* has just built a new ranch-type house, spent years in planning the structure. (*Who* is subject of the verb *has built*.)

It is difficult to see from here *who* the people are. (*Who* is predicative nominative; the people are *who*.)

2. As you have seen in the preceding example, the words in a relative clause are not always in their natural order. The natural word order in English sentences is

first the subject and then the predicate. It may help you
to understand relative clauses if you rearrange the word
order so that the subject comes before the verb.

The following examples show the use of the objective
case form *whom* in relative clauses. In studying these examples, rearrange the word order so that the subject precedes the verb.

> He is the boy *whom* we met at the game. (We met *whom*
> at the game. *Whom* is the direct object of the verb
> *met*.)
>
> Ernest, whom I told this story, did not believe me. (I
> told *whom* this story. *Whom* is the indirect object of
> the verb *told*.)
>
> The child to *whom* I gave the ring thanked me gravely.
> (I gave the ring to *whom*. *Whom* is object of the prep-
> osition *to*.)
>
> You are not the person *whom* I expected you to be. (I
> expected you to be *whom*. *Whom* is the objective com-
> plement after the infinitive *to be*.)

3. Sometimes a relative clause is interrupted by expressions such as *I feel certain, I think, he says, they believe*.
If such an expression can be omitted without interfering
with the thought of the relative clause, it is not a part of
the clause and does not affect the case of the relative pronoun.

> Mr. Scott is the salesman who I believe has the highest
> sales record.

In this sentence, *I believe* may be omitted without
changing the meaning of the relative clause *who has the
highest sales record*.

> Mr. Scott is the salesman who has the highest record.

The relative pronoun *who* is now easily recognized as
the subject of the verb *has*.

4. The following sentences show the use of the nominative form *whoever* and the objective form *whomever*.

The medal will be given to *whoever* has the highest grades. (The object of *to* is the whole clause *whoever has the highest grades*. *Whoever* is the subject of *has*.)

Send to the main office *whomever* you employ this morning. (*Whomever* is the object of *employ*.)

He tells the same old story to *whomever* he meets. (*Whomever* is the object of *meets*.)

4m. In using the case forms of the interrogative pronoun *who* (*who*, *whom*, *whose*), be sure that you understand how the pronoun is used in the sentence.

Who rode away from the ranch in the night? (*Who* is an interrogative pronoun used as subject of the verb *rode*. It is the nominative case form.)

Whose horse shall I ride? (*Whose* is the possessive case form of *who* and modifies the noun *horse*.)

The words in an interrogative sentence (See Section b) may not be in the usual order. Therefore, to understand their relation, rearrange the sentence, if necessary, so that the subject comes before the verb.

Whom did you send to the corral?

Rearranged, this sentence would read:

You did send *whom* to the corral?

In the preceding sentence, the interrogative pronoun is used as the direct object of the verb *did send* and is therefore in the objective case. Read the following sentences:

Whom is the saddle for? (The saddle is for *whom*? *Whom* is used as object of the preposition *for*.)

Whom did you think me to be? (You did think me to be *whom*? *Whom* is the objective complement after the infinitive *to be*.)

The sentences in the preceding examples are direct questions. In indirect questions (see Section 30b), the pronouns *who, whose,* and *whom* look like relative pronouns, but are interrogative pronouns.

I asked *who* was coming. (*Who* is an interrogative pro
noun used as subject of the verb *was coming*. Th
clause *who was coming* is a noun clause, object of th
verb *asked*.)

We wondered *whom* he would choose. (The interrogativ
pronoun *whom* is used as object of the verb *woul
choose*.)

EXERCISE 11

Most of the following sentences contain errors in th
use of relative or interrogative pronouns. Write on you
paper the number of each sentence and the necessary cor
rection or corrections. Write also an explanation of wh
you have made each correction. If no correction is neces
sary in a sentence, write C beside the sentence number

1. Who are you going to invite to the party?
2. That is the boy who we met at the game.
3. The guide who we hired in Washington showed u
   the Lincoln Memorial.
4. We could not decide who had made the best play.
5. I tried to get in touch with the carpenter who yo
   recommended.
6. Has William told you who the class selected as pre
   ident?
7. This is the man who I believe has promised to spea
   for us.
8. Whom could it have been?
9. Please let me know whom should be notified in cas
   of accident.
10. The woman has a child who she has not seen for fiv
    years.
11. Mrs. Corcoran is a very capable woman whom w
    think is doing a good job.
12. Who did you apply to?
13. He appeared with his brother and the girl who th
    latter is going to marry.
14. Your organization will be responsible for all prisoner
    no matter whom they are housed by.
15. Because the border was being changed constantl
    the people did not know who the land belonged to

16. In Beatrix, the author created a character whom the reader feels is alive and real.

17. I am sure that I could handle any children whom you would entrust to my care.

18. One of the counselors who you employed last year has trained me.

19. They gave the messages to all people who they thought should receive them.

20. In many countries people have so few privileges that they cannot even marry who they please.

21. An autobiography is a book written by the person who it is about.

22. The book was written by Dickens, whom, you know, is my favorite author.

23. Of all the famous literary characters, whom should you like to be?

24. Mr. Henderson is always fair to anybody who he works with.

25. That is the boy who I think you could use on the team.

EXERCISE 12

Most of the following sentences contain errors in the use of relative, interrogative, or personal pronouns. Write on your paper the number of each sentence and the necessary correction or corrections. Write also an explanation of why you have made each correction. If no correction is necessary in a sentence, write C beside the sentence number.

1. Whom did you say will ride your horse in the race?

2. How can a toad have the power to cause the growth of a wart on whomever touches it?

3. I should like to communicate with Major Eric Holdon, whom I understand is with the Ninety-fifth Division.

4. We carried word of the meeting to all the ranchers who we found at home.

5. We can secure coaches for whomever needs help with his work.

6. Mr. Sutton Ames is an honorable man respected by all those who he has any business with.

7. There was no doubt in the minds of the people about whom should be elected.

8. The company will give an award to whoever is the most rapid typist.

9. Can you recommend the man as one who I can trust?

10. We challenged the students of Newton High, who we thought we could beat easily.

11. Are you sure it was him who you saw downtown?

12. Whom do you consider to be the best writer in the class?

13. The carpenter who I employed was very rude to my mother and I.

14. Choose whoever you want; I am tired of the whole question.

15. We sent notices to all of our customers who our records show have purchased something in the last six months.

16. Two great women who the world will always remember are Florence Nightingale and Marie Curie.

17. Einstein said Marie Curie was the only one of all celebrated people who fame has not corrupted.

18. Marie Curie was one of a group of Polish girls for who learning had a great appeal.

19. She married Pierre Curie, whom everybody knows later won the Nobel Prize with her.

20. When she was about to be married, a friend who she was very fond of offered to give Marie a wedding dress.

21. The young scientist asked the friend who had made the offer to give her a dress that could be used later in her laboratory.

22. I shall be glad to employ whomever you feel sure will be best fitted for the job.

23. Mr. Cornell is a man who we regard highly because three of us, David, John, and I, know that he would do anything to help we three boys.

24. I have never known a man who people thought to have a greater chance of success, but he has failed

miserably because of misfortunes that came to both he and his family.

25. I employed the man who you recommended, but I later found both he and his brother to be thoroughly unreliable.

15. PRINCIPAL PARTS OF VERBS

Every verb has three *principal parts:* the present, the past, and the past participle. With these parts or the infinitive, every tense of verb can be formed. (See Section 3f.)

15a. Do not misuse the past tense and the past participle.

The past tense is used without an auxiliary (*have, has, is, was,* for example). The past participle is the third principal part of the verb and is used as a finite verb only with some part of *have* or *be.*

Present	Past	Past Participle
see	saw	seen
do	did	done

Right: I *saw* the flames reach the top of the building.
Right: The fireman *did* something very brave.
Wrong: I *seen* the flames reach the top of the building.
Wrong: The fireman *done* something very brave.

Seen and *done* are past participles and form tenses only with the aid of some part of the verb *have* or *be.*

Right: I *have seen* several cock fights.
Right: Herbert was praised because *he had done* a good job on the yearbook.
Wrong: I *have saw* several cock fights.
Wrong: Herbert was praised because he *had did* a good job on the yearbook.

Be careful not to use *of* for *have.*

Right: I could have gone to the circus last week.
Right: I could've gone to the circus.
Wrong: I could of gone to the circus.

17

15b. Do not confuse a strong verb with a weak verb.

Verbs which form the past tense and past participle by adding *ed*, *d*, or *t* to the infinitive are called *weak* or *regular*. Other verbs are *strong* or *irregular*. It is easy to make the mistake of adding *ed* to all verbs.

Right: He *drew* a bucket of water from the well.
Wrong: He *drawed* a bucket of water from the well.
Right: Last night the wind *blew* at thirty miles an hour.
Wrong: Last night the wind *blowed* at thirty miles an hour.

EXERCISE 13

Most of the following sentences contain errors in the use of the past tense and the past participle. Write on your paper the number of each sentence and the correction or corrections necessary. If no correction is necessary in a sentence, write C beside the sentence number.

1. We went to the hospital to see Mary, who had broke her arm.
2. What is the name of the girl who swum across the English Channel?
3. I never done a thing like that in my life.
4. She has tore the whole sleeve out of her dress.
5. I seen him go down the street just a few minutes ago.
6. I should of told you the whole story.
7. The letter was wrote on thin white paper.
8. I had already bit into the apple when I seen that it was rotten.
9. The boys had drunk all the milk that was in the icebox.
10. You should of gave him enough money.
11. Sue had never wore the dress before, and now it was tore to pieces.
12. The old woman taken a huge basket and set out for the store.
13. If you have broke the test tube, you must pay for it.
14. I have hid him in the closet so that Jerry cannot find him.
15. We rung and rung, but nobody came to the door.

16. We are worried about Anna because she hasn't eat a thing all day.
17. His balloon lay on the floor, bursted and tore.
18. "How far have you drove in this car?" asked the policeman.
19. We were sure that Angelo had stole the money.
20. When you have wrote the letter, put this stamp on it.
21. Jack was badly beat by another boy in the neighborhood.
22. When I heard of him last, he had become a great physician.
23. Have you ever rode in an airplane?
24. You must of knew that the chair would break.
25. He done the work so carefully that no corrections were needed.

15c. Learn to use correctly *lie* and *lay*, *sit* and *set*.

The principal parts of *lie, lay, sit,* and *set* are as follows:

lie	lay	lain
lay	laid	laid	(There is no word *layed.*)
sit	sat	sat
set	set	set

Lie and *sit* mean "rest" or "recline." They do not take an object.

I have been *lying* on the beach all day.
Yesterday I *lay* on the beach for only a short time.
Mother *lies* down every afternoon for an hour.
I *had* just *lain* down when the telephone rang.
Please *sit* here.
How long have you *sat* there?

Lay and *set* mean "place." They take objects.

Mr. Burke *laid* the notes on the desk before me.
I *set* the can of paint on the window sill.

NOTE: The sun *sets*.

The *setting* hen is a hen that has been placed on eggs.

EXERCISE 14

In the following sentences, choose the correct form of the verb *lie* or *lay*. On your paper write the number of each sentence and beside it write the correct verb form, if an incorrect form has been used. Write an explanation of every correction that you make. If a sentence is correct, write C beside the sentence number.

1. She laid down for an afternoon nap.
2. That paper has been lying on the lawn for a week.
3. Where did you lay the book? I can't find it.
4. Please excuse me. The doctor says I must lay down and rest every afternoon.
5. How long have you laid there in the sun?
6. The three silver dollars were laying on the counter.
7. Blown over by the wind, the little house lays on its side.
8. I never have the time to lay down during the day.
9. The wash was found laying on the porch.
10. The trash has laid in the alley for a week.
11. I had just laid down for a little rest when the telephone rang.
12. It was time to start for the station, but Tony still lay asleep under the tree in the yard.
13. A foreign ship has laid on its side in the harbor for two weeks.
14. Lay down, Rex. Be a good dog.
15. When I entered the room, the little boy laid with his face turned to the wall.

EXERCISE 15

In the following sentences, correct errors in the use of *sit* and *set* in the way that you corrected the sentences in Exercise 14:

1. If I set here much longer, I'll go crazy.
2. I wanted to sit out a row of plants before the sun was too high.
3. Set the basket on the table and come here.
4. Those women will set on the porch all day.

5. His eyes are so bad that he must set in the front row at the moving pictures.
6. Let's sit where we can see the harbor.
7. In Shakespeare's day, the people sometimes brought boxes to the theater to set on.
8. I was setting at the window crocheting when I saw Hilda coming up the path.
9. I sat my bundle on the ground and went after the boy.
10. Jervis used to set for hours listening to the water flowing into the cave.
11. While setting in his wheel chair with his drawings by his side, he collapsed.
12. Did you set the plants in straight rows?
13. I have never been so tired of setting in one place.
14. I had just set down to sew when Albert arrived.
15. He sat on the porch and rocked for two hours.

16. TENSE OF VERBS

Tense shows the time of the action. Unless the tenses are carefully used, the reader or listener will not understand what happened first or how long action continued. (See Section 3f.)

16a. The present tense is used to show action happening now.

He *hits* the ball.
I *see* Sally coming across the campus.

This tense is also frequently used for statements that are permanently true, or true at the time of the writing.

In *As You Like It*, Shakespeare *presents* the question of love at first sight. (Permanently true; the question continues to be presented whenever *As You Like It* is read.)
Unfortunately, we found that your credit rating *is* not up to our standards. (Although we *found* this fact in the past, it is still true.)

CAUTION: Although the present tense is occasionally used to make dramatic something that happened in the past, the tone of the material is often cheapened by the use of this device. *Never* tell a story by saying, "Then he says to me. . . . Then I says. . . ." Use "He *said* to me. . . . Then I said. . . ."

16b. The past tense shows action that was completed in the past.

We *won* the game.

Be careful when you tell a story not to shift from past to present.

> When Judy *appeared*,¹ she *was dressed*² in a filmy blue dress cut very low. We all *thought*³ she *looked*⁴ beautiful. In a few minutes the doorbell *rings*⁵, and in *comes*⁶ Stanley. (Verbs 1, 2, 3, 4, are in the past; 5 and 6 are in the present.)

16c. The present perfect (*have seen, has done*) is used for action that began in the past and has continued.

Bob *has written* to us every week for several years.
The ice *has been* too thin for skating.

CAUTION: Use the present perfect tense, not the simple present tense, to indicate time starting in the past and continuing to the present.

Wrong: He is studying French for several years, but he cannot say a word of the language.
Right: He *has been studying* French for several years, but he cannot say a word of the language.

16d. The past perfect (*had written, had finished*) indicates action that occurred in the past before some other action that happened in the past.

All the roads were blocked because the snow *had fallen* fast. (It *had fallen* before the roads were blocked.)
In April they *repaired* the streets which *had cracked* during the storm.

Notice the three different tenses required in the following sentence:

> I *wrote* (past tense) to Helen to tell her that Edith *had been* (past perfect) very ill, but I *have heard* (present perfect) nothing from her.

16e. To express a simple future (expectation) use *shall* with *I* and *we*, and *will* with all other subjects. (*Should* is usually used like *shall*, and *would* like *will*.)

> Be careful; the fireworks *will burn* your hand.
> I *shall* be twenty in July.
> I *should* be very glad to come for an interview at your convenience.

To express strong feeling, determination, promise, command, use *will* with *I* and *we,* and *shall* with all other subjects.

> He *shall* not go to the party unless he has finished his work.
> I *will* not go to that school; I don't like it.

NOTE: In informal English *will* is frequently used with all subjects in the future tense.

16f. *Should* is used with all subjects to express obligation or duty or to express a condition in an *if* clause.

> I *should* read more than I do.
> If I *should* win the contest, we could go to Bermuda.
> If he *should* win the contest, he would have a good career ahead.

16g. Use *would* with all subjects to express habitual action.

> He *would* go to the gardens day after day.
> When we were in Paris, we *would* always have coffee at a little sidewalk cafe.

16h. The future perfect tense is used to indicate that an action or a condition will have been completed by some time in the future.

> I *shall have learned* to ride by the time that you come.
> The snow *will have melted* before we start.

16i. Use a present infinitive unless you wish the infinitive to express time before the main verb.

I intended *to see* (not *to have seen*) you about the exam.

16j. A present participle expresses action which takes place at the same time as the action expressed in the predicate verb. The present perfect participle usually expresses action which began before the action in the predicate verb.

Illogical: *Starting* school at eight, he finished at eighteen. (He did not start at the same time at which he finished).

Logical: *Having started* school at eight, he finished at eighteen. (Present perfect participle)

Illogical: Moving to Charleston, we found the town delightful.

Logical: Having moved to Charleston, we found the town delightful.

EXERCISE 16

In the following sentences, correct any errors in verb tense by writing the correction and the reason for the correction beside the sentence number on your paper. If a sentence contains no error, write C beside the sentence number.

1. My son rushed into the room, grabs his coat, and goes dashing down the hall.
2. A few minutes elapsed; then as suddenly as the storm appeared, it disappeared.
3. It has been very cold since we are here.
4. I am waiting for this dance for three weeks.
5. When we entered our cabin, we found some thief made off with our supplies.
6. Terry lives in New Mexico now. He is there for nearly two years.
7. I expected to have gone to Richmond for the holidays.
8. On Saturday, I discussed with Mr. Kelpert the material which he presented to the committee on Friday.
9. From 1934 until now, he was director of the James Newell Hospital.

10. After some discussion, we decided that real happiness did not lie in material things, but in things of the spirit.

11. Leaving the Capitol, we went to the National Art Gallery.

12. Lady Castlewood thought that her husband's coldness was due to the fact that she lost her beauty when she had smallpox.

13. If they realized how ridiculous it was to believe in superstitions, people could save themselves many worries.

14. When I reached home yesterday, I was greatly surprised to find the pair of ice skates you sent me.

15. If anyone found out what Samuel Pepys said in his diary, the writer would have been beheaded.

16. When Alex came of age, the Cossack society of free people was no longer so free as it once had been.

17. People in white seemed to be everywhere in the hospital, but no sound is heard.

18. When the respirometer started, the surgeon nods to the nurse, and she hands him the instruments.

19. Being built a hundred years ago, the hotel was finally considered unsafe.

20. I fed the lost dog as I fed my country dogs ten years ago, and he come along all right.

21. I preferred to have told her nothing, but she dragged the information from me.

22. Since the days of Adam, one of the most common of human pastimes is the criticism by old people of the habits of the young.

23. Starting out on foot, Sue reached Tampa at dusk.

24. Today is Sarah's birthday. I intended to send her a card.

25. The Cossack later enjoyed better food and better clothes than he ever could in the poverty-stricken village from which he fled.

EXERCISE 17

In the following sentences, correct all errors in the use of *shall, will, should,* and *would.* Follow the method of correction given for Exercise 16.

1. I think I shall see Doris tomorrow.
2. If you are not careful, you shall burn your fingers.
3. John will be present tomorrow if I have to drag him to the meeting.
4. I am determined that he will not go to the game.
5. I would be very grateful for any assistance which you can give me.
6. I am sure that my committee shall present a sensible bill to the Senate.
7. I promise that I shall write to you every day.
8. We will be pleased to discuss the plans whenever you are ready.
9. I will be very happy to make an appointment for you with the governor.
10. Before we move, we will have a sale of all the stock in our old store.
11. I assure you we shall do everything in our power to make your visit in our hotel a memorable one.
12. If there is any special service that will make your stay pleasant, I will be happy to arrange for it.
13. I would think that you would find it very pleasant to live in the hotel where you work.
14. We will send your order as soon as possible.
15. As soon as the shoes are repaired, we shall send them to you with the bill.
16. We will be very glad to have you consult with us at any time.
17. We would like to ship your order at once, but a shortage of materials prevents our filling new orders at this time.
18. If you will write your name and address on the inclosed card, I shall send you a copy of our booklet.
19. We will need some information concerning your credit standing before we can open an account for you.
20. I am afraid that I will fail in French.
21. We would be very grateful for your prompt payment.
22. Since I am familiar with the apparatus used in a dentist's office, I should not have to be taught how to use it.

23. We will be pleased to place your name on our mailing list.
24. I would like to apply for the job advertised in yesterday's *News*.
25. I shall consider it a personal favor if you will permit me to send you samples of our merchandise.
26. We hope that we will hear from you and wish to assure you that we will give you our best services on all occasions.
27. We would like to see you; so why not pay us a visit?
28. If you cannot get tickets for the first balcony, get them in the orchestra; and I shall pay you when I see you.
29. If we win the game this afternoon, I will receive a star to place beside my major letter.
30. I shall definitely stick to tennis this summer, and maybe in the fall I will be able to enter the club tournament.

17. MOOD

The mood of the verb indicates the manner in which a statement is made. Every verb has three moods, the indicative, the imperative, the subjunctive. (See Section 3e.)

17a. Use the indicative mood to state a fact or to ask a question of fact.

The maple tree *is* tall.
Jane *sang* a song.
Who *started* the rumor?

17b. Use the imperative mood to express a command or a request (*go, open, shut, sing*).

Shut the door.
Open a window.

17c. Learn to recognize the subjunctive forms.

Present Indicative		*Present Subjunctive*	
I am	we are	(if) I be	(if) we be
you are	you are	(if) you be	(if) you be
he is	they are	(if) he be	(if) they be

The past indicative of the verb *to be* and the past subjunctive of that verb can be seen below:

Past Indicative		*Past Subjunctive*	
I was	we were	(if) I were	(if) we were
you were	you were	(if) you were	(if) you were
he was	they were	(if) he were	(if) they were

In most verbs, the difference between the present indicative and the present subjunctive shows in the third person singular. In the forms given below, notice that in the third person singular, the present subjunctive does not end in *s*.

Indicative		*Subjunctive*	
I come	we come	(if) I come	(if) we come
you come	you come	(if) you come	(if) you come
he comes	they come	(if) he come	(if) they come

17d. Use the subjunctive mood to express a wish.

> I wish I *were* a good driver.
> He wishes he *were* tall.

17e. Use the subjunctive mood to express a condition contrary to fact.

> If I *were* you, I'd refuse to let her use my work.
> If we *were* at home, we could consult our unabridged dictionary for the derivation of the word.

(I am not you. We are not at home. Hence the statements in the preceding examples are contrary to fact.)
NOTE: The subjunctive is used also to suggest a condition that is improbable, though not completely contrary to fact.

> Suppose he were to tell the whole story!

CAUTION: Not every clause that begins with *if* requires a subjunctive.

> If the actress *is* limited, still in her field she is very talented. (Statement of fact)

17f. Use the subjunctive after *as though*, *as if*, to express doubt or uncertainty.

> He talks as if he *were* the only intelligent person in the group.
> She looked as if she *were* completely exhausted.

NOTE: Do not use a subjunctive after every *though*. The clause must express doubt or uncertainty.

> Even though he *is* deaf, he doesn't have to shout. (Indicative)

17g. Use the subjunctive in *that* clauses expressing necessity, mild command, or a parliamentary motion.

> I move that the committee *be* appointed by the president.
> It is essential that he *appear* at the meeting.
> The committee insisted that he *tell* the whole story.
> I suggest that the topic *be* considered at our next meeting.

17h. In parallel constructions, do not shift the mood of verbs.

> Wrong: If I were in your position and *was* offered a trip to Europe, I'd certainly go. (Change *was* to *were*.)

EXERCISE 18

Correct errors in the mood of verbs in the following sentences. On your paper, write the correct form beside the sentence number and write your reason for the correction. If no correction is necessary in a sentence, write C beside the sentence number.

1. If I was Sandy, I'd train that spaniel.
2. Many times he wished he was back in his old job.
3. If her mother was well, she would go with us to the picnic.
4. If I was transferred to the Polytechnic Institute, I could get the algebra which I need.
5. If I was you, I'd stay away from Jane.
6. I could do the job more quickly if I was not annoyed constantly by my neighbor's radio.
7. I move that he is reinstated at once.

8. My neighbor, who is eighty-five, acts as if she was a woman of thirty.
9. She looked as if she was frightened to death.
10. I request that my son is released from the army as soon as possible.
11. If he rides broncos, he must expect some falls.
12. The law requires that he signs the papers.
13. He acts as if he was president of the university.
14. If your work was done carefully, you would get a promotion.
15. The company wishes that it was able to fill the order at once, but the materials are not available.
16. If Mother's health were better, we could make some plans for the summer.
17. He wrote his autobiography just as if he was writing about somebody else.
18. If he was elected, why didn't you tell me?
19. I insist that I am given a new assignment.
20. Often I wish I was able to sing as Todd can.

EXERCISE 19

Follow the directions in Exercise 18.

1. If Howard was a college student, he would be accepted by the medical school.
2. The company requests that he pays his bill at once.
3. Though he works hard, he does not get promoted.
4. I am sure that Catherine is not married. Her mother would tell us if she was.
5. If I was not so nervous, I should not mind speaking before an audience.
6. Mr. Sommers asks that action is delayed until more information can be obtained.
7. The man's face was so red that he looked as if he was going to have a stroke of apoplexy.
8. Eloise insists that her sister is told at once the news of the tragedy.
9. I wish Elinor was taller. She grows very slowly.
10. There was so much noise that it seemed as if everybody was shouting at once.

11. If he is such good company, why don't you invite him to the party?
12. If the situation seem a bit absurd, remember that there are stranger things in life than in novels.
13. If our committee were more serious-minded, we should accomplish more than we do.
14. As the people looked out over the Mediterranean, it seemed as if Corsica was rising from the sea.
15. If the country is interested in wise laws, it must send men of wisdom to its law-making body.
16. If I was sure to fail, I think I should have been told.
17. If he was sorry for Ed, he showed no evidence of his feeling.
18. If he was sorry for Ed, he would help the boy in some way.
19. If the states be serious in a desire to establish peace, let their sincerity be evinced by their public conduct.
20. If the machine was shipped on Tuesday, I should have been notified.

18. ADJECTIVE AND ADVERB USAGE

Most errors in the use of adjectives and adverbs are the result not of ignorance, but of carelessness. They are made because people develop bad speech habits as a result of what they hear among careless friends or co-workers. Remember that whenever you want a word that tells *how* something is done, you need an adverb. Most adverbs telling *how* end in "ly." (See Section 4.)

The President acted *wisely* in the crisis.
Scientists have worked *carefully* in their search for new drugs.
We must walk *rapidly* if we are to reach the station in time.

18a. An adjective modifies a noun or pronoun.

A *free* ticket
A *careless* speaker
Tired but *cheerful*, we reached the top of the mountain.
  (The adjectives *tired* and *cheerful* modify the pronoun *we*.)

18b. An adverb modifies a verb, an adjective, or another adverb.

We want you to speak *freely*. (Modifies infinitive)
He spoke *carelessly*. (Modifies verb)
Sue has a *very* free manner. (Modifies adjective *free*)
Morton spoke *too* carelessly. (Modifies adverb *carelessly*)

18c. Do not use an adjective to modify another adjective.

Wrong: I *sure* am glad to see you.
Right: I *surely* am glad to see you.
Wrong: He's *some* fat.
Right: He's *very* fat.
Wrong: I'm so tired that I'm *most* dead.
Right: I'm so tired that I'm *almost* dead.
Wrong: The poor fellow looked *real* happy when he saw us.
Right: The poor fellow looked *very* happy when he saw us.

NOTE: Not all words ending in *ly* are adverbs. *Lovely* and *holy*, for example, are adjectives.

EXERCISE 20

Correct errors in the use of adjectives and adverbs in the following sentences. On your paper, write the correct word or words beside the sentence number and write your reason for each correction. If no correction is necessary in a sentence, write C beside the sentence number.

1. Some people take life too serious.
2. Everything went off perfect, but we sure were worried.
3. He rides a horse real wild.
4. A student must watch his grammar very close.
5. Why don't you speak plain?
6. We tried to bring the plane in and have it land smoothly.
7. The woman was dressed poor and unattractive.
8. We are afraid that Tom won't make the team because he doesn't play very good.
9. I think she sings lovely.
10. Doesn't Howard skate beautiful?

18d. After verbs such as *smell, taste, feel, sound, look,*
appear, become **(used intransitively), use an adjective if**
the word describes the subject and an adverb if the word
describes the action in the verb.

He looked *cold* standing in the snow. (Describes *he*)
He looked *coldly* at me and left the room. (Tells how he
    looked)
I feel *awkward* when people look at me.
I felt *awkwardly* in pocket after pocket.
The cake tastes *good.* (Adjective)
The flower smells *sweet.* (Adjective)

NOTE: Badly is often misused after *feel.*

Right: I feel *bad.* (*Sick* or *wicked*)
Right: Arthur spells *badly.*

Some words may be either adjectives or adverbs:
cheap, fast, deep, wrong, well, tight, hard, fair, first, slow,
loud. Some of these also have forms in *ly: slowly, loudly.*
The *ly* forms are preferred as adverbs in formal English.
Do not say *firstly, secondly; first* and *second* are preferable. *Well* is an adjective when it means the opposite of
sick. It is an adverb when it tells how something is done.
Never use *good* to tell how something is done.

Right: You acted *well* in the play.

18e. Be accurate in the use of comparatives and superla-
tives.

Most adjectives and adverbs change their forms to
show a greater or smaller *degree* of the quality they indicate. This change is called *comparison.* There are three
degrees of comparison: *positive, comparative,* and *super-*
lative.

Positive Degree	Comparative Degree	Superlative Degree
cool (adj.)	cooler	coolest
soon (adv.)	sooner	soonest

In comparisons that indicate *less* of a quality, the words
less and *least* are used with all adjectives and adverbs
that can be compared.

	Comparative	Superlative
Positive Degree	Degree	Degree
fast (adj. or adv.)	less fast	least fast

Most adjectives and adverbs of one syllable form the comparative and superlative degrees by the addition of *er* and *est* to indicate *more* of a quality.

Adjectives and adverbs of more than one syllable often form the comparative and superlative degrees with the use of *more* and *most*.

	Comparative	
Positive Degree	Degree	Superlative Degree
necessary (adj.)	more necessary	most necessary
awkward (adj.)	more awkward	most awkward
handsomely (adv.)	more handsomely	most handsomely
intelligently (adv.)	more intelligently	most intelligently

However, some adjectives and adverbs of two syllables may also form the comparative and superlative degrees by the addition of *er* and *est* to the positive degree.

heavy (adj.)	heavier	heaviest
early (adj. or adv.)	earlier	earliest

(See Section 39g for an explanation of the change of *y* to *i* in the preceding examples.)

Some adjectives and adverbs are compared irregularly.

good (adj.)	better	best
bad (adj.)	worse	worst
badly (adv.)	worse	worst
well (adv.)	better	best

1. The comparative is used when two persons or objects or actions are being compared; the superlative is used when more than two are compared.

> I bought two new dresses. Which do you think is *more becoming?*
> Which of your eyes has *better* vision?
> The sorrel horse galloped *faster* than the bay.
> He is the *most brilliant* student in the class.

2. Avoid double comparatives and superlatives; that is, do not use *more* or *most* before a word to which *er* or *est* has been added to form the comparative or the superlative.

> Wrong: He is more happier than his brother.
> Right: He's happier than his brother.

3. Choose the comparative form carefully. Do not confuse the comparative of an adjective with the comparative of an adverb.

> Wrong: He learns things easier than Gertrude does.
> Right: He learns things more easily than Gertrude does.

4. A few adjectives like *round, square, unique,* are logically incapable of comparison because their meaning is absolute. An object is either round or not round. It cannot logically be rounder. However, because these words have, in a measure, lost their superlative force, they are often compared in informal English, and even good writers use adverbs like *quite, completely,* before them.

5. Avoid including the subject compared, if the subject is part of a group with which it is being compared. Use *other* or *else* in such cases.

> Illogical: Butte is larger than any city in Montana.
> Better: Butte is larger than any *other* city in Montana.
> Illogical: Andrew is younger than anyone in the school.
> Better: Andrew is younger than anyone *else* in the school.

18f. *These* and *those* **are plural forms and should not be used to modify singular nouns.**

> Illogical: *These* kind of dogs are fine for hunting.
> Better: *This* kind of dog is fine for hunting.
> Better: *These* kinds of dogs are fine for hunting.

Do not use *here* or *there* after the adjectives *this* or *that.*

> Wrong: This here man is guilty.
> Right: This man is guilty.

The use of *a* or *an,* after *this kind* or *this sort* is not desirable in formal English.

Undesirable: This kind of a day always depresses me.
Better: This kind of day depresses me.

NOTE: *These kind of people* is accepted by some writers as standard informal English.

18g. Be careful of the adjectives *fewer* and *less*.

Less refers to quantity and is used with singular nouns (*less money, less food, less sugar*). *Fewer* refers to number and is used with plural nouns (*fewer people, fewer animals*).

18h. In formal English *due* is used as an adjective modifying a noun.

The old woman said that her good health was *due* to careful exercise. (*Due* modifies *health*.)

The woes of the world are *due* to poor thinking. (*Due* modifies *woes*.)

The expression *due to* is often used as a preposition, especially in news reports, radio talks, and business letters.

Informal: We have been unable to ship your order *due to* a strike in the factory.

Informal: The business has expanded *due to* the energy and hard work of our salesmen.

18i. Be careful not to use too many adjectives or adverbs.

The overuse of adjectives and adverbs will weaken your writing. Try to use strong, colorful verbs which will express your meanings without the help of many modifiers.

EXERCISE 21

Follow the directions in Exercise 20.

1. When you go to look for a job, act natural.
2. Jerry learns so quick that I am sure he will make a good salesman.

3. My dog Smoky sure has cost me a lot of money this summer.

4. Everybody at the party was dressed real nice.

5. Did you sleep good last night?

6. When I send for you, I expect you to come prompt.

7. After the war, the people in England had to live very frugal.

8. If any of the pictures turn out good, I'll send them to you.

9. This here picture is not very clear.

10. The new office is arranged so effectively that no steps are wasted.

11. An army must do its planning thorough in order to demolish the enemy.

12. Rachel is more patient than anybody in her class in school.

13. Do you think that any of the comics are written good?

14. The sports comics try to teach the lesson of how to live healthy.

15. One of our big problems today is whether the schools are educating young people satisfactory.

16. There would be less absentees if the students took their work more serious.

17. I always write faster than Lew, but his penmanship is more clearer than mine.

18. Most all filling stations do general repair work on automobiles.

19. I surely do feel bad today.

20. The spaghetti tastes appetizingly if it is cooked with tomato sauce.

21. You came into the room so sudden that you frightened me.

22. Our sales campaign has been extraordinary successful.

23. Matilda looked uneasy; I'm sure something was worrying her.

24. Ted looked around uneasy as if he thought he was being watched.

25. These kind of people are always ready to criticize others severe.

EXERCISE 22

Follow the directions in Exercise 20.

1. The surgeon performed the operation as skillful as he could.
2. My cousin's manners improved considerable during his stay in camp.
3. Trenton has just built a large, municipal-owned stadium.
4. The most favorite book of George Eliot was the Bible.
5. The success of a democratic nation is dependent upon citizens who vote intelligent.
6. We wish to educate our voters to think independent and not be attached secure to the political bosses.
7. I think this paper is arranged much neater than yours.
8. The store has ordered these two types of material. Which do you consider most durable?
9. Every year there are less opportunities in the business world for people over fifty.
10. By now, I suppose the Florida sun has tanned you wonderful and given you a real healthy appearance.
11. Stephen has been extraordinary successful with his engineering experiments.
12. I'm not near so tired as I was yesterday.
13. I was brought up so strict that I never had a date until I was twenty.
14. The cantaloupes of our state are uniform good fruit, but they are not always graded careful.
15. I never understood the war situation because I was real young at the time.
16. Your invitation sounds very pleasantly, but Mother has felt badly all day and I cannot leave her.
17. I feel very strong about all questions involving the relationship between labor and capital.
18. My violin sounds different from yours.
19. One of the salespeople was reprimanded because she was acting impertinent to customers.
20. Because we have had no ice all day, the milk tastes sour.

21. The cook tasted the soup careful and then added more pepper.
22. The Italian lecturer spoke English plainer than some of my friends do.
23. The posters used by the advertising department of our competitors are not near so attractive as ours.
24. Does the decision appear sudden to you?
25. International ethics used to require a declaration of war before fighting began, but now the attacking nation simply walks in unexpected on its prey.

19. PREPOSITION AND CONJUNCTION USAGE

The most common errors in the use of prepositions and conjunctions are made in two ways:

1. By confusing a preposition with a conjunction in usage. The choice between *like* and *as,* or between *without* and *unless,* is an example.

2. By choosing the wrong preposition to accompany certain words. Use *different from,* not *different than,* for example.

19a. In written English use *like* as a preposition or a verb, not as a conjunction.

Although *like* is frequently used as a conjunction in colloquial, casual English, the best speakers and writers still prefer to use *as* or *as if* when a clause follows.

Colloquial: The aviator opened his parachute and dropped to the ground just *like* he had wings.
Formal: The aviator opened his parachute and dropped to the ground *as if* he had wings.
Colloquial: Sarah's friends were interested in books and travel *like* she was.
Formal: Sarah's friends were interested in books and travel *as* she was.
Right: Jane looks *like* her father. (Preposition)
Right: You are behaving *like* a baby. (Preposition)

As is a preposition when it means "in the role of." Notice, however, the difference in meaning:

Right: He acts *like* a madman.
Right: He acts *as* the madman in the play.
Right: He acts *like* the chairman of the club.
Right: He acts *as* the chairman of the club.

Like should not be used in place of the conjunction *that*.

Right: I always felt *that* Roger would be successful.
Wrong: I always felt *like* Roger would be successful.

19b. Use *unless* as a conjunction, *without* as a preposition.

Right: The crops will die *without* rain.
Right: The crops will die *unless* we have rain soon.
Right: We will not rent the apartment *without* a redecoration.
Wrong: We will not rent the apartment *without* you redecorate for us.

19c. Use the correct preposition with special words.

Agree	*To* a proposal
	On a plan
	With a person
Differ	*With* a person
	From something else
Compare	*To* something like the subject
	With something to show differences and likenesses
In regard to	(not *in regards to*)

The Blank, Rischler Company *agreed* to our suggestion to begin the work on January 1.

Mr. Southern *differs with* you. He thinks that we are not ready for expansion.

This plan differs *from* the first one in many details.

In the book review, Steinbeck was compared *to* Chekhov.

Compare Steinbeck *with* Chekhov and write a paragraph on your conclusions.

NOTE 1: A good dictionary will show the correct prepositions to be used with many words.

2: In casual English, it is all right to use a preposition at the end of a sentence, but it should not be an unnecessary preposition.

Wrong: Where are you going to?
Right: Where are you going?
Right: What are you writing with?

EXERCISE 23

From each pair of words or expressions in parentheses in the following sentences, choose the correct word or expression and write it on your paper beside the sentence number. Write also your reason for each choice.

1. He cannot pitch well (without, unless) he warms up thoroughly.
2. Did you have my suit cleaned (like, as) I told you to do?
3. We didn't feel (like, that) this city was large enough to handle the convention.
4. The Sewells are really just neighbors, but they act (like, as if) they were part of our family.
5. The company has said nothing (in regards to, in regard to) the repair of my watch.
6. The poor man never answers (without, unless) he first knows what his wife is going to say.
7. The team is shaping up nicely, but it doesn't yet look (like, as if) it will be a championship team.
8. The doctor says that the patient will die (unless, without) he gets better attention.
9. The awnings will be torn to pieces (without, unless) you pull them up at once.
10. Your answer to the problem looks (like, as if) it should be correct.
11. Joel was eighteen, and (as, like) most boys his age, he was looking for excitement.
12. The scenery in Puerto Rico was different (than, from) anything I had ever seen.
13. He feels (like, that) the world is against him.
14. We rode the first five waves (like, as if) we were on a roller coaster.

15. My Canadian friends at camp were very much (like, as) me. They didn't seem to come from a country different (than, from) mine.

20. ACHIEVEMENT TESTS IN USAGE

20a. Achievement Test I (Sections 11–14).

Write on your paper the number of each sentence. Beside the number, write the correction or corrections necessary and give the reason for each correction. Write the whole sentence only when a complete revision is necessary. If a sentence contains no errors, write C beside its number.

Examples:
1. Every one of the students have their own lockers.
2. Hazel lives near Bernice and I.

Correction:

1. has	1. subject and verb agreement
his own locker	pronoun and antecedent agreement
2. me	2. object of preposition *near*

1. One of my favorite actors is Alfred Lunt, whom you know often performs with his wife.
2. The violinist who I should select as my favorite was a child prodigy.
3. Since the cause of many diseases are unknown, a number of medical men is kept busy in research.
4. There's many ways to solve a problem, but everybody thinks that their way is the right one.
5. The company announced that every employee could receive their bonus by stopping at the cashier's desk.
6. The first coffee house in London was established in 1652, but they didn't reach their peak of popularity until the eighteenth century.
7. Everybody packed their own lunch and met the bus at Tenth Street.
8. I am sure that the party will be a success and every one will enjoy themselves.
9. Why don't you come to spend a few days with Mother and I?

10. The business, including the shop, the goods on hand, and all the fixtures, were sold for $50,000.
11. I don't know who he could be.
12. You are expected to send the papers to Mr. Henderson and I at once.
13. This town can say that as far as they know, every one of the inhabitants are employed.
14. The transit company is replacing cars with busses and therefore have many more vehicles to keep in repair.
15. Unless payment is made in ten days' time, we must turn it over to our attorneys.
16. It must have been him who told you the story.
17. The air was impure which was caused by smoke.
18. Florence Nightingale, who we recognize as the founder of the nursing profession, faced unbelievable difficulties.
19. The garden has been completely rearranged, which ought to give Jane and I a chance to win the contest.
20. Dan went with his brother to the office, where he told the whole story to the principal.
21. The fact that the stories are illustrated by pictures make the magazine interesting.
22. Rickets are prevented by butter and cod liver oil, which contains vitamin A.
23. Mr. Sherwood is studying the question of who we should appoint as director.
24. Every one of us were told that we must pay for the laboratory materials which we lost.
25. At the end of the book it tells that two of the girls was married.
26. Mother decided to let Carol and I go to the circus.
27. Many people are today admirers of swing music, which explains why a concert of this music is given each year at the Lyric Theater.
28. The beautiful scenery with its snow-capped mountains, green pastures, and blue lakes remind him of Switzerland.
29. The number of people who attended the meetings regularly were only fifty.
30. The electron, as well as the proton, were shown to carry electrical charges.

31. The privilege of voting is ignored by many people, and consequently there is in many legislative bodies corrupt politicians sent there by the bosses.

32. If between you and I no compromise is possible, there seems little chance of us doing any business.

33. The prize will be given to whoever makes the largest number of sales.

34. Enclosed is some of our business reply envelopes on which is printed our new address and the name of our new manager.

35. Fred does not want Henry and I to go with him.

36. Of all the contestants, Bert is the only one whom we think have followed the directions exactly.

37. Do not refer to us, Emma and I, as stage-struck juveniles.

38. I am sure that one of the men who is present is the guilty person.

39. George's father, whom I understand once led a band, taught Frank and I to play.

40. It wasn't until last evening that everyone knew their parts and Jack and myself breathed freely again.

41. When the ballots have been counted, please send a report to the principal, who will forward same to the Secretary of the Youth Commission.

42. I was told to give the message to whomever was in the office.

43. Besides the thrill of seeing a stretch of beautiful land, it is probably interesting from an historical point of view.

44. Cataloguing and arranging our specimens for the exhibit has kept my brother and I busy during the whole summer.

45. While we were playing baseball one Saturday afternoon, Howard and myself was asked to join the Brooklyn Dodgers.

46. After three months in this business, I begin to feel at least like one of the people who really belongs to the organization.

47. An inspection has been made in order to determine whether the size and layout of the new steel plant is likely to contribute to efficiency.

48. Complete meteorological data for the site of the airport is available through the Civil Aeronautics Authority.
49. If each of the members of the committee do their work carefully, we shall have an excellent report.
50. The results of the inspection, as covered by the attached report, indicates that the buildings of the plant is in satisfactory condition.

0b. Achievement Test II (Sections 11–19).

Follow the directions for Achievement Test I.

1. Every cat and dog in five counties were quarantined.
2. If it had been necessary, Jim could have beat any of the men.
3. The party at Goldie's house was better than any party we have had.
4. Sarah has not been well; so she don't go downtown like she used to.
5. This heat would be dreadful if a breeze wasn't blowing.
6. When the Crimean War broke out, the techniques of nursing were out of date dreadful.
7. The doctors worked valiant, but they needed assistence of nurses very bad.
8. Joan says she has felt badly all day.
9. I could of gone if I had knew that you were going.
10. I'm afraid his foot is froze.
11. The gadgets which we invent makes life more and more simpler.
12. If I was him, I'd try a new job.
13. After we helped put up the tents, we carried water for the circus animals.
14. I drunk a huge glass of milk when I come home from school.
15. I heard that the boys were drownded because they swum out too far.
16. We did not think that the experiment would turn out very good.
17. He told Mr. Kenworthy that he was sure to be on the committee.

18. Each of the forty-eight samples were placed in a separate jar.
19. Headlines in the newspaper is arranged so that it attracts attention.
20. Since the T-formation has been used successful, many school teams have adopted it.
21. The eyes of the children told of the horror that laid in their hearts.
22. I wish I was able to tell Jack and she the whole story.
23. Neither Mother nor I are surprised to hear that Edith failed; she don't do her work careful at all.
24. When I left, after being with the board for ten years, I felt like a piece of my life was gone.
25. When you consider that neither of us have did any shooting for a year, we are not doing so bad.
26. It is always Mr. Peters and me who is reprimanded if things go wrong in the office.
27. Digging a hole ten feet deep, the boys went away and left it.
28. A strange man whom, we learned later, knew Gertrude at one time, enters the house and joins the party.
29. He shall not use my money. I will see that he does not.
30. The conference will probably last until five o'clock, so there is no point in you waiting any longer.
31. Since you invited Paul and I for a visit, our father has been terrible sick; so we will not be able to accept your invitation.
32. Ted is so proud of his television set that he wants to show it to whoever comes to his house.
33. Everybody said he acted as a fool at the wedding.
34. New cars don't jump direct from the drafting board to the production room like some people think they do.
35. We recommend that there be appointed an experienced superintendent of water works.
36. Losing his fortune in an investment in oil, he begun life anew at fifty.
37. It was not wise for you to have given him the key.

38. The prize was to be given to whomever made the highest mark in German, but I never thought it would be me who would win it.

39. I worked at the job only two months when I was obliged to leave in order to have accompanied my family to Nebraska.

40. Because of the drop in price, power motors sold last year very satisfactory.

41. Every night there has been some sort of party; and although I would have loved to have gone to all of them, it was physically impossible.

42. It says in this article that the average married person is more healthier than the average single person because they have their meals more regular.

43. Since a good picture can sell a product, advertisers are turning to them to improve business.

44. If you won an election against John Cameron, you have did very good indeed.

45. The directors wish to express their appreciation for your coöperation during the year and welcomes this opportunity to wish you a Merry Christmas.

46. The firm objects to me studying Spanish because every man and woman in the office have wasted their time on some similar subject that have not helped their work.

47. I have always felt like I'd like to be a dancer.

48. This school is different than all of the other schools I have attended.

49. The beach was so pleasant I could of laid for hours in the sun.

50. One of the most interesting sights in Seattle are the Cascade Mountains.

Capitalization

21. USE OF CAPITAL LETTERS

A piece of writing in which capitals are scattered about freely or omitted where they should be used gives the impression almost of illiteracy. It is true that some modern writers have ignored the rules of capitalization, but it is not wise for students to be careless about these rules.

21a. Capitalize the first word of every sentence and the first word of a direct quotation.

> Our new car is dark blue.
> He asked, "Is your new car blue?"

21b. Capitalize the first word of a line of poetry.

> Shall I wasting in despair
> Die, because a woman's fair?

21c. Capitalize the word which follows *Resolved* or *Whereas* in formal resolutions.

> Resolved: An automobile driver's license should be granted to no one under twenty-one.

21d. Capitalize the important words in a title of a book, play, magazine, or musical composition. (See Section 34a.)

> *Harper's Magazine, Romeo and Juliet, The Moonlight Sonata, Death of a Salesman*

NOTE: Capitalize prepositions, conjunctions, or articles only at the beginning or end of a title or when they consist of five or more letters.

124

21e. Capitalize the first word in each topic of an outline and the first word in each item of a list.

1. Causes of slums
   A. Crowded conditions
   B. Poor housing
   Our investigation shows the following:
   1. Poor sanitation
   2. Lack of parks and recreation space
   3. Unpaved streets

21f. Capitalize the pronoun *I* and the interjection *O*.

Usually I find the first ripe chestnuts on the tree.
O mighty river, flow on!

NOTE: *O* is rarely used. The more common interjection *oh* is not capitalized unless it begins a sentence.

21g. Capitalize all proper nouns and words derived from proper nouns. (See Section 1.) They include the following:

1. Names of holidays, months, and days of the week (*Christmas, February, April, Monday*).

2. Names of persons and titles accompanying these names, but usually not the titles alone unless the title is used in place of a name.

NOTE: The words *President* and *Vice President,* referring to the President and Vice President of the United States, are always capitalized.

Fred, Helen, Mr. Brown, Dr. Anderson, Captain Wharton, Aunt Helen, the doctor, the captain, my aunt
Can you hear the whistles, Father?

3. The names of races, languages, nationalities.

Caucasian, the French language, Chinese lacquer, Japanese cherry blossoms

4. The names of cities, states, counties, countries, continents, bodies of water, mountains, constellations, and planets (except the earth).

Tucson, Arizona, United States, North America, Mississippi River, Rocky Mountains, Orion, Jupiter

5. Names of streets, parks, buildings, ships, trains, planes, hotels, orchestras.

Hollywood Boulevard, Yellowstone Park, Equitable Building, the Ritz-Carlton, Philadelphia Symphony Orchestra, *Super-Chief, S. S. American Scout.* (See Section 34a.)

6. Points of the compass (North, South, East, West) when they mean sections of the country or when they precede the name of a street, but not when they mean direction.

We moved to the South when I was a child.
When I saw the thief, he was running south toward the river.

7. The names of political parties, religious groups and their members, and the names of particular organizations or groups.

Democrats, Catholics, Methodists, Bender and Company, American Historical Society

8. Schools, colleges, clubs, departments of the government.

Edison High School, Drake University, East High School Glee Club, Department of Agriculture

9. Events in history, historical periods, documents.

War Between the States, Middle Ages, Declaration of Independence

10. Names of school classes when the word *class* accompanies them.

Junior class, juniors

11. Names of school subjects when they refer to languages or specific classes.

English, Latin, Algebra II, algebra

12. Words referring to the Deity and sacred books, but not the word *god* or *goddess* referring to pagan gods.

Lord, Savior, Master, Bible, Koran, gods of the Romans

13. Pronouns referring to the Deity.

We can be sure that He will care for us.

14. The first word in the salutation and the complimentary close of a letter.

Dear Mr. Evans: Dear Sir: Sincerely yours,

15. The abbreviations of academic degrees.

A. B.   Ph. D.

NOTE: *Do not capitalize the following:*

1. The name of a worker in a particular job.

Wrong: He wants to be a Stenographer.
Right: He wants to be a stenographer.

2. The names of school subjects unless they are names of languages or specific names of courses.

French, physics, mathematics, Journalism II

3. Nouns following the first noun in the complimentary close of a letter.

Wrong: Your loving Nephew,
Right: Your loving nephew,

4. The word *dear* when it follows *my* in the salutation of a letter.

Right: My dear Dr. Harlow:

5. The names of chemical substances.

Wrong: We used some Sulphur.
Right: We used some sulphur.

6. Terms referring to school, if the name of the school is not mentioned.

Right: I go to the junior high school.
Right: I go to Edgar Allan Poe Junior High School.

7. Names of diseases.

Right: He has measles.

8. Nouns such as *father, mother, aunt,* when they are preceded by a possessive.

Right: My father is a fishing enthusiast.

9. The names of the seasons, *earth, sun,* and *moon.*

Right: To me, autumn means blue leaf-smoke.
Right: This is the best place on earth to watch the rising moon or sun.

EXERCISE 1

The following sentences from students' themes contain errors in capitalization. On your paper, rewrite each sentence, using the correct capitalization.

1. At the head of the Student Government, we have a Student President and a Student Vice President.
2. Plutarch discussed a Roman Statesman and then a Greek Statesman and compared them.
3. We studied Sulphur and Hydrogen Sulphide in Chemistry.
4. The author lived for many years in a small cottage in devonshire, England.
5. The President of our organization appointed a committee to consult with the Executive Secretary.
6. I want to go to Business College for nine months and then get a job.
7. We asked the advice of James Hannibal, but he referred us to judge rhynhart.
8. I wish to apply for the position of Counselor at camp coxton.
9. Of all the good times that I had during the Spring vacation, I enjoyed most the dance given by the North High glee club.
10. Marie Curie studied radium and won the nobel prize in physics.

11. The lawyer has his office in the fidelity building at 10 east lexington street.
12. I think that easter comes on april 8 this year.
13. They moved to the west and settled on an iowa farm.
14. Mother sent me to visit aunt sally, who lives in paducah, kentucky.
15. Horace has always done well in physics and mathematics, but he cannot master spanish or french.
16. The chamber of commerce is going to publish a pamphlet called "what to see in cleveland."
17. We went down the danube river from vienna to budapest.
18. If you go west for two blocks, you will find the office of the president of the company at 712 charles street.
19. The renaissance was a period of great development in art and literature.
20. Have you ever read the declaration of independence or the bible completely?
21. The seniors wanted to get an advertisement for their year book from snedden, driscoll and company.
22. The gods of the romans were very human in many ways.
23. There are as many baptists in our town as there are catholics.
24. She was employed as chief file clerk, but she often has to act as secretary to the President.
25. The report describes the work of the sales audit division of a department store.

EXERCISE 2

The following paragraphs contain errors in capitalization. On your paper, write with a capital each word that requires capitalization.

Samuel johnson, one of the most colorful figures of the eighteenth century, was born in lichfield on september 18, 1709. His father, a bookseller, permitted the boy to read the books in the shop so that samuel became very well read. during this period, many people were quite superstitious. they believed that a sick person could be cured by the touch of the queen. consequently, when samuel began to suffer from scrofula, he was taken to queen anne, but the supposed power of a queen to cure the disease failed. the affliction remained with johnson and gave him trouble for years.

because the johnsons did not have enough money to educate their brilliant son, a neighbor sent the boy to pembroke college, oxford. there johnson began his writing career by translating some latin verses. he later wrote *taxation no tyranny,* which argued against the points taken by the american colonists in the revolutionary war and showed johnson as a firm supporter of the tory party.

today we remember johnson chiefly as the author of the first dictionary, a book which showed great prejudice against the scotch, and as the organizer of the famous literary club. members of the latter included the most important intellectual people in london. david garrick, the actor, sir joshua reynolds, the artist, edmund burke, the statesman, oliver goldsmith, the writer, were all members. when johnson was finally granted a pension by the king, he showed great kindness to a number of poor people, whom he kept in his house on fleet street.

EXERCISE 3

Rewrite the following letter, using correct capitalization:

> Marston Brothers
> 52 east twenty-ninth street
> chicago, illinois
>
> dear sirs:
>   please send the following books with bill:
>   1 copy preston, *the growth of american ideals*
>   1 copy anderson, *new criticism*
>   2 copies jackson, *big league baseball*
>   very truly yours,
>   howard sachs

Punctuation

Punctuation is an aid to meaning; but if it is carelessly used, it may distort meaning. The following sentence was dictated by a businessman not long ago. The poor punctuation used by his secretary distorted the meaning and caused the firm some embarrassment. She wrote:

> The house was bought on Monday for five thousand dollars. We can put it in excellent condition and resell it.

Her employer expected her to write:

> The house was bought on Monday. For five thousand dollars we can put it in excellent condition and resell it.

Sometimes careless omission of a comma can lead to humorous results, as in the following sentence:

Wrong: When we cooked the woman in the next apartment complained that we rattled pots and pans.

A first glance at the sentence might tell the reader that we cooked the woman.

Right: When we cooked, the woman in the next apartment complained that we rattled pots and pans.

Literary artists sometimes use punctuation in a very free fashion; but in business and the professions, clarity is important, and following a few simple rules is imperative.

How good is your punctuation? Do your sentences always convey to your reader exactly what you mean to say? Try the diagnostic test to see what you need to study. Then turn to the practice exercises that will help you with your problem.

22. DIAGNOSTIC TEST ON COMMAS, SEMICOLONS, COLONS, APOSTROPHES, QUOTATION MARKS

On your paper, rewrite the following sentences, supplying the necessary commas, semicolons, colons, apostrophes, and quotation marks. If unnecessary marks have been used, omit them in your correction. After each sentence write an explanation of each correction that you have made in that sentence. If a sentence needs no correction, do not rewrite it, but write C beside its number.

1. If you desire any information about the city we suggest that you call on our Personal Service Bureau.
2. When I came home after a years course in business my father gave me Mr. Hopkins old job.
3. Lawrence Biddison the Hopkins lacrosse star was chosen for the Olympic team.
4. The streets were narrow and cobblestoned not paved as they are today.
5. Our prices are always fair Mr. Hathaway said the manager we try to please our customers.
6. How many Ts are in your last name Davy?
7. The adding machine which the First National Bank has just installed is a real time-saver.
8. The road outside Miami was long and straight only now and then did we round a curve.
9. Yes the flowers were from the Allens'.
10. A person applying for a job must be sure to wear inconspicuous clothes and to see that they are clean and neatly pressed.
11. Shelley and Keats poetry occupies a high place in English literature.
12. He is famous however chiefly for his autobiography which people call the best of its kind.
13. In the days of horse-drawn cars fire engines and milk wagons Sam Smith kept a bookshop on Center Street and we boys often went there to talk about literature and politics.
14. We must show that we have grown intellectually that we have increased our interests in current problems and that we can be tolerant of others.

15. Our chef has been in our employ for nearly twenty years and has an excellent staff to assist him as a result we are always sure that the meals will be good.

16. In modern times when one speaks of a fool he is usually referring to a person who has not good sense but in medieval days the fool was a professional jester in the kings court.

17. Pepys' tells in his diary of the bubonic plague that swept England and of the great fire that destroyed a large part of London.

18. My father does not approve of James driving so rapidly but he does not want to forbid him to use the car.

19. The author of the book states no nation least of all the defeated Axis nations should be permitted to select a form of government which does not conform to political democracy.

20. William Harlow who plans to build a large number of prefabricated houses has begun his work in our city.

21. I took the boys to see the Orioles play against Rochester said Uncle Jack and although these teams cannot compare in playing ability with those of New York the game was very enjoyable.

22. Mark Hallam born in Peoria Illinois May 22 1899 traveled to India Persia Java and many other exotic places in order to get information for his book.

23. Failure to take the town resulted in Colonel Blacks losing command of his regiment said the general.

24. Major John Perry son of Mr. and Mrs. Henry Perry of Madison Wisconsin won three decorations for bravery in combat.

25. The report submitted by Mr. Arnold showed that the southwest corner of Fleet and Exeter Streets will be an excellent location for our business consequently we shall begin building the new plant next month.

26. One thing is certain this is not the kind of bill which should be rushed through Congress without serious thought and consideration.

27. A ladys purse containing five one-dollar bills a silver ring and some change was found in the employees rest room.

28. The management aware of efforts among its employ ees to set up a closed shop feebly endeavored to nu lify them by promoting an independent compan union.

29. The Mutual Insurance Company which now occupi one floor of the building will be obliged to move t make room for government offices.

30. We planned to have the party at the Kings house bu on the day of the party Mrs. Kings mother was ill.

31. Most of the cars in the parking lot are new roadste sedans and convertibles although a few are old se ond-hand busses.

32. There are five kinds of phrases prepositional pa ticipial gerund infinitive and absolute.

33. There is a sale of ladies and misses dresses an mens suits at Goodman and Canes new store.

34. Her husbands step was strong and vigorous he fathers feeble and slow.

35. A business which is unwilling to change its practic to suit new conditions will never be very profitabl

36. When Ellen heard the lecturer speak with great e thusiasm about antiques she rushed out and boug a lovely Chippendale sofa.

37. When we received Henton and Hawkins acceptanc of our plan for the reorganization of their busine we began the job by moving the credit manage office to the third floor.

38. Hettie born in 1821 after the death of two oth children was a source of great happiness to her pa ents.

39. Harry Manners who was a war correspondent giv in his short story The Voice Speaks a realistic pi ture of soldiers in action.

40. The steps creaked as I walked on them and the a smelled stale and musty.

41. The no-smoking provisions do not of course appl to the outer lobbies of theaters to restaurants or t other places designated with the approval of th Fire Department as places where smoking is pe mitted.

42. When the quarantine on dogs was lifted dozens of dogs began scampering around renewing old acquaintances visiting scenes of former revelry and showing how happy they were to be free.

43. A person who wants to build a hot rod must watch several things careful grinding of crank shaft bearings removal of metal from the inner bearing surface and reshaping of bearings.

44. As we approached the house said Peter we heard a man say Ill get him if you leave the job entirely to me and we fled terrified.

45. Here is a painter who draws his inspiration directly from life and nature.

46. When the scientist sent the beam of his torch toward the tree he saw suspended from a branch a curious little animal which was hanging upside down.

47. It looked something like a Teddy bear but as it moved along the branch of the tree the scientist could see a row of spines projecting from its neck.

48. This animal the potto can double up with its head between its legs so that it is in an excellent position to use those spines on any attacker that comes too close.

49. Because I love animals reading Sandersons *Animal Treasure* was one of the most pleasant experiences that I have ever had but I should not have enjoyed the rats snakes and frogs that the scientist met everywhere.

50. Flying squirrels scaly anteaters whistling skinks were animals new to me until I read of a scientists trip to the jungle but I soon became acquainted with them and learned much about their habits.

23. THE COMMA

23a. Use a comma before the coördinating conjunction in a compound sentence.

The coördinating conjunctions are *and, but, for, or, nor.* A compound sentence has at least two independent clauses, which usually are joined by a coördinating conjunction. To determine whether a sentence is compound, read what comes before the coördinating conjunction and see if the thought is complete standing alone; then read what follows the conjunction and see if it is complete. If there are two complete thoughts, place a comma before the conjunction. If there are not *two* complete thoughts, no comma is needed.

> There was an elevator for the use of visitors, but we decided to walk up the steps. (Two complete thoughts)
> Norris darted around the corner and halted abruptly. (No comma is needed because the words following *and* are not complete in themselves; they are part of the compound predicate used with the subject, *Norris.*)

NOTE: 1. If the clauses are short, the comma may be omitted. This statement, however, immediately brings up the question "How short is short?" If the independent clauses consist of only subject and verb, then they are obviously short, and the comma may be omitted. Examples: *John studied and Mary played. I laughed and I cried.* Sometimes lack of punctuation between short clauses may cause momentary misreading. In reading the sentence that follows, your first thought may be that the boys ate the hired man.

> The boys ate *bacon and the hired man* ate sausage.

2. If the clauses are long and contain other commas, a semicolon is used before the conjunction. (See Section 24c.)

> When he arrived at college, he was invited to join two different fraternities; and it was only after much discussion with his father, his brother, and his friends that he was able to decide which one to join.

EXERCISE 1

Most of the following sentences from student themes and letters contain errors in the punctuation of compound sentences. On your paper, write the number of each sen-

ence. Beside it, write the word after which a comma
hould be used, and the comma. If no comma needs to be
dded to a sentence, write C beside the sentence number.
As an example, the correction for the first sentence is
given below:

1. late,

1. Often the mother had to work late and the child
   was left to take care of himself.
2. The commercials are very elaborate and sometimes
   take three minutes of a fifteen-minute program.
3. Almost everybody has his pet superstition but some
   people take the matter entirely too seriously.
4. A senator from Mississippi and one from Georgia
   were discussing the poll tax.
5. Most of the critics received the book very coldly but
   the public loved it.
6. The new art museum is a beautiful structure and
   some of the paintings are exquisite.
7. His trip on the ocean was pleasing to Joe for he
   rested most of the time.
8. Suddenly dark clouds appeared on the horizon and
   the sea became rough and wild.
9. We wish to thank you for this opportunity to be of
   service and to assure you of our desire to please you.
10. We tried to get in to see Toscanini conduct but we
    didn't have the strength to fight through the mob.
11. His clothes were ragged but his spirit was as
    haughty as ever.
12. We should like to welcome you to Indianapolis
    and to express a sincere hope that you will enjoy
    your residence here.
13. We could drive into town in the evening and see a
    show at one of the small-town movie houses.
14. It's been a long time since we've seen each other
    and you've probably forgotten all about me.
15. The shouts of the people grew louder and louder
    for the two wrestlers had entered the ring.
16. The living room is comfortably proportioned and has
    a large fireplace at one end.

17. A banquet has been arranged for the evening and many other feasts and festivities will be held during the three-day holiday.

18. I do hope that you haven't made any plans for the summer and will arrange to spend July with us.

19. The family intends to drive to my aunt's summer lodge in Oakland for a few weeks and we'd love to have you join us.

20. Last summer I played tennis almost every day and found that I improved quite a bit.

21. I was assigned the task of examining the method and procedures used by other companies and also the job of adapting these findings to our use.

22. One thousand dollars has already been paid and the balance of seventeen thousand will be paid within sixty days.

23. We are able to obtain adequate chemical supplies but we cannot get enough equipment of other types.

24. She was proud of her beauty and spent much time keeping herself attractive.

25. The sun had now vanished completely and the silver moon peeped through a break in the deep blue clouds.

EXERCISE 2

Follow the directions in Exercise 1.

1. We are holding the freezing units for you and should appreciate your letting us know when you would like to have them delivered.

2. It was interesting to see the Indian dances but was disappointed to find that the costumes of the witch doctors were not like those in the pictures.

3. Streetcars clanged as they traveled to and fro on their daily trips and grass grew between the stones on the street.

4. The story has been told far and wide and will forever be a legend in these mountains.

5. The Trinity River broke through the levees in several places and many people were forced out of their homes.

6. Lucy had many music teachers but scales and rhythm simply would not sink into her head.

7. Calls for service received before 1:00 p.m. were completed the same day and those received after 1:00 p.m. were scheduled for the next day.

8. I invited him for lunch and we discussed the present situation in the stainless steel industry.

9. The Metal Products Company has a supply of stainless steel and has been trying to persuade Mr. Paulson to cancel his order with us and buy from it.

10. Some of the homes were on magnificent estates but most of them were the simple houses of workingmen.

11. The relations between labor and management in the company grew steadily worse and an open clash was prevented only by the outbreak of World War II.

12. The early evening was the best time to walk to the top of the hill and look at the little valley below.

13. Practically every firm states that its machinery costs have been reduced by 25 percent and some claim a reduction of 35 percent.

14. I have not had any experience in the business of selling but I will give the job my best effort and feel certain that I can learn it quickly.

15. He subscribes liberally to the Associated Charities and no good object or worthy enterprise fails to receive his support.

16. He made many speeches from the truck and was so well received everywhere that his political party rewarded him with a good job.

17. Virtually all cottages here are reported rented for the summer and hotel reservations are said to have hit an all-time high.

18. We have usually gone to Carmel for the summer but this year we have taken a cottage at Santa Barbara and hope that you will join us for July.

19. Surf bathing and all kinds of water sports are offered and the resort has a background of pine forests and picturesque bays.

20. The cause of a united Ireland is one which arouses flaming passions and causes violent arguments.

23b. Use a comma to separate an introductory phrase or dependent clause from an independent clause.

The fact that the element is *introductory* means that it precedes the independent clause. Often it is at the very beginning of the sentence. The introductory element may be a clause, a phrase, or, occasionally, merely a word. Failure to punctuate it will interfere with the clearness of the sentence. If the introductory element is a clause, it will probably begin with a subordinating conjunction—for example, *if, as, since, because, although, while,* or *when.*

> When she finished high school, she was determined to be an artist.
> If no dormitory rooms are available, I'll inquire about rooms off the campus.
> Although summer is months away, the girls have started to make plans for their vacation.

If a sentence begins with a phrase containing a participle or an infinitive and used as an adjective or an adverb, a comma should follow the phrase.

> Acting on the advice of Mr. Crawford, we bought some stock in the company. (Participial phrase used as adjective)
> To win the game, you must watch each card that is played. (Infinitive phrase used as adverb)

A long prepositional phrase is usually followed by a comma if it begins the sentence. Even a short prepositional phrase must be followed by a comma if the meaning would otherwise be confused. (See Section 6.)

Common prepositions are *to, for, from, with, between, in, over, under, by, across, after.*

> *In a little country store nearby,* we bought some bread and cheese. (Prepositional phrase)
> After a long walk in the brisk air, we were glad to rest before the fire. (Prepositional phrase, in which the object of the preposition is modified by a second phrase)

CAUTION: 1. Sometimes in a compound-complex sentence the introductory phrase or clause comes in the middle of the sentence. In the sentence which follows, the clause *before anyone could get it* is considered introductory because it precedes the independent clause *he had reached second base*. Therefore, a comma is used after *it*.

> Bill Tucker hit a ball into the hole between short stop and third base; and before anyone could get it, he had reached second base.

2. A gerund or infinitive phrase used as the subject of a sentence is not separated from the rest of the sentence by a comma.

> Planting a garden requires skill and care.
> To spend a month at the seashore was her chief desire.

EXERCISE 3

On your paper, write the number of each of the following sentences. Beside it write the word after which a comma should be placed and the comma. If no comma needs to be added to a sentence, write C beside the sentence number. As an example, the correction for the first sentence is given below:

1. yesterday,

1. While walking home from school yesterday she lost her physics book.
2. Should you desire an interview I can be reached at Madison 3–1724.
3. As you are one of our best customers we want you to have advance information about the sale.
4. If you expect to attend the convention please mail the inclosed card for your reservation.
5. Through the purchase of a retirement policy, you can assure yourself of security in your old age.
6. If you purchase a cottage at Shelby Cove you will own property in an exclusive summer colony.
7. During the years of the German occupation Athens suffered indescribably.

8. As she was coming back with a pail of cool water from the well she noticed a strange movement of the bushes.

9. Thinking that the figure was a ghost we ran as fast as our legs could carry us.

10. To make a good model airplane you must follow the directions exactly.

11. Although I have not had any training as a counselor I have gone to camp for many years and know what a counselor should do.

12. To run a mile a person must be in good physical condition.

13. In order for the laboratory to function properly we need two additional technicians.

14. Under his expert direction the symphony orchestra grew to be one of the most famous in the world.

15. During the past month 6 percent of the work hours was required for machinery repairs.

16. Because he had no parental guidance or home life he began to run wild.

17. Complying with your request of March 10 we are mailing you a membership application blank.

18. After an examination of our easy payment plan you will be sure to want a house in Shelby Cove.

19. If you come to Portland may we have the pleasure of reserving a room for you?

20. Since the capacity of our hotel is limited to one thousand guests you must place your reservation now.

21. Sucking the cool juice of the oranges into their dry throats, the boys discussed the ways of getting home that evening.

22. In addition to the attractive features already outlined Shelby Cove is a paradise for children.

23. Although I have had little experience I can assure you that I am very much interested in the work.

24. Since the establishment of the company in 1921 there have been several reorganizations.

25. As I threw open my window I could see a mass of flames rising from the building across the street.

EXERCISE 4

Follow the directions in Exercise 3.

1. As I look back on the five years which I spent as a clerk in a drugstore I see that I learned a great deal.
2. For some reason that we have not determined Friday seems to be our busiest day.
3. To supply a city like this large power plants are needed.
4. Noticing that it was becoming very dark and thinking that our parents would be worried, we began to gather our bats and balls in order to leave.
5. Having gone without ice cream and candy for two whole months Theresa had finally saved enough money to buy the gloves that she wanted.
6. If you will have your secretary type your name on the enclosed card and mail it to me I will see that you receive one of the first copies.
7. I assured him that as soon as we receive our shipment of twenty-four-gauge steel we will fill his order for 100 water coolers.
8. We guarantee that if you do not find the materials satisfactory you may return them at our expense.
9. We have notified our customers that since the materials are not available we shall be unable to fill their orders until May 10.
10. As the zoologist and his group moved through the jungle, the bushes suddenly parted; and there, in front of the astonished scientists, stood a huge baboon.

23c. Use a comma to separate words, phrases, or clauses in a series.

A series is two or more expressions in the same construction. We may have a series of nouns that are subjects or objects:

Subjects: *Men, women,* and *children* were among the injured.
Objects: We invited *Alice, Sue,* and *Eleanor.*

There may be a series of adjectives modifying the same noun:

Tall, slender, graceful girls modeled the clothes.

CAUTION: 1. If there are only two adjectives in the series, the comma should be used if the adjectives are coördinate; that is, if they can be joined by *and*.

A kind, generous woman

Sometimes the second adjective is so closely joined to the noun that together they almost form a compound noun. Under these circumstances, no comma is used between the adjectives.

The child sat at a small mahogany desk.

In this sentence the word *mahogany* is closely linked to *desk;* no comma is needed between the two adjectives.

2. When one word modifies another, do not separate the two words by a comma.

A bright red dress hung in the cupboard.

Here, *bright* modifies *red,* not *dress.* Hence no series exists.

3. Do not place a comma before the first member or after the last member of a series.

Wrong: We put, apples, peaches, and pears, into the basket.
Right: We put apples, peaches, and pears into the basket.

4. A series of phrases or clauses will require the same punctuation as a series of words.

Phrases: He ran *down the steps, across the street,* and *into the park.*
Clauses: They asked me *how I had arrived in Siam, what I intended to do there,* and *when I should return to the United States.*

Some writers omit the comma before *and* in a series; but because in some sentences this omission may cause

misunderstanding, it is better to use the comma before
and.

5. A semicolon is sometimes used to separate the members of a series if any of them contain commas.

> Down the field came the newly organized, somewhat
> incompetent band; three drum majorettes in white,
> spangled skirts; and the team, muddy and wretched.

EXERCISE 5

On your paper, write the number of each of the following sentences and beside it write the word or words after
which a comma or a semicolon should be placed. Include
the comma or semicolon. As an example, the correction
for the first sentence is given below.

1. students, teachers,

1. The members of the society were students teachers
   and clerks.
2. We are sure that there are many things which you
   would like to purchase for yourself your family or
   your home.
3. A short fat girl came into the room.
4. In my history classes I have learned about my country its government and its people.
5. The tight black silk cap had gay shiny buttons
   sewed around the crown.
6. The propaganda bureau said that the people of the
   western countries lacked spirit true culture and po-
   liteness.
7. At the auction sale she bought a beautiful inlaid
   rosewood table an antique highboy and a wrought-
   iron lantern.
8. The courses in science taught us to question to
   reason and to experiment.
9. The pale yellow porch chairs had dark green cush-
   ions.
10. He mixed sodas delivered prescriptions and made
    himself generally useful in the store.

EXERCISE 6

Follow the directions in Exercise 5.

1. The book tells of her romances her marriages he many interesting, famous personal friends on an off the stage and her war adventures.
2. The girl uttered a piercing, uncanny scream dropped her pail of water and ran for the house
3. Early in the morning we milk the cows churn the butter and pick berries or peaches and string beans
4. It was fun to make new friends to take part in the various activities of the school and to join a few clubs.
5. I believe that the school has taught me to think clearly to converse intelligently and to appreciat beauty.
6. Franklin pioneered in the study of the common cold the conduction of heat by various substances an the prediction of the weather.
7. The club has made arrangements to have on dis play the newest boat models engine equipment an safety devices.
8. The strike shut off the country's power closed it mills and stopped the wheels of industry.
9. Within a few years, the J. M. Salten Co. was doing a million-dollar business had purchased the plant of two competitors and was planning to establish branch office in Pittsburgh.
10. The children came to the vacant lot on warm spring afternoons and played long intense games of dodge ball speed ball or volley ball.

EXERCISE 7

Follow the directions in Exercise 5.

1. The attic was hung with clusters of bats the wooden structure was rotten and the whole effect was one of gloom and despair.
2. They needed to cut down the weeds erect new fences and repair the roof in order to make the place habitable.

3. The girl wore a fleecy, dull green coat and hat brown shoes with tall, fragile, spike heels a beige silk muffler and beige gloves.

4. Standardization of the size of the paper will save space in the main store room in individual office storage cabinets and in file cabinets.

5. The clerk is trained to write legibly to show the necessary information in the proper columns and to add and extend the amount of the sale accurately.

6. Members of the Home Service Corps of the Red Cross receive patients handle case correspondence and assist the professional staff in non-technical duties.

7. According to some statistics, individuals today spend an average of one hour a week at the motion pictures twenty-five hours listening to the radio or watching television and five hours reading.

8. The book profits by the author's ability to describe the battlefield to explain the enemy and to show clearly the courage of the marines in annihilating the defending garrisons.

9. Scientists all over the world will perfect new weapons improve present weapons and make ready the instruments of destruction that man will turn against himself.

10. The investigation is to cover the kinds of samples analyzed by each laboratory the methods used in analyzing the samples and new methods which may save time and money.

EXERCISE 8

On your paper, write this paragraph, placing commas and capital letters where they should be. Number each correction that you make. At the end of the paragraph list the numbers and beside each number, write the reason for the correction.

Last Saturday the northern high school played polytechnic a championship game in football. when we arrived at the benton stadium the stands were filled with girls waving pennants boys shouting for their team and gay parents and teachers. swinging along in perfect time our band entered the field marched once around and seated themselves in the reserved section. I was feeling sure of victory but jack had seen polytechnic in practices and did not think our chances were so good. for the first half we played well. then skippy broke his ankle and our chances of winning declined. when they saw that skippy was out of the game the boys seemed to lose heart. the quarterback miscalled a signal the right tackle pulled out of the line at the wrong time and the ball carrier fumbled as he was tackled. then the opposing team recovered the fumble and scored on the next play. I still hoped but my hopes were in vain. the game ended with a score of 13–7 in favor of poly.

EXERCISE 9

Follow the directions in Exercise 8.

A few summers ago judith went with her mother and father on a cruise to the west indies. it was a beautiful trip. mrs. nolte lay lazily in a deck chair and read most of the time but judith and her father were active. they played deck tennis and shuffleboard sat on the top deck to get a good sun tan and danced at night. when the boat stopped for a day at port of spain in trinidad the passengers had an opportunity to see a new kind of life. because judith's father had a business acquaintance in this town she was able to see the inside of a charming tropical home. it was built around a patio where palm and banana trees surrounded a fountain. when judith came home she talked of nothing but trinidad. I was so enthusiastic that I planned to visit the island myself but the war ended all my plans. now I am looking forward again to a trip to the west indies.

23d. Use commas to separate parenthetical words, phrases, or clauses from the rest of the sentence.

A parenthetical expression interrupts a thought and is not necessary to the meaning of the sentence. Although it often makes the sentence smoother or adds a bit of additional information, the thought is complete without it. Some expressions frequently used in a parenthetical sense are *however, for instance, of course, as we said, for example, to tell the truth.* If these expressions or any others are used parenthetically, they should have a comma before them and a comma after them.

> The task, it is true, is not a difficult one.

The words *it is true* interrupt the thought *the task is not a difficult one.* The sentence is complete without this expression. Hence the expression is separated from the rest of the sentence by commas.

The parenthetical expression may be a rather long clause or phrase. Such expressions frequently give interesting information. If, however, they interrupt the main thought, they are considered parenthetical.

> Kenneth, evidently taking his cue from his brother, answered affirmatively.
> Many professional and business men, even if they have plenty of time, will have nothing to do with politics.

CAUTION: The conjunctive adverbs *however, moreover, nevertheless, consequently, therefore, thus, then, so, yet, otherwise,* are sometimes used as parenthetical expressions. But if one of these conjunctive adverbs joins two independent clauses, the adverb must be preceded by a semicolon.

> Jane, however, stayed at home. (Parenthetical)
> John went to school; however, Jane stayed at home. (Two independent clauses)

23e. Use commas to separate from the rest of a sentence nouns or pronouns used in direct address.

> Mr. Henderson, may I see you for a moment?
> I asked you, Ronald, not to come here today.

23f. The words *yes* and *no* are usually followed by a comma when used at the beginning of a sentence.

> Yes, I have studied French.
> No, nobody was there.

EXERCISE 10

On your paper, write the number of each of the following sentences, and beside it write each word after which a comma should be used, with the comma. As an example, the correction is given for the first sentence:

1. believe, doctor,

1. I cannot believe doctor that the disease is so serious.
2. Have you by any chance a suggestion as to our lodgings at the beach?
3. Yes it will seem strange I suppose to go to the beach and not come to the old cottage.
4. Your delivery promise you may recall was for the first week in April.
5. Billy after realizing what had happened gave a long wail and began to sob bitterly.
6. King Saul fearing the loss of his throne drove David from the palace.
7. No Helene I don't need money, but will you do something for me?
8. Before 1945 Okinawa I am sure was a place of which most of us had never heard.
9. New York as we all know has developed many successful writers.
10. Come here Rex and do your tricks.

EXERCISE 11

Follow the directions in Exercise 10.

1. Don't make so much noise Herbert.
2. The price increases effective immediately apply to moderate-priced shoes.
3. Her later associations as well as the early ones influenced George Eliot's writing.
4. Mother though she wanted very much to go relinquished her seat to Aunt Sarah.
5. Boys and girls you will have this year an unusual opportunity.
6. At present for example we have only three thousand of the five thousand test tubes which we need.

7. Jenny glad of a chance to make the trip tried hard not to think of the unpleasant company that she would have.

8. Some of the evidence it is said by the defense counsel concerns military secrets and cannot be presented at this time.

9. The house designed I believe by Carter and Wells is a French provincial cottage with a charming outdoor terrace.

10. The new airport has three runways two of which are 3,000 feet long and a large, impressive administration building.

EXERCISE 12

Follow the directions in Exercise 10.

1. Our research program begun last year in the interest of improved passenger service has now been completed.

2. Pepys though not entirely an egoist never lost interest in himself.

3. Many perhaps the majority of the people traveling this summer will go by train or try one of the new airlines.

4. One of the greatest galleries in the history of American golf estimated to be from 16,000 to 20,000 fans saw the United States Open Championship yesterday.

5. Four good-looking American girls hailed by everybody as the best balanced U.S. team ever sent to England won the Wightman Cup matches yesterday.

6. Some travel organizations proceeding on the premise that there will be too many travelers to share existing accommodations have planned all-expense tours.

7. The man after many vicissitudes sank into abject and hopeless poverty.

8. Two persons were drowned as rivers swollen by thirty hours of continuous rain swept over their banks and flooded numerous homes.

9. The blunt, straight-speaking diplomat opening a foreign policy debate in the House of Commons said that permanent peace can be obtained only through complete coöperation of all nations.
10. The first two years of high school although they taught me to cope with problems sensibly gave me above all an appreciation of the value of an education.

23g. Use commas to separate appositives from the rest of the sentence.

An appositive is a substantive (noun or pronoun) joined to another substantive that means the same thing.

> Jones, an *Englishman*, was an excellent sailor.
> Robert Frost, the *poet* who wrote "Birches," is one of the finest American poets. (*Jones* and *Englishman* are the same; *Robert Frost* and *poet* are the same.)

A comma or two commas should be used to separate the appositive from the rest of the sentence. If the appositive is at the end of the sentence, it is preceded by a comma and followed by a period.

CAUTION:

1. An appositive which is part of a name is not separated by commas.

> Richard the Lion-Hearted was an English king.

2. Occasionally the appositive is so closely related to the noun that it is considered a part of the noun. This is a *restrictive* appositive. It is not punctuated.

> My brother *Sam* is sick.
> The phrase *to my house* is adverbial.

3. If an appositive consists of several words, dashes (See Section 31d) may be used instead of commas.

> My friends—Tom, Paula, and the others—met me at the train.

EXERCISE 13

On your paper, write the following sentences, placing commas where they are needed to punctuate an appositive, a series, a term of address, a parenthetical expression, or an introductory dependent clause.

1. Bob Coleman the coach at Southern High expects his team to win the cup this year.

2. *Good Night Sweet Prince* is the biography of John Barrymore a well-known much-admired actor.

3. City and Polytechnic our two keenest rivals have lost several of their outstanding players.

4. Mr. Andrews a man of long experience in selling tools will tell you the advantages of buying our products.

5. He sold the business to J. P. David Company an old reliable firm.

6. Dan did you know that the author of the book Dr. Baumgarten was a teacher in Germany before Hitler came to power?

7. One of the persons whom she met was Celeste Armiger an author of considerable reputation.

8. Dr. Nils Peterson director of the hospital is greatly worried about the increased expenses.

9. He opened the icebox and saw something that caught his fancy immediately a dish of macaroni and cheese.

10. When I reached the waiting room I was greeted by Mrs. Sheldon the director of the volunteer workers.

EXERCISE 14

Follow the directions in Exercise 13.

1. The first wrestler a mere youth looks small and insignificant beside the other a rugged large heavy-set man.

2. The speech marked an historic moment the turning of the tide.

3. She was happy because she was leaving Russia and going to America the land of opportunity.

4. Joan's father an important businessman worked for one of the large expensive department stores.
5. Student government gave me a chance to learn public speaking an art which will be valuable to me in later life.
6. When Joanne married Bob a tall handsome marine she did not expect to settle down on a farm.
7. Last week at our Spanish club two guests one from Uruguay and one from Cuba spoke in Spanish to us.
8. In two games yesterday the sixth and seventh of the season Northern High the champion of last year was badly defeated.
9. When he visited *The Poplars* a neighboring farm he found the people greatly disturbed by news of a robbery.
10. Elizabeth became interested in Mr. Darcy an arrogant haughty and conceited person.

EXERCISE 15

Follow the directions in Exercise 13.

1. We landed first on the southern end of the island that part where most of the fighting took place.
2. Winston Churchill British wartime Prime Minister and later leader of the Conservative opposition rebuked the Labor Government for its food policy.
3. In your course Dr. Davis I have learned to distinguish between fact and opinion.
4. Pope the man is far different from Pope the poet.
5. Some scientists have been working on an interesting new product a D.D.T. wallpaper which will kill moths flies and mosquitoes.
6. Henry Bronson one of the most wealthy farmers in the county was married to a kind-hearted pert engaging woman of thirty.
7. Godfrey was often led into doing foolish things that would never have occurred to him had it not been for Dunstan his thoroughly dishonest brother.
8. Two important languages Latin and Spanish about which I had no knowledge before I entered high school are now reasonably well learned.

9. Doing two term papers one on labor problems and the other on the development of American railroads has given me a fine opportunity to develop a technique for handling reference materials a skill in using the library and a method of organizing facts.

10. Surrounded by three hundred distinguished guests the regally robed monarch ascended the throne in a ceremony which lasted fourteen minutes the climax of one of the most important days in the history of the country.

23h. Use commas to separate nonrestrictive clauses and phrases from the remainder of the sentence.

Clauses and phrases are *nonrestrictive* when they do not restrict or limit the meaning of the sentence. Study these examples.

> The *Queen Mary,* which is a large ship, was built in Scotland.
>
> The ship which arrived yesterday is named *Queen Mary.*

In the first sentence, the omission of *which is a large ship* does not materially change the meaning of the sentence. In the second, the clause *which arrived yesterday* is necessary for the full expression of the idea. That is, it tells which ship is the *Queen Mary.* The first clause is nonrestrictive because it is not necessary to the thought of the sentence; it is separated from the remainder of the sentence by commas. The second clause is necessary to the sentence. It is called restrictive and is not set off by commas.

Nonrestrictive clause:	Chapter Ten, *which tells of the rescue,* is well written.
Restrictive clause:	The chapter *which tells of the rescue* is well written.
Nonrestrictive phrase:	The book, *dog-eared and dirty,* had been soaked in the rain.
Restrictive phrase:	The book *on the table* is dog-eared and dirty.

Restrictive phrases and clauses may be further explained as ones which are necessary to identify the word or words they modify. They answer the questions *Who?* *Which one?*

> John Mackay, *who is our postman,* is a former aviator.
> The man *who is our postman* is a former aviator.

In the first of the preceding sentences, *Who is our postman* is nonrestrictive; in the second, the clause actually identifies the word it modifies, *man;* it answers the question, "which man?"

The *context* sometimes determines whether a clause or phrase is restrictive or nonrestrictive.

> The man who mended our tire was a Cuban.
> We had a flat tire just opposite a gate on which a man was sitting. The man, who later mended our tire, was a Cuban.

In the first sentence, *who mended our tire* is restrictive. But in the second sentence, the main point is the man's nationality and not the aid which he gave in mending the tire. Thus the clause *who later mended our tire* is nonrestrictive.

EXERCISE 16

Some of the following sentences require correction by the addition of commas, usually to punctuate nonrestrictive expressions. Other uses of the comma are also required. Some of the sentences are correctly punctuated. On your paper rewrite any incorrect sentence, adding the necessary commas. If a sentence is correct, write C beside the number; do not rewrite a correct sentence.

1. The fifteen dollars that I had so carefully saved was spent in one evening on a date with Sandra.
2. Grandfather who was a huckster wanted to get a stall in the market.
3. Her knees which were normally strong and firm were now weak and shaky.

4. I tried to find a vacation spot which would give me something different from the usual thing.

5. Mrs. Seaman's husband who is in the printing business has promised to print the tickets free of charge.

6. It was suggested by Mrs. Bruce that a committee be appointed to call on members who are ill.

7. Our team which has lost four first-string men through injuries can hardly expect to win.

8. Basketball players who are more than six feet tall have a real advantage over their shorter teammates.

9. Recently I have learned a great deal about the labor problem which was formerly a complete blank to me.

10. Parents who do not provide a home where there are love affection and guidance should expect delinquents to develop.

11. My favorite in the play was Alexander Harding who played the role of the prince's tutor.

12. The second and third floors which were formerly show-rooms are now used as storage space.

13. The other blouse of similar style that I have to offer can be seen on page 372 of our catalogue.

14. The school which I attended was not far from our new house but the mountain road was poorly constructed.

15. He became friendly with the governor who offered to help him start his business.

16. The suit which you ordered Mr. Scott has been shipped by American Express.

17. One of the counselors whom you employed last year has told me of a vacancy in your office.

18. When I heard the price which I think is outrageous I decided not to buy the house.

19. Everybody who goes to Exeter thinks it is one of the finest schools in the country.

20. Taking her "over-month" bag Grandma went to Lynchburg to see her favorite cousins who have a small farm.

21. Our plan was to visit the site of the bridge which was being constructed about four miles from our home.

22. After two long weeks she found herself walking up the gang plank of the ship which was to take her to America.

23. Although I have learned many things which will help me I value my English training above all others.

24. During this interview which was very interesting I learned many things about the business the city and the county.

25. My aunt who is living in Denver wrote to us of an amazing experience which she had last month.

EXERCISE 17

Follow the directions in Exercise 16.

1. The meeting was called to order by Mrs. Frank Ford who called on Mrs. James Robb chairman of the banquet committee for her report.

2. My father's hunting lodge which is set high on a mountain overlooking a lake is as quaint as a picture in a book.

3. The bully was a strong husky fellow of seventeen who spent his time beating the small boys.

4. We knew Roger as a little boy who used to hang on to other boys when they wanted to be rid of him.

5. The success of the organization under my leadership made me impatient with my successor who was a slow easy-going boy.

6. All of a sudden without any warning in advance the truck which was carrying sand went out of control and turned over completely.

7. The machine which we installed last week will cut office expenses and give employees who operate it an easier day.

8. When Joseph had finished the article which he read with great interest he stood up folded the magazine and began to lecture us.

9. The second flood condition in that area within a week followed a heavy downpour of rain which felled telephone wires sent trees crashing upon parked automobiles and backed up countless sewers.

10. Mr. Reever who called on me yesterday had some interesting samples but he was unable to get me any of the fine English wool that I wanted.

23i. Use commas to separate dates, places, initials, or the abbreviation of academic degrees from the rest of a sentence. Such expressions are often called *limiting expressions*.

John left on July 8, 1949, to go to Chicago.
Virginia City, Montana, is a restored mining town.
Jackson, E. T., and Wharton, F., are on the list.
James Norman, D. D., and Frank Hale, M. D., are the owners.

EXERCISE 18

On your paper, write the following sentences, placing commas where they are needed. Most of the commas will be required to punctuate limiting expressions, but some commas will be needed in other uses.

1. On February 12 1809 Abraham Lincoln was born in a log cabin in Hardin County Kentucky.
2. Mr. Saunders testified that on May 9 1943 he was in Athens Ohio on business.
3. Good Friday April 10 1868 was the birth date of a great actor George Arliss.
4. The writer studied at the Sorbonne Paris from September 10 1933 to May 30 1934.
5. On July 20 1942 the first group of women to join the United States Army showed up at Des Moines Iowa.
6. At the age of seven my father spent his first vacation away from home in Chestertown Maryland where he had relatives.
7. Simon Bolivar the great South American patriot was a native of Caracas Venezuela.
8. Florence Nightingale often called the "Angel of the Crimea" was born in Florence Italy and took her name from that town.
9. In the March 1946 issue of the magazine there is an article on penicillin.
10. Your advertisement in the Denver *Post* of Thursday March 12 interested me.

11. On November 14 1936 in Louisville Kentucky Jasper Menton one of the leading citizens of the state indicated his willingness to run for Congress.

12. One night fifteen years ago in Windsor Ontario Martin Banner a steelworker bade his wife good-by and went to a lodge meeting. He was never seen again.

13. Elizabeth Benson one of the pioneers in the movement to educate women visited Hastings Nebraska on May 10 1908.

14. Henry started to school with his cousin Pauline Henderson who lived next door to him on Linwood Boulevard Kansas City.

15. On January 9 1834 in Boston Massachusetts a book by John Carrington was published.

23j. Use a comma to separate contrasted coördinate elements.

My name is John, not Henry.
He struck forcefully, but wildly.

23k. Use a comma to show the omission of a verb in a compound sentence.

Shelley is a poet; Swift, a satirist.
My brother lives in Utah; my sister, in Wisconsin.

23l. Use a comma after the salutation and complimentary close in a friendly letter.

Dear Harold,
Sincerely yours,

NOTE: The colon is generally used after the salutation in a business letter and may also be used after the salutation in a friendly letter.

23m. Use a comma before a direct quotation that is introduced by a verb such as *said, exclaimed, thought.* (See Sections 25b and 27a.)

Morgan said proudly, "I am a Texan."

If the sentence does not end with the quotation, a comma is often required before the closing quotation marks. (See Section 27.)

> The stranger said, "This is the end of our trail," and dismounted.

23n. Use a comma or commas to separate an absolute expression from the rest of a sentence.

> The tide having risen, Ferris floated the sailboat.
> On the island, the fog having lifted, he saw the lighthouse.

EXERCISE 19

On your paper, rewrite the following paragraph, placing commas where they are needed. Number each comma in sequence. At the end of the paragraph, list the numbers and beside each number write the reason for the use of the comma indicated by that number.

Not long ago some of our newspapers reported the development of jet-propelled automobiles and we all thought of the great development that has taken place since the first horseless carriage. Although it seems impossible now to think of a life without cars our grandparents remember those carriage days very well. Grandpa climbed into his buggy took the reins in his hand gave old Dobbin a gentle slap and set off to see his girl. The first horseless carriage was built by Charles and Frank Duryea in Springfield Massachusetts in 1892. It was the Duryeas also who won the first road automobile race ever held in the United States. The other day Jane came to me with a photograph album and said "If you want to see something really amusing look at the clothes worn by those early drivers." Long loose coats big goggles and visored caps were used by the men. The ladies not to be outdone added to this costume long veils which tied their hats on securely. Their speed being seven miles an hour those cars caused a great wind a cloud of dust and wild excitement.

EXERCISE 20

Follow the directions in Exercise 19.

Since the radio has become so popular the average person reads less according to a recent report. If this is true then the average person is missing a great experience that could be his. In the first place reading offers us a chance for vicarious experience. It may be adventure in distant lands the problems of raising chickens on a far-from-modern farm or the struggle to establish a business that pays. However one of the greatest satisfactions that the average man can obtain from reading is the mental stimulation of sharing the ideas of great men and women. Because these are ideas that would seldom occur to an average fellow he would never meet them at all except through reading. Anyone who has read widely knows what fun it is to meet challenging ideas to broaden one's own outlook to grow intellectually. In addition a reader develops his aesthetic sense for he learns the beauty of words and imagery. These things being true it would in the opinion of many people be a great mistake to permit the radio to take the place of reading.

EXERCISE 21

Follow the directions in Exercise 19.

As Ichabod approached the stream his heart began to thump. He summoned up however all his resolution gave his horse a kick in the ribs and attempted to dash briskly across the bridge. Instead of starting forward the perverse old animal ran broadside against the fence. Ichabod whose fears increased with the delay jerked the reins and kicked the horse lustily. It was all in vain. His steed started it is true but it was only to plunge to the opposite side of the road. Ichabod now bestowed both whip and heel upon the ribs of Old Gunpowder who dashed forward sniffling and snorting. In a moment he stopped as suddenly as he had begun. In the dark shadow of the grove Ichabod beheld something huge black and towering. As he looked he realized with horror that the figure was headless; but his horror was still greater when he observed that the head which should have rested on the shoulders was carried before the rider on the pommel of his saddle.

Adapted from The Legend of Sleepy Hollow
by Washington Irving

EXERCISE 22

Follow the directions in Exercise 19.

A moment later a throng of people came pouring round the corner. There could not have been fewer than five hundred and they were dancing like five thousand demons. At first they were a mere storm of coarse red caps and coarser woolen rags but as they filled the square some ghastly apparition gone raving mad rose among them. They advanced retreated clutched at one another spun round in pairs until many of them dropped. While those were down the rest linked hand in hand and all spun round together. No fight could have been half so terrible as this dance. It was so emphatically a fallen sport a healthy pastime changed into a means of angering the blood bewildering the senses and steeling the heart. This was the Carmagnole.

Adapted from A Tale of Two Cities by Charles Dickens

24. THE SEMICOLON

The semicolon is a stronger mark of punctuation than the comma. It signifies a greater break between sentence parts. It is used chiefly between parts of a sentence that have equal rank.

24a. Use a semicolon to separate independent clauses not joined by a coördinating conjunction (*and, but, nor, for, or*).

> Please close the window; the room is cold.
> I entertain my friends by playing the piano; Ellen does tap dancing.
> My companion and I walked down the street; he saw only shop windows; I saw only people's faces.

24b. Use a semicolon to separate independent clauses connected by a conjunctive adverb (*however, moreover,*

nevertheless, consequently, therefore, thus, then, so, yet, otherwise, still, likewise).

> They were of opposite characters; yet they remained friends for many years.

> We regret that we have sold all of the blouses in blue; however, we have the same style in pink.

NOTE: Do not use a semicolon every time that you see a conjunctive adverb. Be sure first that you have two independent clauses.

> John, however, has failed to do the work. (This sentence has no semicolon because *however* is a parenthetical expression and does not connect two complete thoughts.)

24c. Use a semicolon to separate independent clauses joined by a coördinating conjunction, if the clauses are long or contain commas.

> When the scorpion stung the man, he felt a sharp pain in his foot; but since there was no swelling, he thought that he had not been injured.

> Roberta, a very good friend of mine, wants me to go to camp with her; but because I have been to camp for three years in succession, I am undecided.

CAUTION: 1. A semicolon does not usually appear between an independent clause and a dependent clause or an independent clause and a phrase. A semicolon joins only those things which are in the same form structurally.

> Wrong: Whenever I hear from one of the old crowd; memories rush to my mind. (The first clause is a dependent clause. It would not express a complete thought if used alone. The second clause is an independent clause. It would express a complete thought if used alone.)

> Right: Whenever I hear from one of the crowd, memories rush to my mind. (See Section 23b.)

> Wrong: Everything that you sent me is beautiful; especially the white doeskin gloves.

> Right: Everything that you sent me is beautiful, especially the white doeskin gloves.

2. Sometimes it is difficult to recognize two independent clauses because in the second clause, the verb is understood. Watch this construction carefully. A semicolon must go between the clauses. Notice that a comma is used to show the omission of the word.

Right: Mary earns twenty dollars; her sister, ten.

The second clause means that Mary's sister *earns ten* dollars. When such a construction occurs, the semicolon is used between the clauses; and a comma indicates the omission of the verb.

24d. Use a semicolon before explanatory expressions like *for example, namely.*

> The government has given to veterans some special considerations; namely, college training, trade training, and insurance.

EXERCISE 23

Some of the following sentences are correctly punctuated; others are not. On your paper, rewrite the latter, using commas and semicolons where they are required. Write your reason for each correction. If a sentence is correct, do not rewrite it, but write C beside its number.

1. It is painful for me to recall the story I prefer never to think of it again.
2. When I arrived at the dentist's office I was asked to give the history of my life then I was ushered into the main office.
3. I can't imagine what he wants; I never heard of him before.
4. Mr. Howells was born on May 30 1903 in Richmond Virginia but at the age of two he moved to Long Beach California.
5. "Cowards die many times before their death; the valiant never taste of death but once."
6. Some of the vehicles were drawn by rough-looking horses others by beautiful mares.

7. Our income this week was slightly more than $500 our expenses a little over $300.

8. Mrs. Smith is interested in purchasing some of our stainless steel products; however, she thinks our prices are too high.

9. Things back home will seem a bit strange to you in fact everything in the old town has changed.

10. Mr. Mayer noticed that Benito was more alert than the average Indian servant therefore he decided to send the child to school.

EXERCISE 24

Follow the directions in Exercise 23.

1. This year I have my last opportunity to win my letter in basketball and if all goes well I shall soon be wearing the emblem of the school.

2. If any fault in our service has caused your long absence from our store we are anxious to correct it for we want you to be entirely satisfied.

3. While the class gives the salute Henry Brown will hold the United States flag Jacob Fleischman the Maryland flag and Herbert Settle the Baltimore flag.

4. In 1912 the Republican candidate for President of the United States was Taft; the Democratic candidate, Wilson.

5. Johnson hated to be questioned and Boswell was eternally catechizing him on all kinds of subjects.

6. Some people felt that she was satisfied too easily others that she was one of the few people capable of a really great love.

7. Farming seemed to be the chief occupation of the section, for everywhere one could see fields planted with corn wheat and potatoes.

8. No one thought until the deadline approached that the men would strike and it seemed inconceivable that they would strike against the government after seizure of the plant.

9. On our side of the street the lawns are neat and the hedges trim on the other side the lawns have tall weeds and ash cans stand in front of the gates.

10. Jane Withers invited me to a party she is going to give for Mary Lou; and when she heard that you would be in town, she included you in the invitation.

EXERCISE 25

Follow the directions in Exercise 23.

1. During twenty years Boswell continued to worship the master and the master continued to scold the disciple to sneer at him and to love him.

2. When the game started Leroy who had been a great success the week before was not on the field and all of the spectators wondered what had happened to him.

3. In the neighborhood where I lived there were no movies, playgrounds, or nursery schools where children could go for recreation; therefore, the streets and empty lots were used for play.

4. It will in the future not be possible to provide Mr. Schultz with room and board at the building consequently some adjustment in his salary is necessary.

5. The equipment is available for use to anyone that needs it however the laboratory employees are responsible for keeping it in good condition.

6. Not only was there trouble with the chickens but since the farm was far from modern Hilda had to struggle with the stove the plumbing and the heating system.

7. Boswell was very much attracted to Johnson; he made it his business to watch the great man, to discover his habits, and to remember the remarkable things he said.

8. In the files I found data showing that the solvent is a mixture of alcohol and Amsco A a naphtha derivative and is purchased from the B. T. Ford Company.

9. I explained that it would be impossible to fill the order at once because we cannot obtain the necessary materials however I assured the customer that just as soon as the strike is over we would make the shipment.

10. There is to be a meeting with the City Council on Monday, June 11, to consider the budget of the Department of Public Welfare; and representatives of this group are planning to appear to show why the funds are necessary.

25. THE COLON

The colon is used chiefly to introduce lists, series, explanations, or formal quotations.

25a. Use a colon to introduce a list.

Please send by American Express the following:
1 White bathing suit #427, size 14
2 Red beach robes #228, medium size
1 Beach umbrella, red and black, #426

We have notified the following people: Mr. James Montgomery, Captain Richard Stout, Dr. Ezra Watkins, Mrs. Martin Slocum.

NOTE: Do not overwork this introductory function. There is no justification for its use in such a sentence as this one.

Wrong: The three cities are: New Orleans, New York, San Francisco. (No mark of punctuation is needed after *are*.)

25b. Use a colon to introduce a formal statement or a formal quotation.

Robert E. Lee is reputed to have said: "Duty is the sublimest word in the English language."

25c. Use a colon after a statement which is followed by an explanatory clause or expression.

These two things he admired: an honest man and a beautiful woman.

My objection to the plan is this: it will cost a great deal of money, and the returns will be small for many years.

Everything was in good shape for the meeting: chairs placed, pads and pencils ready, and a pitcher of water at the head of the table.

25d. Use a colon after the formal salutation of a business letter.

Dear Mr. Henderson:

NOTE: Some business firms today are using no punctuation at all after the salutation.

25e. Use a colon to separate hour and minute figures in writing time, the act from the scene of a play, the title of a book from the subtitle, the verse following the biblical chapter.

7:35
Hamlet I:2
Principles of Geology: A College Textbook
Mark 6:10

CAUTION: 1. Do not use a colon after *are* or *were* when a simple series follows.

The kinds of dogs to be found at the kennels are terriers, bulls, and collies.

2. When *such as* is followed by a short illustration, usually only a comma is necessary.

He has visited many countries, such as Italy, Switzerland, Austria, and France.

3. The words *namely, viz., i.e., that is,* are usually preceded by a semicolon unless the material following is very long.

We have studied five parts of speech; namely, nouns, pronouns, verbs, adjectives, and adverbs.

EXERCISE 26

Write the following sentences on your paper. Place semicolons and colons where they are needed. Give the reason for each correction.

1. Above everything else he hated one thing hypocrisy.
2. He could barely read the sign "Danger, Explosives."
3. The players came from all over the world Germany Italy Japan Russia China and Canada.

4. Howard had little money therefore he had to walk all the way.

5. The lecturer said that we must do three things balance the budget, go back on the gold standard, and raise tariffs however he would not guarantee an immediate return of prosperity.

6. My father thought that the minister was referring to John 3 16 nevertheless, I was certain that he meant Luke 9 10.

7. This is his program for healthful living drink plenty of milk eat good-sized quantities of fresh, green vegetables take exercise every day, preferably in the open air sleep at least eight hours every night.

8. A football team can be little better than its signal-caller that is to say, its success depends upon the play it uses.

9. There are three things that I wish to do before I die go to Europe bathe in the warm, inviting waters of Waikiki Beach see the Taj Mahal.

10. Stuart Chase once wrote "For the milk of human kindness the most obvious substitute is soft soap."

11. He has a very sore leg consequently, he cannot make the trip.

12. The letter began "Dear President Smith I intended to answer your last letter more promptly than this however, I have been so occupied that I have not had time to give my answer the thought it deserved."

13. At 12 15 last night our telephone rang loudly but when I answered it, nobody replied.

14. The notice had an ominous ring to it "All lights must be extinguished at 10 15 sharp."

15. You should give that chair at least two coats of flat paint, then you should put on one coat of varnish.

16. It has been our experience that success in college depends to a great extent on one trait namely, the ability to concentrate.

17. There is nothing very original about the street names in our town Main Street, Broad Street, Bank Street, and so on.

18. He used to astound his friends by quoting something and then rattling off the source for it, such as Macbeth I 2, or Romeo and Juliet IV 1.

19. Please wipe your feet carefully, our front hall is beginning to look like a pigsty.

20. The Johns Hopkins University has six divisions College of Arts and Sciences, College for Engineers, Graduate School, Medical School, School of Public Health, and McCoy College.

21. My itinerary, which I obtained from the travel agent this morning, is certain to do for me one thing, if nothing else it will take me to all the important art galleries in Europe.

22. When he rose to speak, the president of the university threw back his head and began "Ladies and gentlemen, in the troubled times ahead we shall be called upon to make many adjustments, but there is one principle to which we must cling tenaciously it is freedom of speech."

23. In our modern, complicated society, students must do three things they must ask for the source of all information before they believe it they must learn to recognize bad reasoning they must send to their law-making bodies only well qualified representatives.

24. The train was scheduled to arrive in Milwaukee at 6 45, but when we left the station at 8 30, there was still no definite news of the time of its arrival.

25. Dr. Isaiah Bowman said in his address "The trade school exists for the admirable purpose of putting practically trained men into jobs the university exists, among other things, to create and expand the sciences that provide the jobs."

EXERCISE 27

On your paper, write these sentences, placing commas, colons, and semicolons where they should be.

1. These are the words of Edmund Burke a fine statesman "A great empire and little minds go ill together."

2. I should like to make this motion that we appoint committee to study the whole question and repo the findings to the Board of Directors.

3. When she gave the girl advice Mrs. Martin quote this very appropriate line "Gather ye rosebuds whil ye may."

4. Edmund Burke objected to force as a means of handling the colonies for these four reasons it is un certain it is temporary it impairs the object and Eng land has had no experience in using it.

5. One point which you will all concede is this Wal Whitman is one of the greatest figures in America poetry.

6. The framework of the bill is as follows the commis sion will consist of a chairman and four member appointed by the President subject to the approva of the Senate.

7. We sent him a telegram which said "Meet 8:5 Northern Pacific train from Spokane."

8. The questions which we must decide are these sha we have a committee to plan the improvements an shall this committee be appointed or elected?

9. Scientists do not rely entirely on the evidence of the lie detector for an obvious reason all people are no frightened by a third degree.

10. The train stopped between two white fields ahea the snow had buried the tracks.

26. THE APOSTROPHE: POSSESSIVES AND PLURALS

The apostrophe is used to indicate the possessive cas of nouns and of pronouns like *anybody, someone, one everybody.*

> Carl's book was lost.
> Someone's hat was left in the locker room.

26a. Use an apostrophe and *s* to form the possessive of all singular nouns.

> boy's, dog's, doctor's, lady's, James's, Dickens's, M Jones's

NOTE: 1. The apostrophe comes before the *s* if the word is singular.

2. Singular nouns ending normally in *s* may omit the second *s*. The apostrophe will then be placed after the *s* which is part of the noun.

James' or James's (But not *Jame's*)
Keats' or Keats's (But not *Keat's*)
Dickens' or Dickens's (But not *Dicken's*)

If the addition of an *s* causes difficulty in pronunciation, add only the apostrophe.

Aristophanes', princess'

26b. Use an apostrophe alone to form the possessive of most plural nouns.

Most plurals are formed by adding *s*. Place the apostrophe after this *s*. (See Section 39d.)

boys', dogs', doctors', soldiers', friends'

Nouns that end in *s* in the singular must add *es* for the plurals. The possessive form of these nouns has an apostrophe after the final *s*.

The Joneses' house burned last night.
The ladies' dining room is to the right.

A few plurals do not end in *s*. These must add *s* to form the possessive.

men's, women's, children's, people's

26c. When two or more people possess a thing together, the sign of the possessive is added to the last word.

I'll meet you at Levy and Brown's store.
Henderson, Sellers, and Company's branch office is on
   Second Avenue.
We went into Ed and John's room to see their school
   pennants.

26d. Add the apostrophe to the last member of a com pound phrase.

> somebody else's book
> my mother-in-law's house
> sister-in-law (Singular)
> sister-in-law's house (Singular possessive)
> sisters-in-law (Plural)   I have three sisters-in-law.
> sisters-in-law's (Plural possessive)
> My sisters-in-law's dispositions are all bright and chee ful.

26e. Use an apostrophe with each noun when separat ownership is indicated.

> Sally's and Helen's dates for the dance are both very tal
> Albert's and Roger's sisters are blondes.

26f. Use an apostrophe in contractions to indicate th omission of a letter.

> don't (do not)
> can't (cannot)
> haven't (have not)
> shan't (shall not)

NOTE: Although the *ll* in *shall* and the *o* in *not* ar omitted in *shan't,* only one apostrophe is used.

26g. Use an apostrophe and s to form the plural of letter, figure, or word considered as a word.

> There are two *r*'s in my name.
> Your theme has too many *and*'s.
> He wrote three *2*'s on the paper.

NOTE: Letters, figures, and words used in this way ar italicized. See Section 34c.

26h. The possessive case of a noun or pronoun is use before a gerund.

> Wrong: I do not approve of John playing football.
> Right: I do not approve of John's playing football.
> Wrong: Has Father agreed to you studying German?
> Right: Has Father agreed to *your* studying German?

NOTE: Be careful to distinguish between the gerund and the participle. Although they look exactly alike, the participle is used as an adjective, whereas the gerund is used as a noun. (See Section 3g.)

> I saw John writing a letter. (Correct. John is the object of *saw,* and *writing* merely modifies John.)
> I do not like John's writing without my knowledge. (Writing is the object of *like* and is therefore a gerund.)

26i. Be careful to use the apostrophe only when it is needed.

1. Usually, in formal English, only nouns indicating living things are used in the possessive case. Some organizations composed of living people may be considered possessive.

> Correct: the company's plan
> the city's streets
> Informal: the desk's top
> Correct: the top of the desk

2. Some expressions of time and some idomatic expressions may be possessive.

> A week's pay, a month's rest, today's paper, a hair's breadth, for goodness' sake

3. Be sure that the word is completed before the apostrophe is used.

> Right: Charles's finger, Mr. Jones's hat, Mr. Hopkins's new car
> Wrong: Charle's finger, Mr. Jone's hat, Mr. Hopkin's new car

4. Be careful not to use an apostrophe before or after ending a verb.

> Right: He lives near us.
> Wrong: He lives' near us.

5. Never use the apostrophe to form the nominative or objective plural. (See Section 14.)

Right:　　The Smiths were present at the party.
　　　　　　The Joneses have just come home.
　　　　　　The present was from the Raiders.
Wrong:　The Smiths' were present at the party.
　　　　　　The Jones's have just come home.
　　　　　　The present was from the Raiders'.

6. In contractions be sure to put the apostrophe exactly where a letter has been omitted.

Right:　　don't, haven't, who's
Wrong:　do'nt, have'nt, whos'

NOTE: *Who's* means *who is*. The possessive pronoun is *whose*.

　　　Whose book is this?
　　　Who's at the door?

7. Do not use an apostrophe with pronouns ending in *self*.

　　　Oneself, themselves

8. The apostrophe is never used to form the possessive case of personal pronouns. (*hers, yours, ours, his, its, theirs*)

　　　The dog wagged *its* tail. (Possessive)

Do not confuse the possessive form *its* with the contraction *it's* (*it is*).

　　　It's a beautiful day.

EXERCISE 28

Most of the following sentences contain errors in the use of apostrophes and the possessive case. On your paper rewrite these sentences, adding apostrophes where they are needed, correcting words in which apostrophes have been used incorrectly, or making any other necessary change. Write your reason for making each change. If a sentence is correct, do not rewrite it, but write C beside its number.

1. After Bobs part in the play was over, he collapsed.
2. I like the book because the authors style is clear and stimulating.
3. In high school we learned about various musicians lives.
4. Any educated persons opinion on the matter would be worth considering.
5. Anne Hathaway was Shakespeare's wife.
6. Dickens books are very popular in our class.
7. James brother, Allen, is our new clerk.
8. We all like Frances singing.
9. It's nobodys business what I do with my money.
10. Is that hat yours or hers?
11. My sister-in-laws house has just been sold.
12. The stenographers desks have all been painted.
13. The princess clothes were embroidered beautifully.
14. The firemens struggle to save the building was useless.
15. All requests for tickets must be sent to the womens committee.
16. For pitys sake, do something.
17. My respect for my church and it's beliefs is a result of my home training.
18. Arrangements were made to have the food prepared by the mothers' group.
19. Sue Pinemans parents went to Bismarck last week, and Sue and her brother stayed with us.
20. One of the Tibetan natives dragged away the plane's radio.
21. The Bermans' invited their niece to spend the week end at Atlantic City.
22. On Thanksgiving Day we have the annual game between the two boys high schools.
23. My parents finally gave in and said I could get my drivers license.
24. The neighbor's considered Dunstan a spiteful person, incapable of interest in another persons welfare.
25. The day's end came so quickly that I couldnt believe I had been working for ten hours.

EXERCISE 29

Follow the directions in Exercise 28.

1. In the Shakespearean theater, the womens part
were played by young boys.

2. Pepys diary gives an excellent picture of the time'
in which he lived.

3. The cats leg was broken in the accident, but nobody
seemed to care about its pain.

4. Who's house is this?

5. The policemens white gloves were spattered with
mud.

6. One years work in history and two years work in
mathematics are necessary for graduation.

7. This years *Press* is a real students paper, reflecting
the ideas and thoughts of the student body.

8. There is no record of that officer having been as
signed to the duty mentioned.

9. Mother does not approve of James writing to Char
lotte.

10. The nurses' headquarters are next to Dr. Bright'
hospital.

11. We were surprised to hear of the citizens' decision
to call a buyers' strike.

12. The government should use it's influence to preven
the man being sacrificed to a local quarrel.

13. When Janes house was robbed last night, the thieve
took her mothers fur coat and her two sister
watches.

14. Fifteen years' experience in banking makes it possi
ble for us to handle our clients' investments with
skill.

15. The flowers which came from Hazlitt and Paine'
store were from the Burtons.

16. Somebodys coat has been left on the Clarks' porch

17. At Mr. Carltons suggestion, I am sending you sam
ples of materials for childrens dresses.

18. I cannot undertand Doris' refusing to help you.

19. We had Rivers Chambers orchestra, and the girl
favors were school seals.

20. Conner and Evans' business, including the goods on hand and all the company's fixtures, was sold for $130,000.

21. The United Automobile Company's annual report shows a stockholders' dividend of four percent.

22. In yesterdays mail there was an order from J. M. Hawkins Office Supply Company.

23. A ladies purse with a monogram of two *T* s was lost in Benton and Kings store on Friday.

24. My sister-in-law's wedding dress came from the new women's dress department at Hughes department store.

25. There have been in the papers a great many articles about Houston getting a football franchise in the All-American Conference.

27. QUOTATION MARKS

27a. Quotation marks are used at the beginning and at the end of the exact words which a person says (direct quotations).

Right: Scott said, "I am going home."
Right: Scott said that he was going home.
Wrong: Scott said "that he was going home."

The second and third sentences contain an indirect quotation. The exact words which Scott used are not in the sentence; therefore no quotation marks are necessary.

The first word in a direct quotation is capitalized. If the quotation is introduced by an expression such as *he said,* a comma must precede the opening quotation marks.

Martin said, "It looks as if it will rain."

If the sentence does not end with the quotation, a comma is usually required before the closing quotation marks.

Martin said, "It looks as if it will rain," but Lana disagreed with him.

If the quotation consists of several sentences, quotation marks do not introduce each sentence. Use quotation marks only at the beginning and end of an unbroken quotation.

> She said, "I have promised to go downtown. Perhaps I could change the arrangements. I'll let you know in a few minutes."

> Oliver Wendell Holmes says in *The Autocrat of the Breakfast Table:* "This business of conversation is a serious matter. There are men of *esprit* who are excessively exhausting to some people. They are the talkers that have what may be called *jerky* minds. Their thoughts do not run in the natural order of sequence."

27b. If there is a long quotation which includes several paragraphs or several stanzas of poetry, quotation marks should be used at the beginning of each paragraph but not at the end of each paragraph. They are used at the end of the last paragraph only.

27c. In dialogue, every change of speaker requires a separate paragraph.

> "I've never gone to a better dance," said Jessie.
> "It must have been great fun," answered Ida. "Who took you?"
> "I went with Ed, and Sally and Paul joined us. Afterwards we all went to Saunders' for a hamburger."

27d. If the quotation is broken by an expression like *he said*, *Mary answered*, this expression must *not* be included in the quotation marks.

> "If you go," he said, "be sure to let me know."

If a quotation broken by an expression like *he said* is composed of more than one sentence, be sure to use a period, an exclamation point, or a question mark at the end of each sentence.

> "It's raining hard," Harold said. "There is no fun on a picnic in the rain. Do you want to go home?"

27e. A quotation inside another quotation is enclosed in single quotation marks.

> "When I telephoned her last night," said Cary, "she told me again and again, 'Don't worry. I will not let you down.' "

27f. Commas and periods are placed inside the closing quotation marks; semicolons and colons are placed outside; question marks and exclamation points are placed inside or outside the quotation marks, according to the meaning of the sentence.

> We heard Phyllis say, "Don't wait for me," and then we heard a sudden cry.
>
> Andrew said, "Don't worry."
>
> The postman said, "I never receive any mail"; he looked so depressed that Nancy and I shared our postcards with him.
>
> This is what Jim meant when he said, "Bring everything we shall need": food, feed for the horses, bedrolls, cooking utensils, and warm clothing.
>
> He asked, "Who has my knife?" (The question mark is part of the quotation.)
>
> Did Nancy really say, "I won't go"? (The question mark is not part of the quotation.)
>
> Rob cried, "There goes my hat!" (The exclamation point is part of the quotation.)
>
> How amazed I was to hear her say, "You have won the contest"! (The exclamation point is not part of the quotation.)

27g. Use quotation marks to enclose technical terms in non-technical writing.

> This is a heavily "watered" issue of stock.
>
> The pilot made a "three-point" landing.

27h. In formal writing use quotation marks to enclose words which suggest a different level of usage.

> The prevailing opinion is that President Slade informed the Board of Directors that their decision was "cock-eyed."
>
> The symphony was conducted by a "stuffed shirt."

NOTE: See Section 34a for use of quotation marks with names of magazine articles, short stories, and other titles.

CAUTION: 1. Quotation marks *always go in pairs*. Be careful to indicate both the beginning and end of a quotation.

2. Do not use quotation marks to indicate humor.

EXERCISE 30

On your paper, write the following dialogue, adding quotation marks and other punctuation where necessary, and beginning new paragraphs when required:

Ralph and I had a long talk last night said Betty Lou. He thinks that we should go steady, but my mother is definitely hard to deal with. Parents can be such problems sympathized Jacqueline. My mother always insists upon calling me Jacqueline. Imagine giving a girl such a name. It's only with my own friends, who understand me, that I can be called Jackie. It would be definitely romantic to go steady with Ralph. What did you tell him? What could I tell him? My mother's same old line. Girls should know a number of boys. I'm too young to go steady, et cetera. Jackie sipped her lemonade. It's terrific the way parents behave. If you went steady with Ralph, she said, you'd always have a good date for every dance. If you don't go steady, a boy can always make a date with someone else. Betty Lou sighed. Oh well, there's nothing I can do. My mother even invited some friend of hers to bring her son for dinner so that I'd get interested in somebody else besides Ralph. I didn't like him at all. Hi, Sonny, she called as a blond youth came into the drug store; what's on your mind? Parents answered the boy, joining the two girls. They give a guy more trouble.

28. ACHIEVEMENT TESTS ON PUNCTUATION

28a. Achievement Test I on commas, semicolons, colons, apostrophes, quotation marks.

On your paper, write the following sentences, placing punctuation marks where they are required. If any punctuation marks have been incorrectly used, make any necessary corrections. Write your reason for each correction. If a sentence requires no correction, do not rewrite it; but write C beside its number.

1. When the lecturer arrived at 8 30 the hall was filled.
2. The output of the company was greatly reduced consequently the management was obliged to concentrate on new business.

3. A business letter should be friendly courteous and conservative in statement.

4. If businessmen are really interested in their government they can improve it in many ways.

5. The speakers manner was pleasing but his enunciation was poor.

6. When Joan arrived we were in the midst of great preparations for my grandparents fiftieth wedding anniversary.

7. According to reports made by R. T. McClintook the commissioner of public roads the proposed highway will greatly aid traffic between Easton Maryland and Charleston South Carolina.

8. We are pleased to notify you that in accordance with your request of February 10 we have opened a charge account for you.

9. Dont get excited said Jane, Mother will bring the books when she comes to see you.

10. Martin Williamson son of Mr. and Mrs. Peter Williamson 918 Wendover Road Dover Delaware was selected for one of the scholarships.

11. Its likely that the future airplane will be driven by jet propulsion in its wings.

12. When I heard the policemens whistles I thought that something dreadful had happened.

13. Each of the characters' was presented with great care, as a result the novel was very striking.

14. One fact is clear and indisputable the public and avowed origin of this quarrel was taxation.

15. During this period the first organized resistance began and a number of employees looking for a solution of their problems joined labor unions.

16. Im afraid we cant go to the game Sam said David unless you can get your car. My father is going to use ours.

17. In the nineteenth century men worked for long hours in factories and debtors prisons constantly faced the people.

18. Jim had borrowed his father's car for the occasion, and I felt quite smart when he helped me into the new Buick.

19. Dr. Martin Baum president of the society sent letters of invitation to Dr. Hubert Enders Dr. Mark Candell and Dr. Ellen Harrington.

20. Randolph, Brown and Company new store has a sale of mens womens and childrens clothes.

21. One plane will fly from Baltimore to Rehoboth the other from Cumberland to Hagerstown.

22. Gustavus Adolphus of Sweden is often called the father of modern field artillery because he standardized the calibers of his guns brought into existence lighter carriages and placed powder and projectile together.

23. The captain gave orders for everyone to go below and told the sailors to lower the sails.

24. Girls worked as nurses aids collected materials needed by the government and took care of war workers children.

25. The proposed bridge, which will cost $1,397,000, will be valuable to many businessmen.

28b. Achievement Test II on commas, semicolons, colons, apostrophes, quotation marks.

Follow the directions given for Achievement Test I.

1. I am not sure about Ralph going to college.

2. Fredleys store will be glad to grant credit to new residents who want exclusive tailoring.

3. In Walter Reeds experiment with yellow fever some men were put in perfectly sterile rooms and others slept in a place that contained yellow-fever victims clothing.

4. The pressure groups claimed that if price controls were released production would increase goods would pour into the markets and prices would control themselves.

5. In the final vote, twenty boys expressed a willingness to try the new method; five turned down the plan; and three voted for it with an amendment.

6. As we approached a small desolate farm on the side of a lonely country road we were attracted by the fields which were full of uncultivated cotton and tobacco.

7. Waterview Avenue will play an important part in the city's plans, for Totem Street will be connected to Waterview by a bridge 2300 feet long.

8. When the bully beat up one of Hanks friends a short skinny fellow who limped Hank rushed to the rescue.

9. A course in *Critical Thinking* has taught us the difference between fact and opinion truth and propaganda and good and bad sources of information.

10. As practical as the Greeks were they failed to realize the power of war engines consequently it was not until the time of Alexander the Great that these new agents of destruction were developed.

11. In the morning of one of our last days at camp we had a dress rehearsal which was given for the young children who could not stay up late at night.

12. I want to find out if there is any chance of Jack getting a room in the dormitory.

13. The medical clinics occupied the second floor of the dispensary and consisted of rooms for the treatment of eyes nose throat and childrens diseases.

14. After years of secret work in laboratories and months of limited commercial operation this powerful device was at last ready for the public.

15. My practical experience in selling has been obtained in Green and Hoskins Infant Department and in the offices of the Dalton Motor Company.

16. Among my fellow art majors who shared my zest for art and who liked to spend their free time with the paints and brushes I found my friends.

17. At eight o'clock Marion said cheerfully we got dressed in our best clothes and went to see *South Pacific*.

18. Five-year-old Tommy Lynn and his dog Bozo lost since Thursday in the Coconine National Forest were found this morning but the search continued for his three-year-old sister Estelle who disappeared at the same time.

19. Filled with excitement and joy the child rushed into the living room shouting Uncle John has given me a little white rabbit. May I keep it?

20. I am sending you a sample of Chinese brocade from Nortons shop and should greatly appreciate Helen trying to match it for me Marian wrote.

21. A sale of womens and misses clothes nearly caused a riot at Prestons store yesterday.

22. Simple clear bold and straightforward in mind and action Colonel Settle was one of natures noblemen

23. While she was restrained by her husband a man of sense and firmness her worst offenses were impertinent jokes little white lies and short fits of pettishness but after his death she did many things which worried her friends.

24. Dr. Phelps who will retire at the end of the month said to the nurses at their graduation exercises some nurses training schools in their eagerness for progress are placing too much emphasis on medication and methods. Remember that the care of the patient as a person must be your first concern.

25. Please follow these directions for typing the paper
    Double-space the lines.
    Use a 1½-inch left-hand margin.
    Write all headings in capitals.

29. THE PERIOD

29a. Use a period at the end of every complete declarative sentence.

It was a cold, dismal day.

Although his health was poor, he decided to leave the sanatorium.

You go ahead with your proposed trip; I shall remain at home.

NOTE: 1. Do not punctuate sentence fragments as complete units of thought unless they obviously stand for complete expressions. (See Section 57.)

Correct: "I want to go with you."
             "All right."
             "When do you leave?"
             "Tomorrow."

Incorrect: Walking as fast as he could.
           At an early hour when few are awake.

2. Periods are also used after mildly imperative sentences; exclamation marks are used after vigorously imperative sentences. (See Section 30a.)

> Look before you leap.
> Leave the house at once!

29b. Use a period after a standard abbreviation.

> James Smith, Esq., was director of the enterprise.
> The envelope was addressed to Paul Travin, M. D.; the postmark was London.
> Henry Jones, D. D. (b. 1875; d. 1937)
> Dec. 10; bbl.; n.b.; q.v.; p.m.

30. EXCLAMATION POINTS AND QUESTION MARKS

30a. Use the exclamation point to express surprise, command, emphasis, or strong emotion.

> Help! Help!
> What! Are you certain?

30b. Use a question mark at the end of every direct question.

> Do you really know the whole story?
> Why are you so eager to go to Sea Island?

CAUTION: Do not use the question mark after an indirect question.

> Wrong: I was asked if I wanted to go?
> Right: I was asked if I wanted to go.

30c. Use a question mark, enclosed in parentheses, to express doubt or uncertainty.

> This is a genuine (?) leather bag.
> Richardson was born in 1900 (?) in Selma.

CAUTION: Do not overuse the question mark for this purpose. If it is impossible for you to find the exact information needed, you may use the question mark. But do not use it as a lazy excuse for research. Do not use the question mark to express irony or humor.

31. THE DASH

Too frequent use of the dash makes a sensational style. Careless writers sometimes think that the dash makes a chatty, informal style. As a result, they sprinkle friendly letters with dashes. Never use the dash as a substitute for a period, a semicolon, or a colon.

> Wrong: When we reached home, the house was completely dark—we opened the door and saw Jo-Jo wagging his tail.
>
> Right: When we reached home, the house was completely dark. We opened the door and saw Jo-Jo wagging his tail.

31a. Use a dash to indicate a break or shift of thought.

> Here is a fuller explanation—but perhaps you are not interested.
>
> He is the most despicable—but I should not say any more.
>
> Do we—can we—propose such action to the trustees?

NOTE: Omit the period when a statement ends with a dash.

> Well, if that is how you feel—
> George began, "May I ask—"
> "You may not," snapped the judge.

31b. Use the dash to set off sharply distinguished parenthetical matter or to secure emphasis or suspense.

> I am unalterably opposed—unalterably, I repeat—to this suggestion.
>
> She was aware—she must have known—that the proposal was hopeless.
>
> I was pleased—delighted, I should say—to hear your excellent report.

NOTE: When the parenthetical material set off by dashes requires an exclamation point or question mark, such punctuation should precede the second dash.

> If I should miss the train—heaven forbid!—I'll telephone you.

31c. Use the dash to indicate the omission of words or letters.

> Gen. B—was an excellent soldier.
> The Civil War was fought 1861–1865.

NOTE: The dash used with numbers is a short dash.

31d. The dash may be used instead of the comma to separate long appositive expressions from the rest of a sentence.

> All the dogs in town—dalmatians, dachshunds, deer hounds—lined up for the animal parade.

EXERCISE 31

On your paper, rewrite the following sentences, placing dashes where they are required:

1. Col. John Hudson from Kansas, you know fought in France in 1942.
2. When I looked up my heart misses a beat even now at the very memory I saw a huge beast before me!
3. You are too how shall I say? too matter-of-fact to do such a hot-headed thing.
4. From 1922 to 1925 perhaps it was 1921 1925 the man made a canvass of the city of Los Angeles.
5. As I was walking along Waverly Place but before that I should mention the sight I saw on Twenty-first Street.
6. He was a large man who wore a straw hat and a top-coat a very odd sight, I assure you.
7. The food was excellent, but the boarders
8. I am reasonably certain no, I am positive that you will like this if you will only give it a fair trial.

EXERCISE 32

On your paper, rewrite the following sentences, placing periods, exclamation points, and question marks where they are required:

1. The letter was addressed as follows: "Milton Johnson, M D, Barton, Nev"

2. How feverish you seem Are you certain you are all right Shall I call Dr. Jones You must be ill
3. Ouch Watch where you are going
4. "Why is he leaving Any particular reason"
5. "Please stop that You know crying only makes you feel worse Hush"
6. He asked John if he would go John emphatically said, "Never"
7. Are you quite certain that he holds the degree of M D
8. Fifty percent of the boys left for the holidays on Dec 20; the others all left on Dec 22
9. Isn't it strange that Dr and Mrs Browne were both born on December 11, 1898
10. Bob is in his fourth year at the University of Minnesota, but he is still not quite certain whether, after college, he will work for his father or try to earn a degree of D D S

32. THE HYPHEN AND SYLLABICATION

The hyphen is more a mark of spelling than of punctuation. It indicates that two words or two parts of one word belong together. The hyphen is a mechanical device which is necessary for correct, clear writing. It should be sharply distinguished from the dash, which is longer.

Syllabication is the act or method of dividing words into syllables.

32a. Use a hyphen to join the parts of a compound word.

The use of a hyphen in joining compound words varies greatly. Do not attempt to learn the numerous rules; consult a standard dictionary.

Hyphens are generally used:

1. Between two or more words modifying a substantive and used as a single adjective: *a well-bred person, a never-to-be-forgotten incident*. But when adverbs ending in *ly* occur in such expressions, the hyphen is not used: *a lively sounding tune*.

2. Between the parts of compound numerals (from twenty-one to ninety-nine): *fifty-two; eighty-four.*

3. Between the numerator and denominator of a fraction: *a four-fifths majority.*

4. Between the parts of certain compound nouns, adverbs, and verbs: *actor-manager;* a *well-nigh* hopeless task; to *dry-clean* a dress.

NOTE: Carefully distinguish between the short mark (period, dot) generally used by dictionaries to divide syllables and the longer mark (hyphen) used to link two words. (See Section 37.)

32b. Use a hyphen to indicate the division of a word broken at the end of a line.

The rambling old house, it is true, would look considerably better if it were freshly painted.

NOTE: 1. Do not divide a word at the end of a line if you can avoid doing so.

2. Place the hyphen at the end of the first line, never at the beginning of the second.

3. Never divide a word of one syllable. Such words as *nurse, through, though, ground, death, grace, quick, asked,* and *breadth* cannot be divided. Write the complete word on the first line, or leave a blank space and carry the whole word over to the next line.

4. Consult your dictionary to determine the correct syllabication of words. It is easier to consult an authority than to learn the various rules for dividing words. The following suggestions may be helpful, however:

Prefixes and suffixes may be written separately.

Compound words are divided between their main parts.

Two consonants are usually divided.

EXERCISE 33

1. With the aid of your dictionary, determine which of the following words are compounds and should be written with hyphens: *notebook, motherinlaw, understand, laborsaving,*

airtight, bathroom, foregoing, selfstarter, hangeron, blowout
quietspoken, hardworking, thirtynine, offstage, crazyquilt.

2. Syllabify the following words: *symphony, revolt*
delicious, radiation, carefully, torpedo, chemical, heighten
throughout, grounded.

33. PARENTHESES AND BRACKETS

Do not confuse brackets [ ] and parentheses ( )
Brackets are used to set off inserted matter as extraneous
or merely incidental to the context, especially comments
made by someone other than the author of the text. Such
interpolations may be corrections, comments, or explana
tions. Brackets are used to set apart the writer's *additions*
to quoted material; parentheses are used to enclose the
original author's *own words.*

33a. Use parentheses to enclose parenthetical material which is only remotely connected with the context.

> This punctuation (I am convinced it is important
> should be carefully studied.
> If you find any holly berries (surely they must be nu
> merous now), please bring me some.

NOTE: In such constructions the parenthetical material
merely amplifies the thought. Thus many writers prefer
dashes to parentheses. The marks may be used inter
changeably, although parentheses are more commonly
used when the parenthetical material takes the form of a
complete sentence.

33b. Use parentheses to enclose references and direc tions.

> Agrarianism (See Book I) was the next topic discussed
> Avoid split constructions. (See Chapter X.)

33c. Use parentheses to enclose figures repeated to en sure accuracy.

> He paid ten dollars ($10.00) for the shoes.
> There were thirty (30) claims for damages.

NOTE: Students often have an idea that a number written out *must* be followed by numerals. This is a mistaken notion; except in legal documents, words or figures alone are sufficient.

33d. Do not use parentheses to cancel parts of your writing. Erase or draw lines through the words you wish to delete.

33e. Use brackets to enclose a comment of the writer interpolated in a quoted passage.

> "Next came the Queen of the Mardi Gras [Miss Florence Mueller] dressed in white satin."
>
> "The youth of today [1775] are a forward and unruly lot."

EXERCISE 34

On your paper, write the following sentences, placing parentheses or brackets wherever they are required:

1. It was in December I think it was December that Mrs. Glass became ill.
2. The measurements of the lot ninety by sixty feet were considered small.
3. The mean old ogre he is all of that made the child cry bitterly.
4. "The magazine was first published in the nineteenth century 1878 by Lee and Jones now known as Jones and Bushwick."
5. This article by James Hayes you remember him? has been widely quoted.
6. *Plain Sense* was published in the nineteenth century 1836 by an English firm.
7. Totalitarianism see Chapter 10 was eagerly discussed.
8. This book the one I referred to earlier is an excellent example of sixteenth-century thought.

34. ITALICS

Materials that would be italicized in print are underlined in typed or handwritten papers.

34a. Use italics (underlining) to indicate titles of magazines, newspapers, books, long poems, plays, and musical compositions, and the names of ships, trains, and planes.

> From the library of the *Queen Elizabeth* he borrowed a copy of *Life, The New York Times,* and Sherwood's *Roosevelt and Hopkins.*

NOTE: 1. Titles of magazine articles, short stories, and short poems are usually put in quotation marks rather than in italics.

> Cartwright, Wilburn, "The Motorist Girds for War," *Harper's Magazine*

2. Do not italicize the name of a city used with the title of a newspaper unless the name of the city is actually a part of the newspaper's title.

> The San Francisco *Chronicle* (Name of city is not part of title.)
> *The New York Times* (Name of city is part of title.)

3. Do not omit an article which forms part of the title.

> Correct: *The Ancient Mariner.*

4. Do not add an article to a title if none appears in the original work.

> Correct: Rex Warner's *Return of the Traveler.*

34b. Use italics (underlining) to indicate foreign words or phrases.

> Henry was really an *enfant terrible.*
> He claimed for himself *licentia vatum.*
> Zeitgeist means "the spirit of the time."

NOTE: Some writers now omit the italics for these words

34c. Use italics (underlining) to refer to a word, letter, or number spoken of as such.

> You must note the difference between *whether* and *weather.*

Your *t*'s look exactly like *l*'s.
Form your 7's and 9's carefully.

EXERCISE 35

On your paper, write the number of each of the following sentences. Beside each number, write correctly any word or words from that sentence which should be underlined to indicate italics, or which should be placed within quotation marks. Include the punctuation.

1. Noel Coward's play The Astonished Heart has been received with great enthusiasm.
2. All the way to Europe on the Nieuw Amsterdam Ethel sat on deck reading General Clay's Decision in Germany.
3. In his lecture on Psychology of Humor the dean mentioned an article called National Differences in Humor, which appeared in The American Mercury.
4. The San Francisco Chronicle is a good newspaper.
5. Mr. Samuelson is interested in everything that happens. His chief aim is to be au courant.
6. Don't you ever dot an i in your themes?
7. We enjoyed reading Melville's novel entitled Moby Dick.
8. Henry has written a story called The Vandal.
9. The train we traveled on from Seattle was the Olympian Hiawatha.
10. Have you read Robert Frost's poem entitled The Hired Man?

35. ABBREVIATIONS

35a. Avoid most abbreviations in formal writing.

Incorrect: I asked who the prof. of the lit. class was.
His train arrives Wed. aft.
N. J. lies across the Hudson R. from N. Y.
Correct: Mrs. Scott lives on Primrose Street.
Incorrect: Last wk. I went to see a dr. in the bldg. at Valley & First.

NOTE: Themes are formal writing; that is, they are, or should be, prepared with due form and preciseness. Do not use abbreviations, except in footnotes and bibliog raphies. Especially, do not use the ampersand (&), th abbreviation symbol for *and*.

Certain very common abbreviations are permissible however. *Mr., Mrs., Dr., Ph.D., used with proper names* are correct.

Incorrect: The Rev. was not at home.
Correct: The Reverend Dr. Brown was not at home.
Incorrect: Is the Mrs. here?
Correct: Is Mrs. Anderson here?

35b. Do not use contractions in formal writing.

A contraction is a form of abbreviation: a word writter with an apostrophe to indicate the omission of a letter Such contractions as *won't, don't, can't, shouldn't,* and *wasn't* are usually out of place in formal writing.

In reporting dialogue, contractions are correctly usec to convey the exact words of the speaker. Do not avoic the use of contractions and other colloquialisms to the extent of making your reports of conversation seem arti ficial or forced.

35c. Use a period after every abbreviation.

NOTE: A period is not used with *percent*, an abbreviation of *per centum;* periods are not used with contractions such as *don't, won't,* or with the ordinal numbers wher written *1st, 2nd,* and so on. Periods are not used with nicknames.

EXERCISE 36

On your paper, write the following sentences, correct ing all errors in the use of abbreviations:

1. The sts. run e and w in N. Y C, & the aves. run n & s.
2. The king of G B from 1457 to 1509 was Henry VII; he was followed by Henry VIII.
3. The Pres. didn't make any speeches in Jan or Feb

because he was taking a vacation in Fla during those two months.

4. Tom. said that a large percent. of the boys in school tried out for the swimming team.
5. Last mo I went to see Mrs Wilson.
6. The agent asked to see the Rev. Gilman.
7. He said that he would arrive at eight a m on Mon.
8. "I regret that I shan't be able to accept your kind invit. of the fourteenth inst."
9. Ga. lies just across the Savannah R. from S C.
10. The dr also serves as a prof. at the univ. across town.

36. NUMBERS

36a. Use words to represent numerals when no more than two words are required.

Ten; thirty-six; four hundred; eight thousand; three million; one-third

Betty is *eighteen* years old.

36b. Use figures for numerals when more than two words are required.

$9.25   1,689   208   165

NOTE: Figures are always used with the word *percent* or with the percent sign except at the beginning of a sentence.

36c. Usually numbers are used in dates, street and telephone numbers, chapters of a book, and groups of numbers in the same passage.

June 14, 1936; 150 Valley View Avenue; Parkhurst 4–1963; Chapters 6, 9, and 15; Track 4; Annex 12

The dimensions are 4 feet by 9 feet.

36d. Do not begin a sentence with a numeral.

Wrong: 30 boys are playing tennis.
Right: Thirty boys are playing tennis.

CAUTION: 1. Do not repeat a number in parenthetical figures except where great accuracy is desired. (See Section 33.)

2. Use commas to set off figures in groups of three except in dates and street and telephone numbers: 2,365,189; 365,107.

3. Do not use *st, nd, rd, th* after days of the month or with street numbers.

Correct: May 16, 1911; February 18; 10 West 23 Street

EXERCISE 37

On your paper, write the following sentences, correcting all errors in the use of numbers, expressed in figures or in words:

1. He says that the last time he saw the witness was on Feb. 4th, 1949.
2. His telephone number is Hemlock 4,315.
3. 11 players constitute a football team.
4. There are only 500 women in the school, but there are at least one thousand five hundred men.
5. The Blacks have moved to a new home at 8,634 Avondale Street.
6. On March sixteenth his telephone number was changed to Oregon four-six nine six two.
7. 2100 hundred men were at work on the project when the last check was made on April 2nd, 1949
8. 4 boys and three girls failed the test, although they had studied diligently for ⅓ of the term.
9. Traffic over the bridge was very heavy: between four and four-thirty, 90 cars were counted, and between 4:30 and 5:00, 300 cars passed the tollhouse.
10. On March first, 1950, he received a check for $50, but he has received only twenty-two dollars and fifty cents since that time.

The Word

Are you sure of your words?

High school seniors recently wrote:

> Henry Esmond engaged in literary activities as an alibi for his love for Beatrix.
>
> They glanced across the beach trying to enhance the entire scene in one glance.
>
> I was surprised and delighted to receive your lovely gift for my birthday. The scarf has such lovely colors that I can hardly wait to wear it. It was lovely of you to give it to me.
>
> A coma must follow an introductory subordinate clause.

The writers of the preceding sentences were all having trouble with words. The first boy does not know the meaning of the word *alibi*. The second is mistaken in his understanding of *enhance* and has no ear for the sound of his sentence. *Glanced, enhance, glance* cause monotony of sound. The third student knows only one word that she can use to describe something that pleases her, and the fourth student intends to make us unconscious after each subordinate clause. These students all need work with words.

37. USE OF THE DICTIONARY

In your study of words, you will find it very helpful to use a good dictionary which will give you the following information about a word: pronunciation, spelling, part of speech, other forms (plural, comparative), syno-

nyms, syllabification, definition, and derivation. A goo
dictionary also tells whether a word is slang, obsolete, o
colloquial.

37a. Choose a good dictionary.

A pocket dictionary is practically worthless except a
a guide to spelling. Many very small dictionaries ar
actually false guides. Few of us will have in our home
unabridged dictionaries, like Webster's *New Interna
tional Dictionary,* Funk and Wagnalls' *New Standar
Dictionary* or the *New English* (Oxford) *Dictionary,* be
cause they are so expensive; but an abridged dictionar
will serve very well. Be sure, however, that it is of recen
date.

37b. Learn how to use a dictionary.

Because dictionaries use different systems of present
ing their material, it is wise to buy a good dictionary an
become accustomed to the method used by it. Then us
it regularly. Always read the introductory material i
your dictionary. It will explain the symbols and abbrevia
tions used and tell you how to understand the entries
Do not guess the sound of letters. Consult the chart i
the front of the dictionary or the key at the bottom o
each page. They explain, with examples, the variou
sounds that letters may have.

37c. Learn what information a dictionary will supply.

1. *Principal parts of verbs*

Here is part of an entry from a good abridged diction
ary.

> sink (sĭngk), *v.,* sank or sunk, sunk or sunken, sinkin
> . . . *v.i.* . . . *v.t.*

The small *v.* means that this word is a verb. The let
ters *v.i.* mean that the verb is intransitive or may be use
intransitively. The letters *v.t.* mean that the verb is trans

tive or may be used transitively. The entry shows that either *sank* or *sunk* may be used for the past tense of this verb.

Right: The submarine sank a large vessel.
Right: The submarine sunk a large vessel.

What does your dictionary say about principal parts of the following verbs?

dive, drink, spin, wear, swim

2. *Plurals of nouns*

If the word is marked *n.* (noun) and no plural is given, we can assume that the plural is regular and is formed by the addition of *s* to the singular. Here is part of an entry from a good abridged dictionary:

shrimp (shrĭmp) *n.*, *pl.* **shrimps** or . . . (*esp. collectively*) **shrimp.**

It is correct, then, to say:

We ordered shrimps for dinner.
We ordered shrimp for dinner.

What does your dictionary give as the plural form of each of the following words: *trout, deer, hero, tragedy, quiz?*

3. *Syllabification*

Do you sometimes reach the end of a line and find that a whole word cannot be written on that line? If part of a word appears on one line and part on another, it must be divided at the end of a syllable.

In most dictionaries a dot is used to separate syllables:

ed·u·ca·tion

Different dictionaries use different methods of marking syllabification. Read the introductory notes in your dictionary to see what system it uses.

4. *Compound words*

In a dictionary the hyphen (-) shows a compound word, usually a modifier:

well-known, clean-cut, right-handed

NOTE: Many compound nouns are written as two words without a hyphen.

farm land   water power   land agent

Be careful not to confuse the dot and the hyphen.

see · saw, ice · house, hill · side (These are not compound.

5. *References to places and historical, literary, and mythological figures*

Use your dictionary to identify the following names:

Sutter, Savannah, Medici, Beethoven, Magna Carta
Lima, Limoges, Icarus, Leander, Rigoletto, Maginot
Line, Satyagraha, Clytemnestra, Oedipus, Confucius
Dunkirk.

In some dictionaries, such names may be given in a special section or sections at the end. In others, such names may appear in the body of the dictionary.

6. *Foreign words and phrases*

Do you know these foreign terms used in medicine and law?

medulla oblongata, nolo contendere, rigor mortis, decree
nisi

Such foreign words may appear in the body of a dictionary, or in a special section at the end.

7. *Proofreader's marks*

If you write for publication, proofreader's marks are important. See the table of contents in your dictionary to find where such marks are shown and explained.

8. *Usage level*

The boy who proudly pointed to *ain't* on a dictionary page and said, "The word is in the dictionary; so it must be right," had not learned to use his dictionary. It is important to read what is said about any word that you look up. In one good abridged dictionary, the entry is like this:

ain't (ānt), *Now Illiterate or Dial.*

If a word is illiterate, it does not, of course, belong in the vocabulary of an educated person.

The abbreviation *"Dial."* following a word refers to *dialect* and means that the word belongs to the language of a particular district or class.

Such classifications show what is called the *usage level* of a word or expression. Be sure to notice these labels in your dictionary; they will indicate words that are not part of the language in standard usage.

Some other examples of usage classification commonly used in dictionaries are these:

Archaic (old-fashioned) Example: *eftsoon*
Colloq. (colloquial) used in speaking rather than in writing. Example: *fizzle*, meaning "failure"
Obs. (obsolete; gone out of use) Example: *murther*
Slang Example: *gat* (gun)

For further study of words at different levels of usage, see Sections 41, 42, 44, 45, 46.

Look through the front part of your dictionary to see whether you find a discussion of levels of usage. Read such material, if it is given.

9. *Punctuation and capitalization rules*

Either on the back cover or in the introductory remarks, a good dictionary may summarize rules for the use of punctuation marks and capital letters. Find these rules in your dictionary so that you may use them when you need them.

10. *Spelling rules*

The introduction to many dictionaries contains helpful rules for spelling. Locate these rules in your dictionary.

11. *Synonyms*

If your writing is dull because you use the same words too frequently, you may improve your writing by using synonyms. Be careful, however, in choosing a synonym. Half a dozen words may have a similar basic definition, but each one expresses a slightly different shade of meaning. Study the words and examples in the dictionary carefully before you make a selection.

It should be clear from these few examples that a *good* dictionary will give in brief form an explanation of many things that you may need to have explained in ordinary reading or writing. It will give dates of birth and death of many famous persons, location and population of large cities, tables of weights and measures, and numerous other interesting and valuable facts.

38. PRONUNCIATION

Words are mispronounced because of failure to accent the proper syllable or failure to give the letters the proper sound.

38a. Watch the respelling and diacritical marks.

In many dictionaries, a respelling of the word will help to give you the correct pronunciation. In such a respelling, marks over the vowels indicate the sound of the letters. These are called *diacritical marks*. Notice the following example of respelling with diacritical marks.

> **hay·rack** (hā′răk)
> ā is pronounced like *a* in *mate*.
> ă is pronounced like *a* in *mat*.

At the bottom of each page of a good dictionary is a key or list of common words written with these marks over the letters. The following is a sample from such a key:

ăct, āble, dâre, ärt; ĕbb, ēqual; ĭf, īce

These words are a guide for pronunciation of letters similarly marked. If the word that you are examining contains an *a* marked *ă*, the letter will be pronounced like the *a* in *act*.

If the letter is not explained at the bottom of the dictionary page, consult the full key on the inside cover or in the introductory comments of the dictionary.

38b. Watch accent marks.

In your dictionary, the syllable to be stressed will be indicated by a heavy accent mark (**'**).

ide′a, dir′igible, mis′chievous

If the word has two syllables that are accented, the syllable which should be accented more lightly than the other is followed by a light accent mark (′) or by a double accent mark (″).

in′tellec′tual   chor′eog′rapher   Bes″sara′bia

EXERCISE 1

The words in this list are often mispronounced. Consult your dictionary for the correct pronunciation. Then practice saying the words. Use them in your own conversation.

absurd	candidate	deaf	film
absorb	caramel	diphtheria	forehead
accessories	champion	dirigible	genuine
alias	chic	drowned	government
almond	clique	embroidered	height
athlete	column	escape	heroine
attacked	contrary	experiment	hospitable
attorney	corps	favorite	hostile
bicycle	corsage	fete	humble
biography	cruelly	figure	influence

insane	museum	ptomaine	strictly
instead	orchestra	quadruplets	salmon
Italian	peony	radiator	suite
italics	perspiration	relapse	syrup
laundered	pianist	since	theater
length	portiere	souvenir	umbrella
mischievous	positively	stomach	various
municipal	preferable	strength	wrestle

EXERCISE 2

If you have a good reading vocabulary, you may understand many words that you do not pronounce correctly. Which of the words in the following lists are familiar to you? Pronounce all the words in the list, and check yourself by looking up the pronunciations given in the dictionary. Learn the correct pronunciation of any word that you have mispronounced. Learn the meaning of any unfamiliar word in the list. When you know the correct meaning and pronunciation of all these words, try to use them in sentences in conversation, so that they will all become parts of your speaking vocabulary.

acumen	comparable	incomparable	patronize
amenable	condolence	indisputable	quay
audacious	conversant	inexplicable	reptile
autopsy	debris	intricacy	reputable
bourgeois	decorum	inveigle	sonorous
chastisement	formidable	irreparable	subtle
chiropodist	grievous	irrevocable	syringe
clandestine	grimace	lamentable	ultimatum
combatant	incognito	lingerie	verbatim

EXERCISE 3

Are you sure of the pronunciation of the following foreign words that are frequently used today? Consult your dictionary for the correct pronunciation of each word.

au gratin	boudoir	finis	ravioli
bona fide	chaise longue	per diem	table d'hôte
bon voyage	coiffure	pizza	tête à tête

39. SPELLING

Most poor spelling is a matter of laziness. Although it is not possible to control the spelling of all words by means of rules, a few simple rules will help a great deal.

39a. Pronounce words correctly.

1. Do not add vowels in pronouncing such words as *disastrous, similar, athletics,* and you will not misspell them.

2. Do not omit consonants in pronouncing such words as *eighth, library, government,* and you will not misspell them.

3. Do not omit syllables in pronouncing such words as *miniature, sophomore, accidentally,* and you will not misspell them.

4. Carefully examine words that contain silent letters: *(p)sychology, (p)neumonia, g(h)ost.*

EXERCISE 4

These words are often misspelled because they are mispronounced. Choose the correct form in each numbered pair and write it on your paper, with its number. Check your choices and make another list of the words that you misspell. Keep the list for study, adding to it other words that you misspell in your written work or correspondence. (See Section 39c.)

1. accidently, accidentally
2. artic, arctic
3. arthritis, artharitis
4. asparagus, asparagrass
5. atheletics, athletics
6. attackded, attacked
7. basicly, basically
8. boundary, boundry
9. canidate, candidate
10. chesnut, chestnut
11. children, childern
12. congratulations,
    congradulations
13. cruel, crule
14. disastrous, disasterous
15. distroy, destroy
16. description, discription
17. drowned, drownded
18. drasticly, drastically
19. emotionally, emotionlly
20. February, Febuary
21. goverment, government
22. grievious, grievous
23. heighth, height

24. hinderance, hindrance
25. hunerd, hundred
26. incidentally, incidently
27. interduce, introduce
28. mischievious,
    mischievous
29. modern, modren
30. prespiration, perspiration
31. pernounce, pronounce
32. quanity, quantity

33. realisticly, realistically
34. recognize, reconize
35. sarcasticly, sarcastically
36. sophmore, sophomore
37. surprise, suprise
38. satirically, satiricly
39. strickly, strictly
40. temperment,
    temperament

39b. See the words you use.

Poor spellers, especially, should watch the printed pages which they read and familiarize themselves with the appearance of words. The most frequent error in visualizing words is mistaking one for another.

EXERCISE 5

Some mistakes are made because people confuse words that sound alike or somewhat alike. Use a dictionary, if necessary, to learn the different meanings or pronunciations of the words in each of the following groups. Then choose ten of the following groups which include words that have given you difficulty or that you think might be difficult. For each word in these ten groups write a sentence in which you use the word correctly.

1. accept, except
2. access, excess
3. addition, edition
4. advise, advice
5. affect, effect
6. aisle, isle
7. allusion, illusion
8. ally, alley
9. altar, alter
10. anecdote, antidote
11. angle, angel
12. bath, bathe

13. berth, birth
14. breath, breathe
15. break, brake
16. bridal, bridle
17. capital, capitol
18. censor, censure
19. choose, chose
20. chord, cord
21. cite, site, sight
22. cloth, clothe
23. coarse, course
24. comma, coma

25. conscious, conscience
26. corps, corpse
27. costumes, customs
28. counsel, council
29. descent, decent
30. dessert, desert
31. diary, dairy
32. dual, duel
33. eligible, illegible
34. eliminate, illuminate
35. formally, formerly
36. grate, great
37. hoarse, horse
38. hoping, hopping
39. huge, Hugh
40. idle, idol
41. later, latter
42. led, lead
43. lessen, lesson
44. loam, loom
45. lose, loose
46. mist, midst
47. moral, morale
48. passed, past
49. peace, piece
50. persecute, prosecute
51. personal, personnel
52. precede, proceed
53. prescribe, proscribe
54. principal, principle
55. prodigy, protégé
56. quiet, quite
57. rain, reign, rein
58. rapped, wrapped
59. respectfully, respectively
60. scene, seen
61. shone, shown
62. sole, soul
63. stationary, stationery
64. steel, steal
65. surely, surly
66. tenants, tenets
67. thrown, throne
68. track, tract
69. trial, trail
70. wander, wonder
71. woman, women
72. weather, whether

EXERCISE 6

In each of the following sentences, choose from the parentheses the word that is required by the meaning of the sentence. On your paper, write the number of each sentence, and beside it, write the word that you have chosen.

1. We did not (accept, except) the invitation.
2. A tall, dark (woman, women) entered the room.
3. I do not know (whether, weather) I can go to the game.
4. Many people were (persecuted, prosecuted) under Hitler.
5. Sylvia is such a (quite, quiet) girl that we never learn to know her.
6. Do you understand the theorem about right (angles, angels)?

7. Use a (coma, comma) to separate the members of a series.
8. Jack is much taller (then, than) I am.
9. I was so (scared, scarred) that I ran out of the house.
10. Have you bought any new (clothes, cloths) for Easter?
11. How did you (loose, lose) your money?
12. The man standing on the porch is the (principle, principal) of my school.
13. The (sole, soul) on Bob's shoe is an inch thick.
14. The present was (wrapped, rapped) in silver paper.
15. When we arranged the line, Hazel was to (proceed, precede) me.

39c. Keep your own list of misspelled words.

Most people learn to spell simply by paying close attention to the appearance of words which they see in their reading, but almost everybody has trouble with a few words that are difficult for him. You save time by keeping a record of the words that you misspell and making a special effort to learn them. Your list will differ from the lists of other students, but there are some common words that give trouble to many people. Exercises 7, 8, and 9 contain some of these words.

EXERCISE 7

These are simple words frequently misspelled. Be able to write these words from dictation. Put in your own list the words which you misspell.

absence	amateur	awkward	certain
absurd	anxiety	beginning	cheerful
accepted	anxious	believe	chief
across	apartment	biscuit	choose
afraid	apparatus	brief	coming
all right	argument	business	copies
already	arrival	buying	courtesy
altogether	assemblies	cafeteria	cried
always	audience	captain	decide

definite
descend
desirable
describe
despair
destroy
develop
difficulties
dining room
disabled
disagree
divide
doesn't
during
easily
eighth
embarrass
enemies
excellent
exercise
existence
experience
familiar
fierce
fiery
foreign
forty
fourth
friend
frivolous
fulfilled
furniture
generally
governor

grammar
guard
handkerchief
heroes
humorous
hurried
imaginary
immediately
independent
influence
intellectual
invitation
itself
jewelry
knowledge
laboratory
ladies
laid
library
lightning
loneliness
lying
magazine
marriage
mathematics
meant
messenger
minute
misspelled
mortgage
mountain
muscle
necessary
neighbor

neither
niece
nineteen
ninety
ninth
oblige
occasionally
occurred
offered
omission
opportunity
paid
parallel
partner
perhaps
pilgrim
pleasant
possession
potato
prison
privilege
probably
pronunciation
realize
really
receive
repetition
replied
representative
respectfully
riding
rhyme
running
safety

seize
sense
sentence
separate
shepherd
shining
similar
sincerely
speech
stretch
strength
strictly
studying
summarize
superstitious
surely
toward
thorough
tragedy
tries
truly
twelfth
until
using
usually
village
villain
Wednesday
woman
women
writer
writing
written
yacht

EXERCISE 8

The following words are more difficult than those in
Exercise 7 and have been misspelled in many students'
papers. Write the words from dictation. Add to your own
list of words any that you misspell. For rules to help you
with spelling, see Section 39d–j.

abandon	competition	imprisonment	professor
abbreviate	conceived	inefficiency	prominent
abundance	condemn	inevitable	prosperous
accommodate	continuous	infinitive	pursuit
accompanying	convenient	initiative	questionnaire
achievement	conveyed	interfere	recommend
acquired	correspondence	interpretation	reconcile
advertisement	couplet	interruption	recurrence
agreeing	criticism	invariably	religion
antiseptic	curriculum	irresponsible	reminiscence
apology	denying	jealous	repaired
appealed	dependent	lieutenant	repentance
appearance	disability	literature	resemblance
appetite	disappear	luxurious	restaurant
appreciate	disappointment	maintenance	sandwich
appropriate	discussion	miscellaneous	scarcity
architect	distinguish	mischievous	schedule
ascent	dormitories	monotonous	scheme
association	economically	noticeable	sergeant
attendance	eliminate	optimism	serviceable
banana	emergencies	originally	simile
beneficial	eminent	pamphlet	spaghetti
bicycle	emphatic	paralyzed	specialty
brilliant	encouragement	participle	specimen
bureau	enthusiastic	peasant	sympathizes
calendar	environment	persistence	temporarily
campaign	equipped	persuade	tendency
cancellation	exaggerate	polluted	transferred
carriage	explanation	practically	unanimous
ceiling	extremely	precede	unconscious
cemetery	fascinate	precious	undesirable
changeable	fragrant	preferable	undoubtedly
characteristics	grateful	preferred	unnecessary
chauffeur	guidance	prejudices	valiant
colonel	hygiene	prepared	vehicle
committee	icicle	procedure	vengeance
competent	immensely	proceed	volume

EXERCISE 9

Some of these words will give trouble to even a good speller. See how many of them you can spell.

abhorrence	conspicuous	imminent	picnicking
absorbing	contemptuous	impetuosity	pneumonia
accustom	deteriorate	incredulous	preference
acknowledge	diphtheria	intentionally	prevalent
acquaintance	dirigible	intercede	proffered
aeronautics	discipline	irrelevant	promenade
aggravate	dissatisfied	kimono	recede
analogous	dissipate	legitimate	recommendation
apparent	distinction	leisure	reconciliation
arrangement	ecstasy	liquefy	representative
artillery	excessive	mercenary	rescind
auctioneer	exhilarate	mimicking	reservoir
authoritative	exorbitant	momentous	rheumatism
auxiliary	extraordinary	notoriety	ridiculous
barbarous	facilitate	occurrence	rite
battalion	guillotine	parliament	sacrificing
carburetor	harass	particularly	sacrilegious
coincidence	hesitancy	pasteurization	saxophone
colloquial	hypnosis	perceive	soliloquy
comparatively	hypocrisy	perceptible	specifically
concede	illiterate	peremptory	tyrannically
concentration	imitation	perseverance	vacuum
conferred	immigration	pervade	vaudeville
			visible

39d. Spelling of plurals.

1. The plurals of most nouns are formed by adding *s* to the singular.

     desks   dogs   boys   chairs

2. Nouns ending in *ch, x, z, sh, s,* add *es* to form the plural.

     boss, bosses   sash, sashes   church, churches
     tax, taxes   glass, glasses   topaz, topazes

NOTE: Verbs ending in *ch, x, z, sh, s* form the third person singular of the present tense in this same fashion.

     pushes   passes   fixes   pinches   fizzes

3. Nouns ending in *y* preceded by a consonant change *y* to *i* and add *es* to form the plural.

baby, babies	sky, skies
lady, ladies	family, families
dairy, dairies	memory, memories

NOTE: Notice the same change in the formation of the third person singular, present tense, of verbs ending in *y* preceded by a consonant.

try, tries	marry, marries
study, studies	hurry, hurries
worry, worries	justify, justifies

4. Words ending in *ay, ey, oy* add merely *s* for the plural.

valley, valleys	journey, journeys
donkey, donkeys	attorney, attorneys

5. Musical terms ending in *o* and nouns ending in *o* preceded by a vowel add *s* for the plural.

studio, studios	soprano, sopranos
radio, radios	piano, pianos

6. Most nouns ending in *o* preceded by a consonant add *es* for the plural.

potato, potatoes	hero, heroes
mosquito, mosquitoes	Negro, Negroes

7. Many nouns ending in *f* add *s* for the plural, but others ending in *f* or *fe* have plurals ending in *ves*.

chief, chiefs	wife, wives
dwarf, dwarfs	wharf, wharves
reef, reefs	life, lives
belief, beliefs	loaf, loaves

NOTE: *Believes* is a verb.

Howard *believes* that he is right.
Each religion has its own *beliefs*.

8. Compound nouns usually pluralize the most important word of the compound.

brother-in-law, brothers-in-law
commander in chief, commanders in chief

maid of honor, maids of honor
court-martial, courts-martial
man-of-war, men-of-war

9. Some words retain foreign plurals.

Singular	Plural
alumnus	alumni
alumna	alumnae
analysis	analyses
bacterium	bacteria
crisis	crises
datum	data
parenthesis	parentheses

A few foreign words have two accepted plurals, the foreign plural, and an English plural. In the following list, the foreign plural form is given first for each word:

Singular	Plural
memorandum	memoranda, memorandums
curriculum	curricula, curriculums
index	indices, indexes
radius	radii, radiuses

10. Some words have the same form in both singular and plural.

deer   sheep   grouse   moose

EXERCISE 10

On your paper, write the plural form of each of the following words:

agony	balcony	canoe	crutch
alley	battery	cargo	echo
ally	blackberry	casualty	fox
alto	biography	cello	gypsy
analysis	box	century	hero
apology	buffalo	comedy	lady
army	butterfly	conspiracy	leaf
authority	business	crash	lobby
baby	calf	crisis	loyalty

mosquito	piano	soprano	tomato
Negro	potato	stratum	topaz
palace	process	sympathy	tornado
parenthesis	pulley	synopsis	tragedy
pass	quality	thesis	valley
penny	mother-in-law	thief	volcano

39e. Words contaning *ei* or *ie*.

Write *i* before *e*
Except after *c*,
Or when sounded as *a*
As in *neighbor* and *weigh*.

believe	deceive
relieve	receive
grieve	perceive
siege	conceive
sieve	

Exceptions often misspelled: *leisure, seize, neither*.

39f. Final e.

Words ending in silent *e* usually drop the *e* before adding a suffix beginning with a vowel (*ing, able, ance, ous*).

resemble	resemblance
believe	believing – believable
interfere	interfering
advise	advising – advisable
hope	hoping
desire	desiring – desirous
care	caring
argue	arguing – arguable
amaze	amazing

Such words keep the *e* before a suffix beginning with a consonant (*by, ful, ment, ness*).

pale	paleness
sincere	sincerely
state	statement
care	careful
amaze	amazement

NOTE: Exceptions often misspelled: *argument, truly, dye-ing, canoeing*

Words which end in *ce* or *ge* retain the *e* when *ous* and *able* are added.

notice,	noticeable	change,	changeable
peace,	peaceable	courage,	courageous
outrage,	outrageous	advantage,	advantageous
bridge,	bridgeable		

EXERCISE 11

On your paper, write the words in the following list. Then from each word form as many other words as you can by adding suffixes (*ed, ing, ous, able, ible, ness, ance, ment, ly*). Write these new words beside the words from which they are formed.

adore	debate	hurry	reconcile
advantage	decide	imagine	refute
advise	desire	levy	ride
argue	dine	lonely	sale
arrange	efface	lose	secure
arrive	endure	love	sense
believe	exchange	manage	separate
blame	excite	marriage	service
change	excuse	move	silly
charge	fatigue	note	singe
come	file	peace	store
conceive	force	pronounce	trace
courage	grieve	receive	use
damage	hope	recognize	value

39g. Final y.

Words ending in *y* preceded by a consonant change *y* to *i* before any suffix except one beginning with *i*. Be sure to keep the *y* if the suffix *ing* is added.

happy, happiness	worry, worried	worry, worrying
study, studying	try, tried	mercy, merciful
steady, steadiness		

39h. Words ending in *ible* or *able*.

There is no rule that will tell you how to spell words ending in *ible* or *able*, but careful pronunciation will help.

EXERCISE 12

On your paper, rewrite any word in this list which is not correctly spelled. Consult a dictionary for the correct spelling. Then put on your personal spelling list the ones which you miss.

acceptable	convertible	inaccessable	manageable
accessable	desirable	incomprehensible	movable
adjustable	dependable	incredable	notable
admissible	destructable	indispensable	noticeable
advisable	digestible	inexcusable	perceptible
allowible	discernible	inexpressible	permissable
available	divisible	infallable	plausable
combustible	durable	inseparable	sensible
commendible	eligible	intangable	susceptable
comparible	excitable	invisable	tangible
compatable	excusable	irrefutable	unbearable
comprehensable	feasable	irresistable	valuable
conceivable	flexible	livable	visible
contemptable	imaginable	lovable	vulnerable

39i. Double consonant before suffix.

Double the final consonant before a suffix which begins with a vowel if both of the following conditions exist:

1. The word has only one syllable or is accented on the last syllable.

2. The word ends in one consonant preceded by one vowel.

Examples:

slip (One syllable ending in one consonant, *p*, preceded by one vowel, *i*) slipped, slipping

compel (Two syllables with final one accented) compelled, compelling quarrel (Two syllables with first accented. Do not double final consonant.) quarreled, quarreling

equip (Two syllables accented on final one) equipped (Suffix beginning with vowel) equipment (Suffix beginning with consonant)

confront (Two syllables accented on final one. Do not double consonant *t* because it is not preceded by a vowel.) confronted, confronting

Exception: *crocheted.*

EXERCISE 13

Write on your paper the words in this list. Then add *ed, ing, ment,* where possible. Write the whole word each time you add a suffix.

accuse	confer	grab	refer
acquit	confront	happen	repeal
admire	control	knit	repel
admit	counsel	infer	reveal
allot	deter	interfere	shine
anchor	develop	jam	ship
assent	disappear	occur	step
beg	disappoint	omit	stop
begin	domineer	permit	submit
benefit	drop	plan	transfer
brag	equip	prefer	tramp
combat	exhibit	put	travel
commit	fan	quarrel	trip
compel	fit	rebel	whip
concur	gossip	recur	wrap

39j. Words ending in *ally*.

Words ending in *c* do not usually add *ly* alone to form an adverb. They add *ally*.

realistic	realistically	drastic	drastically
sarcastic	sarcastically	satiric	satirically
basic	basically	enthusiastic	enthusiastically

NOTE: Watch also *accidentally* and *incidentally.*

40. VOCABULARY GROWTH

Vocabulary growth does not mean simply learning new words. It means also discarding worn-out expressions, seeking to make language vivid and colorful, learning to suit the expression to the audience and the occasion. It means making the language work so that it says exactly what you want it to say. Of course, you will not sit down and memorize lists of words; you learn words because they can be useful in speaking, writing, and understanding. With a clever use of words, you make comfortable social adjustments, make other people understand your interests, and read on a higher level. It is important, then, to consider how you can develop a *useful* vocabulary and use it wisely.

40a. Simple words for a growing vocabulary.

No list of words supplied by a book can meet all of the needs of people who wish to understand better what they read or hear. Make your own personal list, composed of words which you find in your reading or your listening and which will be valuable to you. Use new words frequently for several days in order to fix them in your memory. Although nothing can take the place of a personal list, it is sometimes interesting to examine some common words to see whether they are a part of your vocabulary.

EXERCISE 14

Do you know the meaning of the words italicized in the following paragraph? Consult your dictionary for the words which are not clear to you. Be prepared to explain their meaning in the paragraph.

An *eminent* scholar, known for his *eccentricity*, complained recently that he had received a number of *anonymous* letters and had been approached on the street by an *ungainly* creature who made strange *grimaces* and gestures while threatening the learned man. For a time the scholar had ignored the letters because people of refinement do not write anonymous communications, nor do they pay any attention to them; but the notes came so frequently that he was annoyed by their insolence and decided to try to discover the writer of such *malicious* material. A *magistrate* who was a neighbor of the scholar liked to do a little *sleuthing* as an *avocation*. He agreed to work with the scholar at no *pecuniary* gain. Together they examined the notes and made conclusions. The magistrate was an *egotistic* man, who told many *anecdotes* of his *ingenuity* and *prowess* and exacted a kind of *homage* from his friend. Because the evidence at first seemed *obscure*, the men had to display genuine *acuteness* in working out the problem; but they finally decided to accuse another neighbor, an *uncouth* fellow known in the neighborhood as a *hypochondriac*. When this man was threatened with a *libel* suit, he was frightened, and the scholar received no more anonymous mail.

40b. Words from newspapers and magazines.

Do you know what a *bipartisan* foreign policy is?

When the paper speaks of a *gubernatorial campaign,* what is happening?

The man was tried for *perjury*. What had he done?

The italicized words in the preceding sentences appear regularly in newspapers. A democratic government depends for its success upon literate citizens, people who know what is going on and who, consequently, vote wisely. Learn the words which are used frequently in the newspapers and magazines.

EXERCISE 15

These words appear regularly in everyday reading. On your paper write the words in the first list. Then write opposite each word the number of the group of words in the second column that matches it in meaning. Example:

1. abitration   3

    1. arbitration   1. working with another
    2. collaboration   2. make easier

3. facilitate

3. settling a dispute by discussing and coming to an agreement

4. agrarian

4. mutual exchange

5. reciprocity

5. become worse

6. deteriorate

6. having to do with farm matters

7. dilemma

7. dishonest, cheating

8. strategy

8. belonging to the same time

9. ideologies

9. compensation by a defeated nation for damage after a war

10. amphibious

10. contact between military units to get action together

11. contemporary

11. skillful management to get the better of an opponent

12. reparations

12. self-governing, independent

13. liaison

13. a difficult or embarrassing situation

14. autonomous

14. capable of working on both land and water

15. fraudulent

15. beliefs of a political group

EXERCISE 16

Choose fifteen interesting words from your newspaper and write a definition for each. Arrange words and definitions in two lists as in Exercise 15, and see whether your classmates can match them.

40c. Business words.

Everybody needs to know some business terms in order to manage his affairs.

EXERCISE 17

Here are some common words that will be useful. Match each word and its meaning as you did in Exercise 15.

1. disbursements

1. an addition to a will

2. commodity

2. to reduce, diminish

3. allocate

3. decrease in value as a result of wear

4. codicil	4. to make payment for expense or loss
5. curtail	5. sum of money paid to shareholders in a corporation
6. amortization	6. amount subtracted from a bill for prompt payment or other special reason
7. assets	7. the amount by which a sum of money is short
8. depreciation	8. security pledged for payment of a loan
9. dividend	9. an article of trade
10. discount	10. property or cash possessed by a company
11. reimburse	11. paid before material is sent
12. deficit	12. to set apart for a special purpose
13. prepaid	13. an itemized bill
14. invoice	14. wiping out a debt
15. collateral	15. amount paid out

40d. Foreign words in everyday use.

Long ago, the Romans had a little proverb that said:

De gustibus non est disputandum. (There is no disputing about tastes.)

The French say:

Chacun à son goût. (Everyone to his own taste.)

But the Spaniards, with their own sense of humor, say:

Cado loco a su tema. (Every madman to his own idea.)

Our language has been enriched by adopting from other languages expressions like these. Many terms used in everyday living are from Latin, French, Spanish, or German.

EXERCISE 18

Write a sentence containing each of the following words or abbreviations and then read the sentence aloud

with the correct pronunciation. If you have trouble, con
sult your dictionary.

A.D.	ex officio	post mortem
à la carte	finis	pronto
à la mode	gringo	répondez s'il vous
alma mater	hara kiri	plaît (R.S.V.P.)
B.C.	hombre	rodeo
connoisseur	hors d'oeuvres	siesta
corral	kindergarten	sombrero
debris	laissez faire	tamale
ennui	mañana	wanderlust
entrée	mantilla	
espionage	patio	

EXERCISE 19

These foreign words are more difficult than the words
in Exercise 18. Follow the directions in Exercise 18.

ad infinitum	crêpe suzette	noblesse oblige
ad nauseam	divertimento	persona non grata
agent provocateur	esprit de corps	peseta
al fresco	fait accompli	pièce de résistance
antipasto	habeas corpus	savoir faire
au courant	maître d'hôtel	savoir vivre
carte blanche	mare nostrum	summa cum laude
coup d'état	milieu	verbatim

40e. Medical terms.

If your doctor tells you that you have laryngitis, what
has happened to you?

What should you do if you need a tonsillectomy?

It is often necessary to know a few medical terms in
order to understand what your doctor tells you.

EXERCISE 20

Explain the meaning of the following words:

allergy	appendectomy	carcinoma	neurosis
amnesia	arteriosclerosis	insomnia	schizophrenia
anemia	astigmatism	malignant	therapy
anesthetic	benign	myopia	toxic

40f. Musical terms.

Can you read your program at a concert or the newspaper report of a musical event?

EXERCISE 21

What do these terms mean? Pronounce them correctly.

a cappella	coloratura	leitmotif	recitative
acoustics	con brio	medley	scherzo
allegro	concerto	opéra bouffe	sonata
andante	counterpoint	opus	sotto voce
aria	crescendo	overture	staccato
atonal	harmony	percussion	symphony
cadenza	instrumentation	pitch	syncopation

40g. Scientific terms.

Scientific terms appear in newspaper and magazine articles dealing with scientific subjects. Can you understand such terms? The following exercise may help you. As you meet unfamiliar scientific terms in your reading, find out their meaning and pronunciation, and add the words to your personal vocabulary list.

EXERCISE 22

Write sentences using these words. Read the sentences aloud pronouncing the words correctly.

amoeba	bisect	deciduous	horticulture
bacillus	carnivorous	dissect	perennial
bacteria	combustion	erosion	saturated

40h. Art words.

Here are a few words used in discussions of art. Perhaps your art teacher will help you to increase the list.

caricature	chiaroscuro	etching	pastel
ceramics	cubism	impressionism	symmetry

40i. Literary terms.

The following are words which you may need if you are going to talk intelligently about literature:

allegory	denouement	lyric	realism
analogy	discourse	nuance	romanticism
blank verse	elegy	pathos	satire
couplet	epic	protagonist	sonnet

40j. Words for the ambitious.

How good is your vocabulary? Test it by seeing how many of the words in the following exercise you know.

EXERCISE 23

On your paper, write the words in the first column. Then place opposite each word the number of the defini tion which you think suits that word. Write sentences of your own in which you use these words.

1. abscond
2. adamant
3. adroitly
4. ambidextrous
5. ameliorate
6. anachronism
7. antipathy
8. apothegm
9. assiduous
10. bilingual

1. able to use both hands equally well
2. improve
3. dislike
4. to run away to avoid legal process
5. a short, pithy saying
6. constant in application
7. hard-hearted
8. able to speak two languages
9. cleverly
10. something occurring out of its proper time

EXERCISE 24

Follow the directions in Exercise 23.

1. cacophony
2. calumny
3. casuistic
4. complicity
5. concatenation
6. cupidity
7. cynosure

1. great desire to possess some thing
2. formal expression of praise
3. abominable
4. foolish
5. leadership exercised by one state over another
6. lasting only a short time
7. intellectually dishonest

8. discrepancy
9. egregious
10. elucidate
11. encomium

12. ephemeral
13. execrable
14. facilitate
15. fallacious

16. fatuous
17. ghetto
18. grandiose

19. hegemony
20. heretic

8. partnership in wrongdoing
9. state of being linked together
10. harsh sound
11. something that strongly attracts attention
12. inconsistency
13. in glaring taste
14. slander
15. a person who has religious beliefs contrary to the accepted form
16. affectedly grand
17. make clear
18. a place in which Jews have been required to live
19. make easy
20. logically unsound

EXERCISE 25

Follow the directions in Exercise 23.

1. imminent
2. incognito
3. incongruous
4. ingenuous
5. innocuous
6. intrepid
7. intrinsically

8. invective

9. lugubrious

10. mendacious
11. meticulous
12. misanthrope

13. misogynist
14. nebulous

1. out of keeping; not harmonious in character
2. essentially, by nature
3. artless, innocent
4. mournful
5. a hater of mankind
6. likely to occur at any moment
7. a formal expression of great praise
8. disgrace or reproach incurred by conduct considered shameful
9. having one's identity concealed
10. coolly unconcerned
11. characterized by show
12. a theory that identifies God and nature
13. cowardly
14. careless or superficial

15. nonchalant	15. policy of adopting one's actions to whatever circumstances are present
16. onerous	16. impracticable, visionary
17. opportunism	17. not harmful
18. opprobrium	18. careful about small details
19. ostentatious	19. fearless
20. panegyric	20. hater of women
21. pantheism	21. vague, hazy, cloudy
22. perfunctory	22. not easily excited
23. phlegmatic	23. false, untrue
24. pusillanimous	24. an utterance of violent reproach or accusation
25. quixotic	25. burdensome

EXERCISE 26

Follow the directions in Exercise 23.

1. rationalize	1. done by stealth
2. sanguinary	2. waver
3. sophistry	3. brutally harsh
4. supercilious	4. the skill of a person specially talented or clever
5. surreptitious	5. to invent an acceptable explanation for behavior
6. truculent	6. bloody
7. ubiquitous	7. haughtily disdainful
8. vacillate	8. experienced in place of another
9. vicarious	9. present everywhere
10. virtuosity	10. false argument

41. PROVINCIALISMS

When you work to develop vocabularies, you must not only learn new words, but discard old ones that interfere with accurate, effective speech and writing.

A fundamental requirement of formal usage is that words must be in national, not merely sectional, use. A provincialism, or localism, is a word or phrase used and understood in only a particular section or region of the country. Such words are difficult to detect because a writer or speaker may have come to accept them as reputable and to assume that they are nationally understood since he himself has known them from childhood. Some parts of the United States are especially rich in colorful localisms which add flavor to speech but which may not be immediately intelligible in other areas. Such localisms are appropriate in informal writing and conversation but should usually be avoided in formal writing. Examples: *chunk* and *chuck* for *throw; tote* for *carry; tote* (noun) for *load; poke* for *bag* or *sack; fatback* for *bacon; bunk into* for *bump into; reckon* for *think* or *suppose; choose* for *wish; draw* for *gully; chuck wagon* for a *supply wagon; selectman* for a *town official; to home* for *at home; loco* for *crazy*. Linguists may differ among themselves over which of such expressions are localisms and which are merely colloquial. In formal writing, it is advisable to guard against them, whatever their label.

EXERCISE 27

Make a list of provincialisms heard in your neighborhood or vicinity. Then decide which ones should not be used in your formal writing.

42. COLLOQUIALISMS

A *colloquialism* is a conversational expression which is permissible in an easy, informal style of writing and speaking, but it is not appropriate in formal writing or speaking.

Dictionaries mark words as colloquial (*Colloq.*) when in the judgment of the editors they are more common in speech than in writing, or more appropriate to informal than to formal discourse. Since editors differ in the interpretations of their findings, the label *colloquial* may apply to many kinds of words. All contractions, for example, may be considered "respectable" colloquialisms, whereas some other kinds should be guarded against even in informal writing.

The test for the use of colloquialisms is appropriateness. There is no objective test or exact rule to enable you to determine when colloquialisms may be used. Certainly it is better to employ them than to avoid them and make your writing seem artificial and awkward. But in formal, well-planned writing they should be avoided unless they are deliberately used to achieve some stylistic effect. Consult the dictionary to determine what words are considered colloquial.

Examples of colloquialisms: *don't, won't, phone, auto, ad, gumption, cute, flop, in back of, show up, try and, brass tacks* (facts), *take a try at, alongside of, angel* (financial backer), *fizzle* (to fail), *goner* (a person lost or dead), *flabbergast*.

43. IDIOMS

Idioms are forms of expression peculiar to a language. Many idioms defy grammatical analysis; but because they are sanctioned by current usage, they are looked upon as correct. Idioms correctly used make speech and writing vigorous and picturesque.

Although idioms often cannot be analyzed grammatically, the careful writer will not therefore assume that he can use them as he pleases. A good dictionary will contain a statement of idiomatic usage following words which need such explanation. Many idioms involve the use of prepositions. A few examples of idioms follow:

Unidiomatic	Idiomatic
cannot help but talk	cannot help talking
comply to	comply with
die with (a disease)	die of
different than	different from
doubt if	doubt whether
graduated (high school)	graduated from (high school)
identical to	identical with
kind of a	kind of
listen at	listen to
out loud	aloud

Unidiomatic	*Idiomatic*
plan on going	plan **to** go
providing that	provided that
to home	at home
try and	try to
wait on	wait for (to await)

Certain words require different prepositions to express different meanings.

Examples:

agree $\begin{cases} \textit{to} \text{ a proposal} \\ \textit{on} \text{ a plan} \\ \textit{with} \text{ a person} \end{cases}$

compare $\begin{cases} \textit{to} \text{ something similar} \\ \textit{with} \text{ something dissimilar} \end{cases}$

contend $\begin{cases} \textit{for} \text{ a principle} \\ \textit{with} \text{ a person} \\ \textit{against} \text{ an obstacle} \end{cases}$

differ $\begin{cases} \textit{with} \text{ a person} \\ \textit{from} \text{ something else} \\ \textit{about} \text{ or } \textit{over} \text{ a question} \end{cases}$

impatient $\begin{cases} \textit{for} \text{ something desired} \\ \textit{with} \text{ someone else} \\ \textit{of} \text{ restraint} \\ \textit{at} \text{ someone's conduct} \end{cases}$

rewarded $\begin{cases} \textit{for} \text{ something done} \\ \textit{with} \text{ a gift} \\ \textit{by} \text{ a person} \end{cases}$

Avoid: They were confirmed up St. David's Church.
Say: They were confirmed at St. David's Church.

Avoid: We were out the country club yesterday.
Say: We were at the country club yesterday.

Avoid: Marian came over my house last night.
Say: Marian came to my house.

Avoid: I wanted to go down the country yesterday.
Say: I wanted to go to the country.

EXERCISE 28

On your paper, write the number of each of the following sentences. Beside the number, write the preposition which should be supplied for that sentence. Consult your dictionary if you have difficulty.

1. This letter means that he will accede—your request.
2. Contrast this idea—that one.
3. She does not adhere—that theory.
4. Mr. Bullock will compensate you—the work.
5. Your mother is apprehensive—your safety.
6. What do you infer—that proposal?
7. Mrs. Smoak will be—home this afternoon.
8. Please don't meddle—affairs not your own.
9. She will prohibit you—doing that.
10. Jack is now reconciled—living on a small salary.
11. I didn't think him capable—doing such a thing.
12. Jane is too careless—her appearance.

EXERCISE 29

On your paper, write correctly each of the following sentences:

1. What kind of a car did you buy?
2. I can't help but think that Jane has caused all the trouble.
3. When our parents graduated high school, education was different than it is now.
4. We didn't plan on going to the shore so early.
5. I'll try and see you sometime next week.
6. I doubt if you will get any help from Ellen because she is not to home very often.

44. VULGARISMS

Vulgarisms (also called "barbarisms" and "substandard" or "illiterate expressions") are words and phrases not accepted in either colloquial or formal language. Since they are used by uneducated speakers, such expressions are always to be avoided in writing unless you put them into the dialogue of people you are characterizing.

The following words and phrases should be guarded against:

> *hadn't ought, mistakened, this here, anywheres, couldn't of, hisself, being as, concertize, vacationize, still and all, coronated.*

45. IMPROPRIETIES

Improprieties are recognized English words which are misused in function or meaning. The word that constitutes an impropriety is acceptable; it is its misuse which causes an error in diction.

45a. Avoid improprieties in grammatical function.

A word may be transferred from one part of speech to another, but the careful writer will not employ such a word in its new function unless it is sanctioned by good use. Examples of improprieties in function:

Verbs misused as nouns:	*eats,* an *invite,* a *fix,* a *think,* a *combine* (meaning "combination")
Nouns misused as verbs:	to *suspicion,* to *suicide*
Adjectives misused as adverbs:	*real* pretty, *sure* pleased, *some* tall
Prepositions misused as conjunctions:	*like* for *as, except* for *unless*

Avoid: We served eats.
        I suspicioned that the plan would fail.
Use: We served food.
        I suspected that the plan would fail.

45b. Avoid improprieties in meaning.

Although some improprieties in meaning are the result of ignorance, most of them are caused by the misuse of words similar in form. For example, words in the following groups are frequently misused:

accept, except   formally, formerly
affect, effect   healthful, healthy
all ready, already   ingenious, ingenuous
all together, altogether   irritate, aggravate
allusion, illusion   later, latter
avenge, revenge   liable, likely
complement, compliment   noted, notorious
council, counsel   party, person
disinterested, uninterested   principal, principle
elude, allude   respectfully, respectively
expect, suspect   stationary, stationery
farther, further   than, then

EXERCISE 30

1. Use correctly in sentences each of the groups of words listed in Section 45b.

2. Use each of the following words correctly in a sentence: *continual, creditable, practicable, apt, continuous, vocation, consul, can, may, mad, conscious, conscience.*

46. SLANG

Slang is a particular kind of vulgarism. Formerly the term was applied to the cant of gypsies, beggars, and thieves, or to the jargon of any particular class of society. Now slang is defined as language which consists of widely current terms having a forced or fantastic meaning, or displaying eccentricity. It is sometimes very colorful and forceful, but it is often used with such crudeness that it may offend people who are careful of their choice of words and cause the person who uses it to be considered vulgar.

Note these typical slang expressions:

grub, to get away with it, bang-up, to get pinched, a bum hunch, to put it across, so what, spuds, took the count, going some, put on the dog, have a heart, a lemon, attaboy, cut no ice, fall for it, hard-boiled, get the goods on him, talk through your hat, it's the berries, goofy, wacky, off his nut, squawk, dead pan, drip, crab, let it ride, what's cooking, you said it, in the groove, a smooth number, to get hep, a rat race, on the beam, sourpuss, cockeyed, good egg, mike, croak (meaning "to die" or "to kill").

47. TRITENESS

How many times have you heard the following speech?

On behalf of the members of the team, I should like to present to Mr. Anderson this small token of our appreciation.

This is a trite speech. The first time that it was used, it was acceptable; but the person who uses it now shows clearly that he is lazy or unwilling to think for himself.

Trite expressions have been used too often. Avoid them. Make your language fresh and interesting. Here are some expressions to avoid. You will probably notice many other trite expressions in your reading, in public speeches, or in conversations.

abreast of the times
absence makes the heart grow fonder
all in all
all the luck in the world
all work and no play
as big as a house
as luck would have it
add insult to injury
a friend in need is a friend indeed
according to our records
are in receipt of
at an early date
at your earliest convenience
be that as it may
better half
bigger and better
bitter end
brown as a berry

budding genius
by leaps and bounds
checkered career
cold as ice
conspicuous by his absence
deem it an honor and a privilege
deepest gratitude
do justice to a dinner
doomed to disappointment
each and every
esteem it a great honor
exception proves the rule
favor with a selection
festive occasion
few and far between
for better or worse
get away with
goes without saying

good time was had by all
great open spaces
green with envy
heartfelt thanks
hit an all-time low
holding the bag
hungry as a bear
in this day and age
irony of fate
last but not least
level best
makes the world a better
place in which to live
meets the eye
method in his madness
milestone on the road of
life
my best wishes

needs no introduction
none the worse for wear
proud possessor
psychological moment
ripe old age
shot heard around the
world
take this opportunity
the good life
the weaker sex
the worse for wear
time marches on
time of my life
tired but happy
to make a long story short
too full for utterance
where ignorance is bliss
words fail to express

NOTE: Try to avoid trite ideas as well as trite expressions.

EXERCISE 31

On your paper, write an improved version of each of the following sentences:

1. Everybody had heaps of fun at Joe's party last night, but you were conspicuous by your absence.
2. I'm sure that each and every one of you had a fine time, but I didn't get an invite.
3. I suspicioned that you were not coming when I saw Ethel with a short, dark-complected fellow named Lee.
4. I think her mother wants Ethel to set her cap for him. I gave him the once over a few days ago and decided that if he is Ethel's type, I'll beat a hasty retreat while the going is good.
5. Well, keep me posted. Why don't you take her out to trip the light fantastic? You're liable to beat the other fellow out.
6. No, I don't think I'm ready yet to line myself up with a better half.

EXERCISE 32

Follow the directions in Exercise 31.

1. When I reach a ripe old age, I want to get away from the city and go to the great open spaces.
2. If this inflation keeps on, you will be down and out when you reach that ripe old age.
3. It's certainly true that prices are increasing by leaps and bounds. I've worked like a dog and have nothing to show for it.

EXERCISE 33

Follow the directions in Exercise 31.

This morning we seniors face the school for the last time. Soon we shall be sailing the ship of life into the future. I deem it an honor and a privilege to present to you as our speaker, one who needs no introduction. It is fitting that Dr. Edward Terminstumpler should speak to us on this occasion. Before I present him to you, I should like to offer him our deepest gratitude for taking time out of a busy day to join us.

EXERCISE 34

Follow the directions in Exercise 31.

After we had done justice to a good dinner, the speaker rose. "Gentlemen," he said, "I'm too full for utterance."

He was perfectly serious, but this brought down the house. A little red in the face, he went on:

"On this festive occasion, each and every one of you certainly feels the seriousness of the dreadful problems that face us. By herculean efforts, we must overcome them. We must fight until, tired but happy, we are able to withdraw to our domiciles, perhaps a little the worse for wear, but glad in our accomplishment."

48. JARGON

Some inexperienced writers think that they will improve their writing by using long words, elaborate expressions, or involved words recognizable only by a special trade or profession. Actually, the best writing is simple, direct, clear.

Instead of saying, "No," the writer of jargon says, "The answer is in the negative."

Jargon	*Clear Writing*
Pursue his tasks with great dili- gence	Work hard
Unfavorable conditions	Bad weather
Pass away	Die
Enter into the state of matrimony	Get married

Business people are often users of jargon. They should avoid expressions such as *along the line of, with regard to, attached hereto, in connection with, enclosed herewith please find.* Another type of jargon is the circumlocution or descriptive phrase used instead of a celebrity's name; for example, "home-run king." Such expressions are often used in sportswriting.

EXERCISE 35

On your paper, rewrite the following sentences, improving the wording. Substitute other words for jargon.

1. The greatest factor in his success was that he had reached man's estate in a healthy physical condition.
2. In the case of those not present, the nature of their offense will be judged as of a different character.
3. Ruth was one of baseball's greatest assets. He possessed ability to an unusual degree, and thousands of human beings in the environs of New York City thought that no one could ever rival the great Bambino. But by the very nature of things, the Bronx Behemoth entered a declining state over a long period of years. Later the fickle fans were of the persuasion that, with regard to baseball ability, Joe DiMaggio, the former San Francisco star, was of the same quality as the former home-run king.
4. With great diligence the student pursued his studies along the lines of medicine.
5. In this instance, his answer in the affirmative was a distinct asset to our business.

EXERCISE 36

On your paper, rewrite in simple, straightforward English this business letter. (See Section 97.)

Dear Mrs. Jenkins:

In reply to your letter of January 10 with regard to merchandise along the line of slip covers, we are enclosing herewith samples of three types of materials. We should like to advise that our representative will be in your district on Monday, and we are of the opinion that he will be able to assist you re the slip covers as per your request.

Thanking you for your inquiry, we beg to remain

Very truly yours,
J. A. Henderson

49. EXACT DICTION

The following two sentences come from students' themes:

Four great English allergies are *Adonais, Lycidas, In Memoriam,* and *Thyrsis.* (Elegies)

Thackeray wrote of the sallowness of the rich. (Shallowness)

Young writers like to use big words. They are developing their vocabularies and wish to fit the new words into their speech and writing. But great care is necessary to avoid misusing a word, as in the sentences used as examples.

Choose words carefully. An expression is not correct because you have heard it frequently or your favorite radio commentator uses it. Check new expressions in your dictionary.

Do not use inexactly such words as *terrible, ghastly, thrilling, terrific, gorgeous, awful, phenomenal.* These words are correctly used in a superlative sense, but too often they are employed to describe anything that is pleasant. Avoid exaggeration in your speech and writing.

Exaggerated: The game was terrific.
Better: The game was exciting.

EXERCISE 37

What is the difference in meaning of the words in each of the following groups?

argue, debate, discuss
dislike, disgust, distaste
feature, characteristic, peculiarity
color, hue, tinge, shade

50. CONCRETE AND SPECIFIC WORDS

Walk is a general word. It gives no definite picture. There are many ways of saying *walk:*

strut, hobble, stumble, stagger, glide, creep, scurry, stroll, march.

These are specific words. Because they show a special type of walking, they are much more colorful and interesting than the general word *walk.*

50a. Use specific rather than general words.

It was a fine day. (General words)
The sun warmed the gentle breezes of an April day. (Specific words)
In the garden were some beautiful flowers. (General)
Tall purple and yellow chrysanthemums formed a background for white asters. (Specific)

50b. Choose vigorous verbs.

Much of the life of a sentence depends upon its verbs.

Colorless: When the door opened, she went in.
More lively: When the door *yawned* open, she *plodded* in.
Colorless: A man came into the room.
More lively: A man *slouched* into the room.

EXERCISE 38

Write a specific word for each of the following:

house	musical instrument	boat	building
laugh	tree	food	bird
go	dog	beverage	road

EXERCISE 39

On one of the following topics, write a paragraph in which you use specific words:

> The Final Touchdown, A House on the Shore, Enter the Ghost, The Beach Party, A Blind Date, An Old-fashioned Garden, My Sister's Son

51. FIGURATIVE LANGUAGE

Figures of speech help to make writing vivid, but they are not effective if they are forced and strained or if they are mixed. There are a large number of figures of speech, but those discussed in Sections 51a–f are among the most important.

51a. A simile is the comparison of two images which are essentially different, but which are alike in at least one respect. The words as, as if, like are used to point to the resemblance.

> He eats like a wolf.
> The morning hung over us like a great dark mushroom.
> The vultures hung over the village like a storm cloud ready to burst.

51b. A metaphor is a suggested comparison.

> Money is a lens in a camera.
> He is a cur.
> Madeline is a cat.
> All the world's a stage.
> The crime investigation committee was told to stop looking for mice and find the breeding place.

51c. Personification gives human qualities to objects that are not living.

> The wind howled.
> A smiling moon looked down on the lovers.

51d. Hyperbole is exaggeration.

> I was insane from grief.
> I've told you a thousand times what to do.

Hyperbole should be used sparingly and very cautiously.

51e. Metonymy is the use of one word for another that it suggests.

> The kettle boils. (Water in the kettle boils.)
> She sets a good table. (Good food)

The use of figures of speech, when overdone, makes a style florid. It is important that the figures be fresh and original. Many figures that were once effective have become trite. Avoid these.

51f. Avoid mixed figures.

Students who are striving for effect sometimes mix their similes or metaphors; that is, they start a sentence by making a comparison and finish it with another comparison entirely different from the first.

> The road to success is straight, narrow, and strewn with rocks, but the ambitious man must swim through it. (The way to success is a road; then it is a river.)

Good similes and metaphors are valuable in the writing of sales letters or advertising copy because they appeal to the emotion.

52. "FINE" WRITING

"Fine" writing is writing which is affected.

52a. Avoid "fine" writing.

The use of direct, simple words to gain effectiveness in writing is mentioned in Section 48. Avoid artificiality, pretentiousness, affectation.

52b. Use short words.

Short words are usually clearer than long ones. A writer with a mature style will, of course, use many long words; but they will generally be used only to express particular meanings for which shorter words may not exist.

Avoid the following expressions:

> *savory repast* for *meal*
> *retire* for *go to bed*
> *inebriated* for *drunk*
> *obsequies* for *funerals*

In these expressions, the simple words express quite clearly what the writer wishes to say and are in better taste. Big words are for big ideas. Be sure that the idea is worth the word.

52c. Use modifiers intelligently.

Too many adjectives or adverbs make a style seem overdone. Notice the overuse of modifiers in the following excerpt from the description of a wedding:

> As she swept gracefully down the flower-bordered aisle of the old, freshly painted church, the bride smiled graciously and kindly into the eyes of her handsome, stalwart husband.

52d. Be careful in using foreign expressions.

A bit of Latin or French sometimes seems impressive, and the inexperienced writer thinks that he is showing his skill when he uses foreign phrases. Actually they are ostentations and should be avoided except in the very few instances when there is no English equivalent. Businessmen sometimes talk about *per diem* pay when they mean *a day's pay,* or they ship things *via* when they mean *by.* Other people talk of a *faux pas* when they mean a *mistake.*

EXERCISE 40

Rewrite this paragraph in simple language:

Yesterday at high noon Miss Adrienne Sinclair, the lovely youngest daughter of Mr. Gustav Ober Sinclair, was given in marriage to her handsome college classmate, Mr. Spencer Horston-Palmer. The exquisite, radiant bride was begowned in shimmering white satin adorned with old family lace of the utmost delicacy. Her hands, enveloped in spotless white kid, bore a white prayer book, symbol of purity, from which showered fragile lilies of the valley. As the lovely bride moved toward the sanctum sanctorum, she was followed closely by three stunning attendants wearing pale orchid organdy. The tender strains of the wedding march were presented by the talented organist.

EXERCISE 41

The following letter of eighty-three words can be written in clear, simple language in thirty-one words. See how close to that number you can come in your revision.

Dear Sir:

We are in receipt of your favor of the tenth instant in re order for five television sets and wish to advise that according to our records your order was shipped on Oct. 19 via American Express. In as much as the order was carefully checked on this end, we would ask you to wait for three days. If the material has not been received in that time, we would ask that you use the card attached hereto and give us due notice.

EXERCISE 42

These three paragraphs are taken from a student theme. On your paper, write in clear, good English what you think the student was trying to say.

It was during my first year of high school that adolescent reason catapulted a mental conflict of doubtful victory—the attainment of a lifelong friend.

Succeeding years seemed quite remote from the momentum of the impending expectancy of a mutual comrade. Chums, I had plenty, but the seemingly, gripping void that only the reality of a lasting friendship could dispatch, depressed me. I imagined myself forever walking companionless, alone.

In my persistent search I was rewarded with short-lived acquaintances with several of my classmates, but, slowly, the dream images I often found myself unconsciously forming, corporeally and facially resembling their likenesses, would crumble, become indistinct and nebulous, disintegrating into nothingness. Wraithfully vague, one face clung tenaciously, and it was from the pattern of its features that the process of creative reconstruction would begin all over again, fading and dimming, but bravely struggling for substantial visibility.

53. WORDINESS

Wordiness, or redundancy, is the use of more words than are needed to express the meaning.

Writing, to be effective, must be as economical as possible. This does not mean that it must be sketchy or that essential words can be omitted.

Wrong: Shipped order today.
Right: We shipped your order today.

Omit unnecessary prepositions; for example, do not say *meet up with* for *meet,* or *fall off of* for *fall off.*
Be careful not to say the same thing twice.

Redundant: He operates a large 800-acre farm.
Better: He operates an 800-acre farm.
Redundant: When they had spent all the money, they returned back home.
Better: When they had spent all the money, they came home.
Redundant: The bonds were burned and reduced to ashes.
Better: The bonds were burned.

Wordy	*Better*
repeat again	repeat
someone I met up with	someone I met
important essentials	essentials
many in number	many
blue in color	blue
combined together	combined
round in form	round
check up on	check
in my opinion, I think	I think
each and every one	each one
rest up	rest
recur again	recur

Wordy	*Better*
join together	join
connect up with	connect with
refer back	refer
return back	return

Do not use more words than are necessary.

> I am indeed sorry that you were not supplied with the necessary information requested by you in order to assure you of the safest means of traveling to reach Cimarron. (Verbose; 30 words)
>
> I regret that you did not receive information concerning the safest road to Cimarron. (Economical; 14 words)

EXERCISE 43

On your paper, rewrite the following sentences, omitting unnecessary words:

1. Maybe I misinterpreted the story wrong.
2. Gabriel was an adjacent neighbor to the Lukes.
3. The Esmonds wished to restore James II back to the throne.
4. I do not wish one which is square in shape; I want one oval in form.
5. The end of the corridor terminates at a small door, green in color.
6. In this day and age any girl with the necessary financial resources can keep her hair neat and attractive in appearance.
7. After his death he received the award posthumously.
8. Although we were many in number, there were a few of us who felt close; and so we decided to correspond with each other in future years to come.
9. It is undeniably true that once you start to study in earnest, your troubles will be lessened and mitigated.
10. When he combined together the events of the autobiography of his life, he saw that the important essentials would have to be repeated again.
11. The desire to express oneself is a universal craving which is common to all people.

12. The company had a complete monopoly in that territory, but there were unfavorable climatic conditions which prevented the factory from resuming production again.

13. In the case of those culprits, there are not many people who would judge them solely and completely responsible for their cruel, thoughtless, and heinous misdeeds.

14. In my opinion, I think that the check should be returned to the bank.

15. Each and everyone of you must rest up before the game.

54. FAULTY REPETITION

Careless repetition of words or different forms of the same word causes monotony in style.

Weak: The book is covered with a green cover.
Better: The book has a green cover.
Weak: He thought everyone would think his act to be generous.
Better: He thought everyone would consider his act generous.

EXERCISE 44

On your paper, rewrite the following sentences without faulty repetition:

1. The height of the desk is three feet high.
2. The room has not as much room as my former room had.
3. She placed the box in another place.
4. Slowly the Indian edged toward the edge of the river.
5. I mind having you read my mind.
6. Tommy received a birthday present from everyone present.
7. The man loafing in front of the bakery explained that he had come to buy a loaf of bread.
8. He was a likable kind of man, always kind to children and really interested in his fellow man.

9. At the track meet, I met my old friend Marshall.
10. All the tomato plants that we had transplanted were thriving.

55. EUPHONY

Euphony is pleasant sound. Good writers choose their words carefully and arrange them so that the sound of the sentence is euphonious.

55a. Avoid repetition of the same sound.

I hope that you will like the *prize* and that it is the right *size*.

When Mr. Edwards *recovered*, he *discovered* that his money had been stolen.

NOTE: Be particularly careful of words ending in *tion* or *sion*. Several of them used together make a sentence sound heavy.

After Jack's *explanation*, the principal gave the problem careful *consideration*.

55b. Avoid alliteration and rhyme.

Alliteration is the use of several words beginning with the same sound. It is often used in advertising because it attracts attention, but it should usually be avoided in good prose.

He *fought* for *foreign* nations in *four* wars.

EXERCISE 45

On your paper, rewrite these sentences, giving them greater euphony:

1. The balmy winds blew warmly over the bay.
2. The sun rode high in a bright blue sky.
3. In high school I developed a yearning to learn.
4. The intelligence service built morale by sending reports concerning support by the home front.
5. Why should we care if you cut your hair?
6. In a blind fury he flew into the fray.

7. Scenes such as these are best seen at sunset from some lofty parapet.

8. I'm sorry that I was late for the date, but fate just seemed to be against me.

9. When the meetings were resumed, we consumed quantities of refreshments.

10. A good deal of misconception based on unscientific tradition has resulted in the dissemination of much misinformation regarding nutrition.

56. GLOSSARY OF WORDS AND EXPRESSIONS OFTEN MISUSED

The following glossary contains words and expressions often misused. The list is not comprehensive, but it does contain some of the most common violations of good usage.

Many of the words and expressions in the list are acceptable in formal English, when used correctly. A few are always to be avoided, but many are incorrect only on the level of formal English. Especially remember that no stigma attaches to the label "colloquial"; it merely indicates that a given expression is more appropriate in conversation and in informal discourse than in formal writing. In your formal theme work, however, you should think carefully before using a word or expression on the following list which bears a restrictive label.

Usage is so constantly changing that expressions which are now restricted in some way may later be considered standard. Furthermore, because no dictionary or grammar is a final authority, some usages are disputed. No two linguists would agree on all the comments which follow.

1. A, AN. *An* should be used before an initial vowel sound; *a*, before a word beginning with a consonant sound: *an adult, a problem*.

2. ACCEPT, EXCEPT. *Accept* means "to receive"; *except* (when used as a verb) means "to exclude."

He *accepted* the nomination.

> I agree to the conditions if I may *except* the fourth in the list.

3. ACCIDENTLY. A vulgarism (see Section 44). Use *accidentally*.
4. AD. Colloquial abbreviation for advertisement. In formal writing avoid such colloquialisms as *ad, exam, phone,* and *prof.*
5. ADVISE. "To give advice." Use sparingly for "inform," "tell." (Note that *advise* is used as a verb, and *advice* is used as a noun.)

> Questionable: I *beg to advise* you that your letters have been received.

6. AFFECT, EFFECT. Affect means "to influence" or "assume"; *effect* means "to cause" and, as a noun, means "result." (*Affect* is not used as a noun.)
7. AGGRAVATE. Used colloquially for "irritate," "provoke," or "annoy." Specifically, *aggravate* means "to make more severe or intense."

> His disease was *aggravated* by this recent accident.

8. ALIBI. Used colloquially to mean an excuse or any kind of defense; properly, "a plea or fact of having been elsewhere when an offense was committed."
9. ALL RIGHT, ALRIGHT. *All right* is overworked to mean "very well." *Alright* is not an acceptable word.
10. ALL TOGETHER, ALTOGETHER. The former means "everybody (or everything) in one place"; *altogether* means "wholly."
11. ALLUSION, ILLUSION. *Allusion* means "an indirect reference," "a hint"; *illusion* means "a misleading image or vision."

> The speaker made an *allusion* to the strike.
> "Your security," he said, "is but an *illusion.*"

12. ALMOST, MOST. See MOST.
13. ALREADY, ALL READY. *Already* means "previously";

all ready (two words) means "everything (or everyone) ready."

14. AMONG, BETWEEN. *Among* shows the relation of more than two objects; *between* refers to only two.

> He distributed the prizes *among* the five winners.
> He divided the prize *between* Jack and Joe.
> That is the road *between* Fort Worth and Dallas.

15. AND ETC. Redundant. *Etc.* is the abbreviation for *et cetera,* meaning "and so forth." (In formal writing, such abbreviations should usually be avoided.)

16. ANY PLACE, EVERY PLACE, NO PLACE, SOME PLACE. Faulty. Use instead, *anywhere, everywhere, nowhere, somewhere.* Do not use *any wheres* or *somewheres.*

17. APT, LIABLE, LIKELY. *Apt* suggests "fitness" or "tendency"; *liable* implies "openness or exposure to something burdensome or disadvantageous"; *likely* means "expected," "probable." *Apt* and *likely* are often interchangeable.

> She is *apt* in mathematics.
> You are *liable* for damages.
> It is *likely* to rain.

18. AS. (1) *As* is overworked as a conjunction meaning "since," "because," "when," "while."

> Overworked: *As* it was raining, we waited.
> Better: *Since* it was raining, we waited.

(2) *As* is misused as a substitute for *that* or *whether.*

> Misused: I doubt *as* I can go.
> Better: I doubt *whether* I can go.

(3) In formal English, use *not so . . . as* in negative comparisons.

> Correct: He is *not so* wealthy *as* she.

19. AWFUL, AWFULLY, ABOMINABLE, ABOMINABLY, TER
RIBLE, TERRIBLY. These are inaccurate, overworked
intensives, sometimes substituted for *very*.

20. BESIDE, BESIDES. *Beside* is a preposition meaning "by
the side of"; *besides* is both a preposition and an
adverb meaning "moreover," "except," "in addition."

> Correct: Jane sits *beside* me.
> Who is going *besides* Harold?
> I don't know the boy; *besides,* I don't
> want to know him.

21. BURSTED, BUST, BUSTED. Vulgarisms for *burst*. The
principal parts of *burst* are *burst, burst, burst.*

22. CAN, MAY, MIGHT. *Can* suggests ability, physical and
mental. *May* implies permission or sanction.

> Correct: He *can* make good grades if he tries.
> The teacher says you *may* leave.

The distinction between *can* and *may* is shown
in this sentence:

> I doubt that you *can,* but you *may* try.

May also expresses possibility and wish.

> It *may* rain today. (Possibility)
> *May* you have a good trip! (Wish)

Might is used after a governing verb in the past
tense; *may,* after a governing verb in the present
tense.

> He *said* that you *might* go.
> He *says* that you *may* go.

23. CANNOT HELP BUT. A double negative (*cannot help*
and *cannot but*).

> Correct: I *cannot help* believing the story.
> I *cannot but* believe the story.

24. CAN'T HARDLY. A double negative.

> Avoid: I *can't hardly* hear you.
> Correct: I *can hardly* hear you.

25. COMPLECTED. Colloquial.

> Formal: He was a dark-complexioned man.
>   or, better
>   He was a man of dark complexion.

26. CONTACT, CONTACTED. Overworked business terms. Use such expressions as "get in touch with."

27. CONTINUAL, CONTINUOUS. The former implies a "close recurrence in time," *continuous* means "without interruption."

> Correct: The ticking of the clock was *continuous*.
>   They refused her *continual* requests.

28. COULD OF. Illiterate. Use *could have* or *could've*.

29. CREDIBLE, CREDITABLE, CREDULOUS. *Credible* means "believable"; *creditable* means "praiseworthy"; *credulous* means "gullible."

> Correct: The story is *credible*.
>   This is a *creditable* effort.
>   You are too *credulous*.

30. CUTE. An overworked colloquialism for *attractive, pleasing*.

31. DISREGARDLESS, IRREGARDLESS. The prefixes *dis-* and *ir-* are superfluous. Avoid these two words and use *regardless* instead of either of them.

> Correct: *Regardless* of what he says, I think the book was good.

32. DUE TO. An adjective phrase, which should not be used adverbially in formal English. The same principle applies to *owing to, caused by*.

> Correct: His hoarseness was *due to* a cold.
>   He was hoarse *on account of* (because of) a cold.

33. EITHER . . . OR, NEITHER . . . NOR. *Either* and *neither* are correlative conjunctions. *Or* is used with *either; nor,* with *neither. Either* and *neither* are also used as singular indefinite pronouns.

34. ENTHUSE. A colloquial substitute for "to be enthusiastic."

35. FARTHER, FURTHER. *Farther* is preferably used to indicate "space"; *further* indicates "greater in degree, quantity, or time," and also means "moreover," "in addition to."

> Correct: He walked one mile *farther.*
> Let us speak *further* on this topic.

36. FELLOW. Colloquial for "individual," "person," "one," "man."

37. FEMALE. Always stresses the idea of sex and applies to animals, plants, and human beings. Its use as a synonym for *woman* is generally tabooed.

38. FINE. A colloquial term of approval. It specifically means "delicate," "refined," "sensitive," "subtle."

39. FOLKS. Colloquial for "relatives," "people."

40. FORMALLY, FORMERLY. *Formally* means "in a formal manner"; *formerly* means "in the past."

41. FUNNY. Colloquial for "strange," "queer," "odd," "remarkable."

42. GOOD, WELL. *Good* is an adjective: "to have a good time," "to give a *good* performance." *Well* functions as either adverb or adjective.

> Correct: I feel *well.* (Adjective)
> He plays the violin *well.* (Adverb)

43. GOT, GOTTEN. *Got* is colloquial in the sense of "must" or "ought."

> Colloquial: He *has* got to go.

> *Got* is redundant in such an expression as "I've got a cold." *Gotten* is rarely used as the past participle of *get.* Use *got* instead.

> Correct: Have you *got* your mail?

Got is correctly used as the past tense of the verb *get*.

> Correct: I *got* good news yesterday.

44. GUESS. *Guess* means "conjecture" and is colloquial when used to mean "believe," "think," "suspect."
45. HEALTHFUL, HEALTHY. *Healthful* means "conducive to health"; *healthy* means "possessing health."

> Correct: He is a *healthy* person.
> She lives in a *healthful* section of the state.

46. HISSELF. Faulty. Use *himself*.
47. HOME, HOMEY. Do not loosely use *home* for *house*. Do not omit the preposition in such an expression as *He was at home. Homey* is a provincial substitute for *homelike*.
48. IF, WHETHER. Use *if* in conditional sentences; use *whether* in stating alternatives.

> Correct: *If* he is in, I mean to call on him.
> I don't know *whether* he is ten or twelve years old.

49. IMPLY, INFER. *To infer* is to draw a conclusion from statements, circumstances, or evidence. *To imply* is to suggest a meaning not explicitly stated.

> Correct: The detective *inferred* from the position of the fingerprints that the man who fired the shot was left-handed.
> What you say *implies* that you think me a liar.

50. IN, INTO. Verbs indicating movement into a place are generally followed by *into*.

> When he walked *into* the room, he found us ready.

In is used to indicate motion within a place.

> She paced up and down *in* the classroom for the whole period.

In is used when the place is not mentioned.

> He came *in* after we had finished the dishes.
> The train came *in*.

51. INGENIOUS, INGENUOUS. *Ingenious* means "talented," "resourceful"; *ingenuous* means "frank" or "naive."
52. IRREGARDLESS. *See* DISREGARDLESS.
53. ITS, IT'S. *Its* is the possessive form of "it"; *it's* means "it is."
54. KIND OF, SORT OF. Colloquial when used in such expressions as "I am *kind of* weary tonight"; "he is *sort of* glad you spoke."

> Correct: He is an unusual *sort of* person.

Do not use *kind of a, sort of a.*

55. LET, LEAVE. *Leave* means "to go away." *Let* means "to permit." "Let me alone" means "stop annoying me!" "Leave me alone" means, "I wish to be here by myself."
56. LIABLE, LIKELY. *See* APT.
57. LIE, LAY. *To lie,* meaning "to recline," is an intransitive verb; *to lay,* meaning "to place," is a transitive verb. (See Sections 15 and 16.)

> Correct: I shall *lie* down.
> Please *lay* the book on the desk.

58. LIKE, AS. *Like* is a preposition and is followed by an object. *As* and *as if* are conjunctions and may introduce clauses. (See Section 19.)

> Correct: He looks *like* his grandmother.
> It looks *as if* it will rain.

59. LOAN. As a verb, *loan* is a synonym for *lend.* Either may be used, but *lend* is preferred in most formal writing.
60. LOCATE. A provincialism when used to mean "remember" or "settle." Use the exact word.
61. LOTS, A LOT OF, WHOLE LOT. Colloquial for "many" or "much."

62. LUXURIANT, LUXURIOUS. *Luxuriant* refers to abundant growth; *luxurious* pertains to luxury.

> Correct: The undergrowth was *luxuriant*.
> The hotel was *luxurious*.

63. MAD. *Mad* means "insane." It is colloquial when used to mean "angry."

64. MAY, MIGHT. *See* CAN.

65. MOST, ALMOST. *Most* is an adjective; *almost* is usually an adverb.

> Correct: We have *almost* finished the work.
> *Most* games are entertaining.
> He *almost* decided to leave.
> *Almost* all politicians are used to speaking in public.

66. MUCHLY. A vulgarism. Substitute *very, greatly*.

67. NICE. Colloquial for "agreeable," "pleasant." *Nice* actually means "precise," "fastidious."

68. NOTORIOUS, NOTEWORTHY, NOTABLE. *Notorious* means "infamous"; *noteworthy* and *notable* mean "remarkable," "worthy of note."

69. NOWHERE NEAR. Colloquial. Use *not nearly*.

> Correct: I have *not nearly* finished the job.

70. O. K. Greatly overused. Use a more exact expression.

71. PARTY, PERSON, INDIVIDUAL. *Party* implies a group and, except in legal and telephonic language, should not be used to refer to one person. *Individual* refers to a particular or single person.

72. PASS OUT. Slang in the sense of "faint."

73. PEP, PEPPY. Slang. Use *zest, energy, vivacity, animation*.

74. PLENTY. A noun. As an adverb or adjective, *plenty* should be avoided in formal speech or writing.

> Incorrect: He was *plenty* angry.
> Correct: The dairy has *plenty* of milk.

75. PRACTICABLE, PRACTICAL. *Practicable* means "capable

of being put into practice"; *practical* means "concerned with practice rather than theory."

Correct: The housewife should be *practical*.
The proposal is not *practicable*.

76. PRETTY. Provincial or colloquial for "rather," "mod-
erately," "somewhat."

Questionable: That is a *pretty* large order.
I feel *pretty* good today.

77. PRINCIPAL, PRINCIPLE. *Principal* is used as a noun
("sum of money" or "teacher") and an adjective
meaning "chief" or "main." *Principle* is used as a
noun meaning "a governing rule or truth."

78. PROPOSITION. Business jargon for "proposal" (offer,
affair).

79. QUITE A. Colloquial in phrases such as *quite a few,*
quite a bit, quite a lot.

80. RAISE, REAR, BRING UP. *Raise* in the sense of "rear"
or "bring up" is frequently used, but it is still considered provincial by some of the best writers.

Preferable: The mother *reared* (brought up) the
children.

81. RAISE, RISE. *Raise,* as a verb, may be used transitively; *rise,* as a verb, is used intransitively, and
should therefore not be used with an object.

Correct: As I *rise* from the chair, I shall *raise* my
hat.

82. RECEIPT, RECIPE. *Receipt,* as a noun, means "an
acknowledgement of payment"; *recipe* means "a
formula," "a set of directions."

83. REFER BACK. *To refer* means "to direct attention" or
"to make reference": *back* is therefore superfluous.
(The same kind of faulty diction is evident in
repeat again.)

84. RELATION, RELATIVE. *Relation* used to refer to a

member of one's family is colloquial. Use *relative* in this sense.

85. RESPECTFULLY, RESPECTIVELY. *Respectfully* means "in a respectful manner"; *respectively* means "severally," "each in the order given."

86. RIGHT ALONG, RIGHT AWAY, RIGHT THEN. Colloquialisms. Substitute *directly, immediately.*

87. SAID, SAME, SUCH. *Same* and *such* are adjectives. *Said* is usually a verb.

> Objectionable: Although the *said* plan was feasible, I decided not to adopt *same.*

Use *it, that,* or *this* instead of *said, same,* or *such.*

88. SHALL, WILL. The distinctions in the use of *shall* and *will* have broken down somewhat, but a few careful speakers and writers still observe them. (See Section 16e.)

89. SHOULD, WOULD. (See Section 16e.)

90. SIGN UP WITH, SIGN UP. Colloquial for *join, enroll, hire, engage.*

> Faulty: He has not *signed up* with any club.
> The coach *signed up* two assistants.

91. SIT, SET. *Sit* is usually an intransitive verb; *set,* transitive.

> Correct: I shall *sit* down.
> Please *set* the vase on the table.

92. SO. Avoid overuse of *so* as a conjunction; excessive use of *so* is a mark of immaturity, of childishness. Use more exact connectives. If a clause shows purpose, use *so that:*

> Correct: Martha went with Fred *so that* she could be sure to catch the bus.

Do not use *so* as a general substitute for *extremely, indeed,* or *very.*

> Correct: He is very kind. (Not *so kind*)

93. SOME. Do not use *some* as an adverb.

> Incorrect: He was some glad to see us.
> Correct: He was very glad to see us.

94. SURE. Colloquial for "certainly," "surely," "indeed."

95. UNIQUE. *Unique* means "having no like or equal" and logically should not be accompanied by *more, most, very.*

96. WAIT ON. *Wait on* means "to attend," "to serve"; it is provincial when used to mean "wait for."

> Incorrect: I *waited on* him for an hour before he came.

97. WHERE AT. Colloquial (and redundant) for *where.* Avoid such a statement as "He did not know *where* he was *at.*"

98. WORST KIND, WORST SORT, WORST WAY. Misused for "very much."

99. WOULD OF, COULD OF, MIGHT OF. Vulgarisms for "would have," "could have," "might have."

100. YOU ALL. In the sense of "all of you," this phrase has a recognized plural meaning. When used to refer to one person, it may be considered provincial.

EXERCISE 46

On your paper, rewrite the following sentences, using good diction:

1. I don't understand your illusion to that poem, but I guess it must be some clever.
2. I disremember what grub we had, but I can't ever forget the dame that fixed it.
3. I couldn't of figured out what funny doings were going on in town if you hadn't fetched me this paper.
4. The player, Red Russell, was the goofiest guy I ever saw.
5. The farmer was plumb tuckered out after his day's work, but he managed to enthuse a little over the chow his old lady had fixed for supper.

6. As soon as you give me your ascent, I'll pop the question to her.

7. I think you'll find the fellows concertizing in back of the house.

8. He doesn't cut a bit of ice in this burg, but on the campus of the state univ. I reckon he must be pretty hot stuff.

9. The prof's council was good, but Henry was a stubborn egg except you treated him easy and confidential-like.

10. I never was much good at telling antidotes, but I'll take a try at this one anyway.

11. Melton had all ready left for the barn, where the vet was trying to doctor a sick calf.

12. Many people have suspicioned him, but he ain't let on that he knows a thing about it.

13. I know you are intrigued with the car, but it's too expensive for you; and I don't calculate on loaning you the money for it.

14. I don't care if he is a good fellow; he's a sucker to let himself be taken in that away.

15. He remained perfectly stationery while I toted in the whole load of packages.

16. He was a dark-complected, smark-alecky fellow, and the girls were all crazy over him.

17. The mare looks as if she feels right poorly, but she looked alright this morning.

18. He went and did it even though we all told him the principal of the thing was wrong.

19. The foreman got the goods on him, and he was laid off with nary a chance to defend himself.

20. She was real pretty accept for stringy hair, which she tried every which way to fix so it would look tolerable well.

EXERCISE 47

On your paper, rewrite the following sentences, correcting the errors in diction:

1. In spite of the favorable factors in your case, I shall have to answer in the negative.

2. In the sea of ruthless competition, one can climb to success only by seizing the golden flower of opportunity.

3. In connection with the degree of his guilt, I am of the persuasion that we are not certain as to whether we are fully conversant and acquainted with all the facts of the case.

4. The president's attention was arrested by Mr. Blaine's ability to cope with any situation that might arise.

5. Before giving the glass of milk to the little lass, I placed a box of crackers before her.

6. My fellow classmates average in height a height of sixty-eight inches.

7. In these respects, laboratory sciences are of a notoriously trying nature.

8. With bated breath we watched that miserable specimen of humanity go to his doom.

9. The comestibles served in this refectory possess a high degree of noisomeness.

10. Concentrate on the coverage and do not concern yourself with minor, petty details.

11. As soon as I saw that sleek roadster in the showroom, I felt a weak moment coming on.

12. Those who take rooms in this house will have more than enough room in which to house their appurtenances.

13. The sheer force of his personality beggars description.

14. In connection with her other traits I should mention her pulchritude, which is of a very high order.

15. With regard to gardening facilities, there is an empty, vacant piece of unused land in back of the house.

16. The good benefits one receives from camp are perfectly all right, but excess laziness has a toe hold on the minds of most campers.

17. Ellen is the sort of girl with whom one likes to have a date with.

18. There were many of us who thought that he was an exceptionally unique person.

19. A goodly number of voters, perhaps more sinned

against than sinning, wrought havoc by staying away
from the polls in droves.

20. Please refer back to the minutes of the last meeting,
where you will find a new angle along the lines
which we have been corresponding with each other
about.

EXERCISE 48

The following sentences contain provincialisms, improprieties, colloquialisms, vulgarisms, slang, and mis-
spelling. On your paper, rewrite the sentences in correct,
formal English.

1. We have et every one of the sandwiches.
2. Will you be in the dorm then?
3. The poor student always gets it in the neck.
4. He never let on he knew about it.
5. She was an earthly angle, but one without wings.
6. I could of gone if I had worked on Saturday.
7. They walked up to the alter and got married.
8. What do you reckon he meant by that?
9. Dick had a bad case of the jitters.
10. Please proceed me into the room.
11. She took on when I told her of the accident.
12. I never would have suspicioned it.
13. He had to accompany a dumb bunny to the dance.
14. The latch is broken off the gait.
15. George should never have took her skating.
16. Leave go of me at once.
17. He was peaceful ordinarily, but sometimes his choler
rose.
18. I've been invited to the Hopkins formal in June
Week.
19. Why did you fall for that?
20. Now you will have to work extra hard.

EXERCISE 49

The following sentences contain examples of triteness,
"fine" writing, jargon, mixed figures, wordiness, faulty
repetition, lack of euphony. On your paper, rewrite each

sentence, keeping as close as possible to the intended meaning.

1. Rod decided to seize the bit in his teeth and come down like a wolf on the fold.
2. At the institution of higher learning which he favored with his presence, he was justly proud of his rugged individualism.
3. After spending much time preparing to leave, and after many fond goodbyes, we decided to proceed on our journey.
4. Although he ordinarily liked the succulent bivalve, he picked up one of the delectable morsels in a gingerly fashion and devoured it with a wry smile.
5. Not all widow women regard their lot with apprehension, but those who are left with small children are prone to view their status with alarm.
6. Sitting in his room alone by himself, he repeated her name over again and again.
7. A raging conflagration all too soon destroyed the edifice which with loving hands we had erected.
8. Sweetly-scented school sashes worn by the fair sex added to the riot of color on the crowded dance floor.
9. Full steam ahead! In this storm of controversy, you must not let your hand falter on the plow.
10. After serious financial reverses, he attempted to misappropriate funds from the bank.
11. We followed the speaker's line of reasoning to a very great extent.
12. Our gridiron warriors were tendered a banquet at the conclusion of their victorious season, and after the sumptuous repast each gladiator spoke a few well-chosen words.
13. The nature of the outside reading in English composition is something of an added attraction.
14. When asked if he wished to be the recipient of our offer of a position, he replied in the affirmative.
15. We beg to state that your valued order will receive prompt attention, along the lines which you suggested.

16. At the groaning table I forgot that I was supposed to have a delicate and birdlike appetite.

17. He was caught in the immutable wheels of fate and never reached the goal of his ambition.

18. I may have gone a little too far, but I was simply impelled to get it off my chest.

19. Among those present were included only a paltry few who voiced the sentiments of the players themselves.

20. All nature seemed engaging, but the sight of the crimson orb setting behind the lofty mountain was a delightful feature which beggars all description.

The Sentence

Do you write *gobble-de-gook?* This is a type of writing
that rambles; it uses ten words where five would do a
better job; it is awkward in structure and unpleasant in
sound. As a result, the reader must examine it three or
four times before he knows what it means. Recently the
Air Matériel Command sent to all its employees a little
pamphlet called *Gobble-de-gook or Plain Talk?* In the
pamphlet there are quotations from an article on annual
leave and from other military notices—all written in
gobble-de-gook. Then the author begs for clear, simple
sentences. But the clear sentence is important not only
to the military forces. It is vital in business. It is effective in the club and in your social life. The problems of
writing good sentences may be considered under three
heads: Correctness (Sections 57–60), Clearness (Sections
61–69), and Effectiveness (Sections 70–74).

57. PERIOD FAULT

A sentence is a group of words that expresses a complete thought. Do not write a part of a sentence and put
a period at the end. Such punctuation is known as the
period fault.

Wrong: To a trapper, a fur coat means hours of back-
breaking work. Also the joy and thrill known only
to the hunter. (The words beginning with *also* do
not make a complete thought. They are only part
of a sentence).

266

Right: To a trapper, a fur coat means hours of back-breaking work; but it means also the joy and thrill known only to the hunter.

Wrong: After a time, I began to find value in the sport. A value appreciated chiefly by the man who follows the trail. (The words beginning with *a value* form an appositive, not a complete thought. They are part of a sentence, not a whole sentence.)

Right: After a time, I began to find value in the sport, a value appreciated chiefly by the man who follows the trail.

Wrong: The hunter sees the beauty of the morning sun. Throwing a path of light across the lake. (The words beginning with *throwing* form a participial phrase, not a complete thought. They are only part of a sentence.)

Right: The hunter sees the beauty of the morning sun throwing a path of light across the lake.

Wrong: The hunter loves life outdoors. Especially in the fall and winter. (The words beginning with *especially* do not form a complete thought. Be careful of expressions beginning with *especially, for example*. They should often be joined to the independent clause that precedes.)

Right: The hunter loves life outdoors, especially in the fall and winter.

CAUTION: Don't relax because you are writing a friendly letter. Your correspondent deserves the courtesy of careful work.

Wrong: Was very happy to hear of your promotion. (No subject)
Right: I was very happy to hear of your promotion.

NOTE: There are two kinds of incomplete sentences which are permissible, elliptical sentences and fragmentary sentences used for stylistic effect.

In elliptical sentences, the complete thought is implied but not stated.

> "Did you buy it?"
> "Yes."
> "For how much?"
> "Five dollars."

Skilled writers sometimes obtain special effects by using fragmentary sentences for stylistic effect, but only people skilled in the use of language can use sentence fragments cleverly. Poor use of sentence fragments gives the effect of illiteracy. High school students, unless they are very talented writers, should avoid the fragment.

EXERCISE 1

On your paper, rewrite these sentences, correcting the period fault:

1. The room was filled with flowers. Some of which were very expensive.
2. She put on her best clothes and went to the movies. Instead of sitting at home worrying.
3. The airship was put into its hangar. So that curious spectators could not damage it.
4. Have shipped your order and billed you for July 1.
5. First of all, the training which is required.
6. Everything was new and interesting. Mainly the clothes.
7. He told many jokes at the party. Some of which were not at all funny.
8. Swimming and fishing in the ocean in the daytime and dancing on the boardwalk at night.
9. While Julius was in the army, he received many medals. One of these being the Purple Heart.
10. Dignitaries of both governments attending in official uniforms and medals.

58. COMMA FAULT

Do not write two sentences with only a comma between them. Such punctuation is known as the *comma fault.* Sentences that are separated only by commas are called *run-on sentences.*

> Wrong: I hope that you can get the house that you spoke about, it sounds great.
>
> Wrong: I have some good news for you about the bowling team, we have won three straight matches.

Each of these groups of words is composed of two complete thoughts with only a comma between them. A comma is not a strong enough mark to use between two complete thoughts. Use a period instead.

> Right: I hope that you can get the house that you spoke about. It sounds great.
>
> I have some good news for you about the bowling team. We have won three straight matches.

If the ideas are closely related, these run-on sentences may be combined in one sentence. Here are three ways of making one sentence out of them:

1. Use a semicolon.

> I hope that you can get the house that you spoke about; it sounds great.

2. Use a coördinating conjunction (*and, but, for, or*) and a comma.

> I hope that you can get the house that you spoke about, for it sounds great.

3. Subordinate one idea.

> Because the house that you spoke about sounds great, I hope that you can get it.

The method that you choose depends upon the emphasis that you wish to make. If both of the ideas are equally emphatic, you will use a period or a semicolon. The two ideas will then stand out with equal strength. The use of a subordinating conjunction makes one idea dependent upon the other. In order to make your style interesting and vivid, you must give some attention to the impression that you wish to make and the type of sentence that will fit that impression.

NOTE: Be particularly careful if the two clauses are joined by a conjunctive adverb (*however, moreover, nevertheless, therefore, thus, then, so, yet, otherwise*). If these words join two independent ideas, a semicolon must precede the conjunctive adverb. (See Section 24b.)

Wrong: You did not complete your work, consequently you will receive no credit.

Right: You did not complete your work; consequently you will receive no credit.

EXERCISE 2

On your paper, rewrite these run-on sentences, which appeared in students' papers. Choose for each sentence the form that in your opinion suits it best.

1. Thank you very much, it was sweet of you to invite me to your party.
2. This is my own fault, if I had done my work in the winter, I should not have to go to summer school.
3. Some shops are using lucite boxes for a display of jewelry, their tops are transparent.
4. You will have to give the chair two coats of white paint, otherwise the dark color of the old paint will show.
5. In South America a businessman must talk sociably for at least fifteen minutes, then he can introduce a business matter.
6. He was not dependable in his former position, therefore we cannot employ him.
7. Do come to see us in our new home, we have missed the pleasant evenings we used to spend with you.
8. Ten tanks had left our ship, only eight had landed on the beach.
9. The next thing to work on is the motor of the car, this is the part of the work that runs into money.
10. There were three political parties in Burke's day, they were Tories, Old Whigs, and New Whigs.

59. FUSED SENTENCES

Do not write two sentences with no punctuation between them. Such sentences are known as *fused sentences.*

If the two sentences combined in this way are both statements, the methods suggested in Section 58 may be used in correcting them. Sometimes, however, an inexperienced writer combines a question and a statement. Then, the only way to correct the sentence is to end one of the complete ideas with a period, a question mark, or an exclamation point. Be very sure that you have *two* complete ideas before you use this method of correction.

Wrong: What kind of year book are you going to have, will it be anything like ours?

Right: What kind of year book are you going to have? Will it be anything like ours?

Wrong: He is a great lacrosse player, don't you think so?

Right: He is a great lacrosse player. Don't you think so?

Wrong: Who is going to pay for the propaganda films? The government or private film companies? (The words beginning with *The government* do not express a complete idea. (See Section 57.)

Right: Who is going to pay for the propaganda films, the government or private film companies?

EXERCISE 3

On your paper, rewrite the following sentences, using periods, question marks, or exclamation points where they are needed:

1. Are you going so soon I'll walk to the corner with you.
2. Criticizing the candidates gets you nowhere you should vote.
3. Turn out the lights they will see that we are here.
4. Have you been affected much by the water shortage if so, I guess your sister is glad, for she won't have to take a bath every day.
5. On Saturday I saw Susan Peters in *The Barretts of*

Wimpole Street I wish hoop skirts like hers would be fashionable again.

EXERCISE 4

On your paper, rewrite these sentences, correcting the period fault, the comma fault, or the fused-sentence fault. (See Sections 57–59.)

1. Was glad to hear that you made the team.
2. Suppose we had lived long ago when there were no radios just think what we should be missing.
3. In Mexico, the mistress never goes shopping in the market, the maid does the laundry, the cleaning, and the shopping.
4. When they found a piece of ground that suited them. They built a beautiful ranch house.
5. I enjoyed very much seeing June Randall again, she asked to be remembered to you.
6. We drifted down the Grand Canal. Listening to the music and enjoying the beauty of Venice spread out before us.
7. When we took off, not a man knew our destination, we were to be signaled when to jump from the plane.
8. Only one thing will give us peace. The willingness of countries to work together.
9. The lie detector does not detect lies, it merely records the emotional excitement of the victim.
10. First cream the butter and sugar thoroughly, then you should stir in the eggs and milk.
11. I like all the ties. One particularly because it goes so well with my new suit.
12. The most interesting part of the book has to do with the Atlantic Charter. Especially the part in which the Charter permits each nation to choose its own government.
13. There is a great deal of fun in gardening, my neighbor and I always have friendly arguments about whose crops are better.
14. At the age of nine, I was enrolled in The Children's Experimental Theater. A drama group that teaches free expression.

15. When the great day came, I was not too anxious to be in the play, in fact I had a terrible feeling that I was going to be sick.

16. All was quiet, then the man in the glass booth raised his hand and dropped it, we were on the air.

17. There was a tense feeling among the crew. When all of a sudden a cannon shot burst into the air.

18. There was another girl in whom he was interested, she had dark hair and big black eyes.

19. At Garrison Boulevard we didn't see the policeman, it was a dark night, and the street light on the corner was out.

20. Last week was a memorable occasion for me, I purchased my new communications receiver.

21. I surely wish I could get you interested in "ham" radio, it is a fascinating hobby.

22. Last Saturday night the two teams lined up against each other. One like David and one like Goliath.

23. When the crops are sold, all of the money is not profit, a great percent is overhead. Such as labor, repairs to machinery, and freight charges.

24. In the Shakespearean theater, the poor people sat on the ground. While the rich sat in boxes on the side of the theater.

25. To prove my point, let's go back a few years. When Henry Ford started his revolutionary idea of producing cars in great numbers.

60. MISUSE OF DEPENDENT CLAUSES

A child writes simple sentences beginning with the subject; but as a person's style matures, he uses dependent clauses to show the relationship of one idea to another, and he varies the structure of sentences in order to give strength and rhythm to his writing. A knowledge of the proper use of dependent clauses is necessary for the development of a mature style.

60a. Do not use an adverbial clause as a noun clause.

Wrong: I read where the weather forecaster said a snowstorm was coming.

Right: I read that the weather forecaster said a snow-
          storm was coming.
Wrong: The reason why the automobile stopped was be-
          cause it had run out of gasoline.
Right: The reason why the automobile stopped was that
          it had run out of gasoline.

60b. Do not use an adverbial clause in place of a noun.

Adverbial clauses beginning with *when* and *where* are
often used incorrectly as noun clauses.

Wrong: Plagiarism is *where* you take the work of another
          and pass it off as your own.
Right: Plagiarism is *copying* the work of another and
          passing it off as one's own.
Wrong: Anemia is *when* the blood is deficient in red cor-
          puscles.
Right: Anemia is an *illness* in which there is a deficiency
          of red corpuscles.

60c. Do not use an independent clause as the subject of *is* or *was*.

Faulty: I had sprained my ankle was the reason I could
          not go to the dance.
Better: The fact that I had sprained my ankle was the
          reason I could not go to the dance.
          I could not go to the dance because I had sprained
          my ankle.

EXERCISE 5

On your paper, rewrite these sentences, correcting the
misuse of dependent clauses:

1. I see in the paper where the weather has been un-
   usually cold this winter.
2. The train left by daylight time is why I missed it.
3. In the game of baseball, a strike is when the player
   tries to hit the ball but misses it.
4. He did not concentrate was why he failed the course.
5. The reason the mower did not cut the grass was because its blades were dull.

6. Perjury is where a man swears to tell the truth and then tells a lie.
7. Because I bought a new suit is why she thinks I have money.
8. My father was a lawyer was the reason why I studied law.
9. His definition of freedom is when you can look any man squarely in the eye.
10. His home is where you can always have a good time.

61. USING ONLY RELATED IDEAS IN A SENTENCE

In order to be clear, a sentence must have unity and coherence. Sections 61–63 deal with ways of obtaining sentence unity. Sections 64–69 deal with methods of making a sentence coherent. Clear reference of pronouns, which is important in any study of the clear sentence, has been treated in Section 13. A sentence has unity when every idea in it is closely related and contributes to a single impression.

Wrong: 1. Bill was a good basketball player, and he was a graduate of the Erie High School.
2. Vaslav Nijinsky was one of the greatest dancers the world has ever known, and he was in a mental hospital for many years.
3. I hope that you will visit me next summer and tell June to write to me.

Sometimes unity can be obtained by making one idea subordinate to the other and using a connecting link that makes clear the relationship between the ideas. See the improved form of Sentence 1.

Improved: 1. Bill is a graduate of Erie High School, where an excellent basketball coach made him a good player.

Sometimes, however, the ideas are so completely unrelated that only a complete separation of them can establish unity. Occasionally they should be in another paragraph. See the improved form of Sentence 2 and Sentence 3:

Improved: 2. Vaslav Nijinsky was one of the greatest dancers the world has ever known. Unfortunately he was in a mental hospital for many years and could not show the world his art.

Improved: 3. I hope that you will visit me next summer. Please tell June to write to me.

EXERCISE 6

On your paper, rewrite the following sentences so that they are unified. If the ideas in any sentences cannot be related, omit one of them.

1. We believe that our club is the best in the school, and it was founded ten years ago.
2. *The Saturday Evening Post* is my favorite among weekly magazines, and it is published in Philadelphia.
3. I made 93 in the last history test, and I decided to go to the movies instead of studying.
4. Last Saturday, I went on my first blind date, and I lost my school ring.
5. My sister wants to be a florist, and she is only twelve years old.
6. He is a much better dancer than his brother, who took lessons for several years and works in a grocery store.
7. Woodrow Wilson was an eminent statesman, and he had a prominent chin.
8. People in North Carolina like hot breads, and the largest city is Charlotte.
9. The father of the family was a physician, having studied at Jefferson Medical College in Philadelphia, the third largest city in the United States.
10. He is a very clever person, his sister having studied in Paris for several years.

62. RAMBLING SENTENCES

Avoid rambling sentences which introduce too many details.

Rambling: Beethoven, who is considered one of the great masters of music, was the son of a court musician and a cook, and he became deaf at thirty-two, but he composed some magnificent symphonies.

Revised: Beethoven, one of the great masters of music, was the son of a court musician and a cook. Although he became deaf at thirty-two, he composed some magnificent symphonies.

EXERCISE 7

On your paper, rewrite the following selection in unified sentences:

1. Nijinsky was a great dancer. 2. His tremendous leaps seemed to defy gravity, and his grace, probably inherited from his mother, who was a dancer, especially in "Scheherazade," in which he dances the part of a slave in love with a princess, caused him to be applauded by throngs of people in all countries. 3. One of his greatest successes was his debut in New York in a dance called "Specter of the Rose," now a part of the repertoire of several ballet companies, in which thousands of rose petals floated over the stage as the great dancer performed. 4. Later he danced in Paris with the famous Pavlova and came to England in 1948 with his wife, a Hungarian actress, and his daughter lives in Rome and is also a dancer.

63. CHOPPY SENTENCES

Students who have been taught not to write rambling sentences sometimes go to the opposite extreme. They become afraid to join any ideas in one sentence. As a result, they write each thought as a separate unit. This procedure, however, can destroy the unity as thoroughly as rambling sentences do, for in choppy sentences, you cannot see how the ideas are related.

Choppy: Many trees die each year. They have had bad treatment. In our neighborhood, some people whitewash the trunks. They think that whitewash will keep insects away. Tree doctors say that whitewash will damage the bark. In some states there are laws against stripping blossoming trees like dogwood. Every spring a few people evade the law. They want to please themselves. They have no thought for the beauty of the woods. They are unconcerned about the destruction of a tree. They break off large branches. Then the tree dies.

EXERCISE 8

On your paper, revise the choppy paragraph in Section 63 by making sentences that show the relationship of one idea to another.

EXERCISE 9

On your paper, rewrite the following selection in unified sentences:

1. We are bombarded on all sides by propaganda. 2. We don't know what to believe. 3. We have been taught a few ways in which to test what we hear on the radio or read in the newspaper, and it is important to know who the speaker or writer is and what he knows about his subject. 4. Some people try to make us act by stirring our emotions. 5. They do not think clearly themselves. 6. They expect to make us do what they want done. 7. They don't give us logical reasons for acting. 8. Some people present only one side of the question discussed, and no question has only one side; so we suspect those people of being prejudiced and we do not put too much faith in what they say because if they were honest, they would tell the whole story, not simply a part of it. 9. It is important also to know what methods a speaker or writer used to gather his facts because sometimes investigations are carelessly made and the conclusions drawn are not valid conclusions and yet many people believe these conclusions without inquiring whether the facts have been carefully gathered. 10. In a democratic country, it is important for people to think.

64. INCOMPLETENESS

To be coherent, a sentence must be complete. Sometimes words are omitted when the writer understands so well what he wants to say that he thinks he has made his meaning clear to the reader.

64a. Be sure to include all necessary verbs.

Doubtful: The lawn is mowed and the hedges trimmed.

Correct: The lawn is mowed, and the hedges are trimmed.

Correct: The lawn is mowed and the fence repaired.

NOTE: The auxiliary verb can be understood when it is in the same form that has been expressed in the sentence. If another form is grammatically necessary, it should be expressed. *Is* can be understood before *repaired* in the preceding sentence.

Doubtful: He has never done any work and never will.

Improved: He has never done any work and never will do any.

NOTE: If the verb *to be* is used as an auxiliary and as a main verb, it must be expressed both times.

Doubtful: She was a fine girl and liked by everybody.

                main verb   auxiliary

Improved: She *was* a fine girl and *was* liked by everybody.

64b. Include necessary articles, pronouns, and prepositions.

We needed a clerk and typist. (One person)

We needed a clerk and *a* typist. (Two persons)

Doubtful: He built an automobile which could go ninety miles an hour and pleased many people.

Improved: He built an automobile which could go ninety miles an hour and *which* pleased many people.

Doubtful: I am neither interested nor concerned about his welfare. (Interested about his welfare?)

Improved: I am neither interested *in* his welfare nor concerned about it.

64c. In formal writing, do not omit *that* if the subject of the subordinate clause might seem at first glance to be the object of the verb preceding.

Informal: I think the boy is a singer (At first glance, *boy* seems to be the object of *think*).

Formal: I think *that* the boy is a singer.

See Section 69 for omission of words in a comparison.

64d. Be sure to express every idea essential to the sense or structure of the sentence.

Do not begin a sentence with one structure and shift, before finishing it, to another structure. (See Section 71.)

Not clear: An automobile, unless you take good care of it, you will soon have to repair it. (No verb to complete the structure begun with *automobile*.)

Improved: An automobile will soon have to be repaired unless good care is given to it.

Not clear: With these eleven men working together as a team is the reason for our successful season.

Improved: With these eleven men working together as a team, we had a successful season.

or

Because these eleven men worked as a team, we had a successful season.

64e. In formal writing, complete the thought after *so, such, those*.

Informal: I was so bored.

Formal: I was so bored that I left the party.

Informal: He is one of those eccentric philosophers.

Formal: He is one of those eccentric philosophers who prefer to be alone.

EXERCISE 10

On your paper, rewrite the following sentences so that they are complete and unified:

1. I have not spoken to Judith about your decision, nor will I.
2. All the money I spent for repairs, I could have bought a new car.
3. The secretary and treasurer were both so excited by the election.
4. It was a night that if one wore a sweater and skirt, she could feel comfortable.
5. He was such a pleasant man and so universally admired.

6. The soldier asked us would we please tell him the road to Washington.
7. Anybody who could get 100 on that history test, the whole class would think he was a genius.
8. I shall always be so grateful and appreciative of his kindness to me.
9. Betty had so much trouble with the stove, pressure cooker, and heating system.
10. Bob asked Arthur was he sick yesterday.

65. WORD ORDER

A sentence is not clear if its parts do not fit together. Notice the word order in the following sentence from a student's theme:

> In the days of Leeuwenhoek, anyone who was working with science was thought to be "cracked" by the public.

Because the phrase *by the public* is misplaced, the preceding sentence has a ridiculous meaning.

> Improved: In the days of Leeuwenhoek, anyone who was working with science was thought *by the public* to be "cracked."

65a. Do not misplace words such as *only, hardly, even*.

Vague: I *only* want to say a few words.
Improved: I want to say *only* a few words.
Vague: We were *even* victorious in our game against Southern.
Improved: We were victorious *even* in our game against Southern.

65b. Place phrases and clauses as close as possible to the words which they modify.

Vague: Silas Marner lived with a friend whom he trusted *in a small apartment*. (Misplaced prepositional phrase)
Improved: Silas Marner lived *in a small apartment* with a friend whom he trusted.

Vague: It gives me great pleasure to send you a little souvenir with my compliments, *which I hope you will find useful.* (Misplaced adjective clause)

Improved: It gives me great pleasure to send you with my compliments a little souvenir *which I hope you will find useful.*

Vague: New kitchen units will be installed, which will include built-in cabinets, electric stoves, and dishwashers. (It is often possible to improve sentences of this kind by putting the verb first.)

Improved: There will be installed new kitchen units, which will include built-in cabinets, electric stoves, and dishwashers.

65c. Avoid a "squinting" modifier.

A modifier is said to be "squinting" when it may refer to either of two parts of a sentence.

Awkward: Because inflation is dangerous *when it begins to develop,* the government should check it at once.

Does the sentence mean that inflation is dangerous when it begins to develop, or that when it begins to develop, the government should check it at once?

Improved: Because inflation is dangerous, the government should check it as soon as it begins to develop.

NOTE: In a structure involving *neither . . . nor* (*either . . . or*), the same part of speech that follows *neither* (*either*) should follow *nor* (*or*).

Vague: She had neither *completed* her English nor *her Spanish.*

Improved: She had completed neither *her English* nor *her Spanish.*

EXERCISE 11

On your paper, rewrite the following sentences, placing modifiers correctly:

1. We can only supply two of the items which you ordered.
2. In an effort to amuse me, the nurse put a hat on my head made of a towel.
3. I worked for the Sewell Company during the entire vacation in the Boys' Department.
4. A small native boy was balancing a basket on his head held down by a stone.
5. My turn finally came to bowl.
6. I prepared for the trip by putting the most comfortable shoes I had on.
7. New houses will be built in our country which will be heated by the sun.
8. There were three children injured yesterday by busses on their way home from school.
9. Some of the dancers carried huge baskets on their heads which were filled with bright flowers.
10. I wanted my mother to purchase a television set costing a small fortune for me.
11. We got a ride with Pete in his truck to Annapolis.
12. You cannot write a good report of an experiment in physics unless you know how to arrange what you have to say in clear sentences.
13. Your reply to our previous letters has not been received concerning the $48.95 that still remains unpaid.
14. One night Silas fell into a mysterious sleep during a prayer meeting which was mistaken for death.
15. The clown was wearing a bright blue and yellow sign on his back advertising the side show.
16. The new manager settled himself behind his desk and told the boys how he had made his fortune after dinner.
17. Most cars have sun visors above the windshield, which can be adjusted to shade the eyes.
18. We have the shirts in stock that you inquired about in your letter of May 15.
19. In order that the job may be done efficiently, large bins are distributed on this floor in which are placed different kinds of cotton.

20. The manufacturer can only use the four pelts which you sent to patch others.

21. I sent invitations to a party on Saturday, two weeks ago.

22. She told us to come at nine o'clock, and at ten she rescinded the invitation.

23. There are three letters in this file which are poorly written.

24. I am sorry that you were refused the information that you requested by a member of our company.

25. A representative is always on the grounds who will gladly show the cottages.

EXERCISE 12

Follow the directions in Exercise 11.

1. In this new history of art, a number of artists are excluded whom no editor can afford to neglect.

2. The book contains excellent reproductions of paintings by many artists to the great delight of the reader.

3. The end of the war released 2,000,000 Poles from forced labor, who could only get home by means of international agreement.

4. Please excuse Jane's absence from school which was a result of a cold accompanied by a fever on Friday, March 5.

5. We cannot stress the advantage of traveling with an established firm too forcibly.

6. Driver-education classes are being taught in high school in which any student may enroll.

7. More than a hundred inmates of the city mental hospital escaped today during a strike of the attendants, roaming the streets and looting stores.

8. A careful study of these figures shows that there are 7,500,000 people in this state that use chewing gum.

9. Norms have been developed for some jobs that are indicative of the possibilities of success which an individual may have.

10. We have made a tracing of the signature on the checks you enclosed for our files, and we shall pub-

lish a warning about this man's activities in our bulletin.

EXERCISE 13

On your paper, rewrite the following excerpt from a travel itinerary. Place the modifiers in the positions that make the sentences clear.

1. Cars will call at the hotels indicated when booking at about 9 A.M. 2. At the first stop, the party will embark in a "canoa" propelled by the natives of the vicinity with long poles, for a picturesque trip on the canals. 3. Then you will see the famous palace built in 1530 by Cortes which is now the seat of the local government. 4. You are requested to either touch anything nor sit in the old chairs. 5. The shopper will find something either to please himself or the folks at home, with ease. 6. Each resident of the United States is entitled to bring one hundred dollars' worth of articles free of duty home.

66. SPLIT CONSTRUCTIONS

Parts of a sentence which are closely related grammatically should not be carelessly separated. No tight rule about this principle can be made because sometimes it is necessary to separate these parts. In general, however, these rules can be followed.

66a. The parts of a verb phrase should usually be kept together.

Awkward: After he made a decision, he would, *no matter what the consequences might be,* stick to his point.

Improved: After he made a decision, he would stick to his point, no matter what the consequences might be.

Awkward: This tree has, although you would not think so, been here for thirty years.

Improved: Although you would not think so, this tree has been here for thirty years.

66b. Avoid *unnecessary* separation of subject and verb object and verb, preposition and object.

> Awkward: He, in one sweeping motion, threw both book and newspapers on the floor.
>
> Improved: In one sweeping motion, he threw both book and newspapers on the floor.

66c. Keep parts of an infinitive together.

Many good writers use and defend a split infinitive. I is true that in some constructions the split infinitiv makes a smoother or more emphatic sentence, but it ma often make an awkward sentence. Clearness and natura ness must be the test.

> Permissible: After we had caught a beautiful rainbo trout, we went home to *proudly display* o prize. (*Proudly to display* or *to displa proudly* makes the sentence stiff.)
>
> Unnecessary: The radio announcer told the audience t *vigorously applaud* when he raised his hand
>
> Improved: The radio announcer told the audience t *applaud vigorously* when he raised his hand

66d. Keep coördinate sentence elements together.

> Awkward: *Although he was a good tennis player,* he neve was ranked among the first ten, *although h practiced daily.*
>
> Right: Although he was a good tennis player and prac ticed daily, he was never ranked among the firs ten.

EXERCISE 14

Rewrite the following sentences, avoiding split con structions:

1. Shirley had, instead of doing her job, kept looking ou of the window.
2. When the war was over, Vincent bought a farm, afte he had come home.
3. In 1937, we added a new top story which was care

fully designed to, both in style and material, follow the original structure.

4. When he instead of building a house, built a barn, Mrs. Perkins rebelled.

5. One man in the group told, when he saw Corsica, a story of life on that island.

67. DANGLING MODIFIERS

A modifier is *dangling* when it is not clearly attached to the word to which it refers. Many of these dangling modifiers appear at the beginning of the sentence. They may be phrases beginning with the present participle (*arriving late, walking across the campus*) or the past participle (*exhausted by the trip, overcome by his trouble*); they may be phrases that contain a gerund (*after copying my schedule, in examining the plans*); they may begin with an infinitive (*to give better service, to finish the job*). Logically, they should be attached to the subject of the clause which follows.

67a. Avoid dangling participial phrases. (See Section 6.)

Dangling: *Opening the door,* the odor of strong perfume struck me at once. (The subject of the clause is *odor,* but the odor did not open the door.)

Right: *Opening the door,* I smelled strong perfume. (The subject of the clause is *I;* so the phrase is connected logically with the word which it modifies.)

             As I opened the door, the odor of strong perfume struck me at once. (The dangling phrase is changed to a clause.)

Dangling: *Exhausted after the day's work,* it was difficult for Betty to enjoy the evening. (Phrase with past participle. See Section 6.)

Right: *Exhausted after the day's work,* Betty found it difficult to enjoy the evening.

             Because she was exhausted after the day's work, Betty found it difficult to enjoy the evening.

Dangling: *Sung by a good contralto,* we thought that the music was beautiful.

Right: *Sung by a good contralto,* the music seemed beautiful to us.

When the music was sung by a good contralto, it seemed beautiful to us.

67b. Avoid dangling gerund phrases.

Dangling: *On examining* the goods, they were found to be defective.

Right: *On examining the goods, we* found them defective.

When we examined the goods, we found them defective.

Dangling: *After convincing Mr. Pressman of my ability,* he gave me a job.

Right: *After convincing Mr. Pressman of my ability,* I was employed by him.

After I had convinced Mr. Pressman of my ability, he gave me a job.

EXERCISE 15

On your paper, rewrite correctly any of the following sentences that contain dangling phrases. If a sentence contains no errors, write C beside the sentence number on your paper.

1. After worrying my parents for two months, they agreed to let me learn to drive.
2. Arriving late at night, all the lights in the house were out.
3. Seeing a storm coming, we pulled down the sails.
4. Examining all the plans with care, the one presented by the Benders Company seemed best.
5. Being Saturday morning, the bus was crowded.
6. Hoping to overcome her awkwardness, Isabel went to dancing school.
7. Walking across the dark road, the driver did not see me.
8. Having lost his fortune in some bad investments, his life seemed completely ruined.

9. Handled carefully, a clever propagandist could make great use of television.

10. After being told to take my morning bath, the clanging trays announced breakfast in the hospital.

11. Looking inland, the first thing that we saw was a church tower.

12. Reserved for high dignitaries, we could not occupy the seats.

13. Instead of realizing a return on our investment, it is costing us money to run the department.

14. By filing our cards according to the new system, another clerk will have to be hired.

15. Before going to bed and upon arising, clothes and shoes had to be examined for scorpions.

16. Established in 1890, the inn has always been owned by the Pembroke family.

17. Pressing the button, the elevator went up to the tenth floor.

18. Respected by everybody who knows his work, we shall have as candidate for governor Mr. Jameson Harkness.

19. After forcing all opposition groups to withdraw from Parliament, a new constitution was imposed on the people.

20. Repelled by our army, the enemy withdrew to form a new defense line.

21. Having been named chairman of the committee, a meeting was called by Albert Delton.

22. Being interested in aviation, my course in physics has helped me very much.

23. After seeing the circus, there was always pink lemonade for the children.

24. By locating the factory on the third floor and the repair department on the second floor, greater convenience can be given to our customers.

25. Drunk with power, it was impossible for the people to curb their leader.

67c. Avoid dangling infinitive phrases.

Wrong: *To avoid scrapping such expensive material,* an adjustment was made in the condenser.

Right: *To avoid scrapping such expensive material,* we
          made an adjustment in the condenser.
Wrong: *In order to keep the car in good condition,* it was
          washed every week.
Right: *In order to keep the car in good condition,* we
          washed it every week.

67d. Avoid dangling elliptical expressions.

An elliptical expression is one from which something
has been omitted. Many of these elliptical clauses begin
with *while* or *when.*

Wrong: *While swimming in a river near our farm,* my
          clothes were stolen by a tramp. (The italicized
          expression means *while I was swimming.* In this
          sentence the clothes were swimming.)
Right: While I was swimming in a river near our farm,
          my clothes were stolen by a tramp.
Right: While swimming in a river near our farm, I had
          my clothes stolen by a tramp.
Wrong: When still a small child, his first appearance was
          made on the stage.
Right: When still a small child, he made his first appear-
          ance on the stage.

EXERCISE 16

On your paper, rewrite correctly any sentences containing dangling infinitive phrases and dangling elliptical
clauses. If a sentence contains no error, write C beside its
number on your paper.

1. While eating his lunch one day, land was sighted.
2. While walking home, her name was frequently mentioned.
3. When startled, the animal will fight fiercely.
4. In order to communicate with the president of the
   company, a cablegram was sent.
5. Unless desirable, we do not list apartments.
6. While talking to a friend one day, he told me where
   I could get a summer job.

7. While studying bookkeeping, Elaine was offered a job with Crandon, Wells and Co.
8. To serve our customers more promptly, a new information service has been set up.
9. When ten years old, his uncle died and left him a small fortune.
10. As an employee of the Illinois Motor Club, we expect you to follow the rules.

NOTE: The word *due* in formal English is usually considered an adjective. Some writers today, however, are considering the expression *due to* as a preposition.

Adjective: His illness was *due* to overeating.
Preposition: He was ill *due to* overeating.

CAUTION:

1. Final participial modifiers beginning with *thus* often make awkward constructions.

Awkward: We have just introduced a new filing system, thus making everything easy to find.
Improved: Because we have introduced a new filing system, we can now find everything more easily.

2. The absolute construction (noun or pronoun and participle) is often awkward at the beginning of a sentence if it contains a pronoun.

Awkward: He *being a good salesman,* we sent him to see Mr. Eckels.
Improved: Because he is a good salesman, we sent him to see Mr. Eckels.

3. The participle *being* should not be followed by *that;* nor should it be used as a conjunction.

Wrong: *Being that it is a clear day, we can go for a hike.*
Wrong: *Being it's a clear day . . .*
Right: Since it is a clear day . . .
Wrong: *Being we lived at our shore all summer,* I could practice swimming every day.
Right: Because we lived at our shore all summer, I could practice swimming every day.

NOTE: When a verbal is used to specify a general action, it is not considered a dangling modifier: *In diving,* the feet should be kept together. *Generally speaking, considering everything, judging from past experiences,* and similar expressions are often used without being attached to any specific noun.

EXERCISE 17

On your paper, rewrite correctly any sentences containing dangling modifiers or awkward expressions. If a sentence contains no error, write C beside its number on your paper.

1. After leaving the ship, the first thing that we noticed was the strange birds.
2. In addition to being interesting work, I feel that I am making a contribution to public health.
3. While walking into the quiet office to apply for a job, my shoes began to squeak.
4. Skilled in all kinds of executive work, it was easy for him to get a job.
5. When making a golf stroke, the back swing is the first motion.
6. In order to progress, it was necessary for business to do mass production.
7. After ceaselessly searching the newspapers and getting assistance from several agents, we finally found an apartment.
8. One day while looking at the newspaper, my eyes fell on a page that told of dreadful conditions in mental hospitals.
9. Looking back on my years in the army, my last assignment was decidedly the most stimulating.
10. Besides being a beautifully designed car, a business man with a small business can cut his delivery expenses in half.
11. By teaching in the schools an understanding of our government, it will be possible to develop wise voters.

12. Being that the strike has interfered with production, we cannot fill your order until March.

13. Looking at random through the many plans submitted, there is a splendid one offered by the Chamber of Commerce.

14. He being one of our best customers, I should not want to disappoint him.

15. Overcome by his numerous problems, his health failed rapidly.

16. Acting on the advice of Mr. Sellers, Henry's report was presented to the Board of Directors.

17. Having grown up in the business, it was hard for him to leave.

18. We arrived very late due to an accident on the road.

19. After having checked each item against the order, it is packed in cartons and shipped.

20. She being our best stenographer, we gave her an increase in salary.

21. Everything was measured with great care, being sure not to make the smallest mistake.

22. The business had been completely reorganized, thus making it necessary to employ more people.

23. He was experienced in many kinds of business, thus helping him to manage a business of his own.

24. We believe that by appropriating larger funds for education, the legislature would improve instruction in the schools.

25. Huge lights play like searchlights on the tops of people's heads scampering to their places.

68. MIXED AND ILLOGICAL CONSTRUCTIONS

Every part of the sentence must agree with the other parts in some logical way so that a clear meaning is presented.

68a. Be sure that the subject makes sense in its relationship to the verbs.

Vague: 1. The first case of smallpox dates back more than a thousand years before the birth of Christ and has gone unchecked until recently.

This sentence lacks logic because it says that the first case of smallpox has gone unchecked until recently.

Vague: 2. The time will be eight o'clock at my home and will be informal.

(The time will be informal? If it will be eight o'clock at my home, what time is it elsewhere?)

Improved: 1. The first case of smallpox dates back more than a thousand years before the birth of Christ. Yet only recently has the disease been checked.

2. The party will be at my home at eight o'clock and will be informal.

or

2. I shall have an informal party at my home at eight o'clock.

68b. Every verb must have a clear-cut subject.

Vague: With medals on his chest or publicity in the paper makes a man attractive to some women.

In this sentence, the verb *makes* has no subject. In addition, the prepositional phrase beginning *with medals* has nothing to which it can attach itself.

Improved: A man is attractive to some women merely because he has medals on his chest or gets some newspaper publicity.

68c. Adjust the form of an indirect quotation to the rest of the sentence.

Awkward: The boy asked us would we give him a lift to Easton.

Improved: The boy asked us if we would give him a lift to Easton.

68d. Avoid mixed constructions.

Mixed: Despite of what you say, I think you are wrong.
(*In spite of* is confused with *despite*.)

Improved: In spite of what you say, I think you are wrong.

or

Despite what you say, I think you are wrong.

68e. Avoid double negatives.

Awkward: I can't hardly see you.
Improved: I can hardly see you.
Awkward: He hasn't scarcely any money.
Improved: He has scarcely any money.

EXERCISE 18

On your paper, rewrite the following sentences, making them logical:

1. Seeing youngsters running through the streets in dungarees and loose shirts has become a familiar sight.
2. Eighteenth-century literature was a new and exciting period.
3. Eleanor wanted to know was I ever in China.
4. *The Snake Pit* is the story of a woman who lost her mind and her experiences in a mental hospital.
5. Her hair is blond, and her eyes are a clear gray with a cute little nose and a dimpled chin.
6. I really don't know how to express the wonderful time I had at your house.
7. During the night we were reinforced with one hundred men and orders to attack in the morning.
8. The Senator read a letter from David Carlton, a fighter pilot who spent much time among Mihailovic's Chetniks and "have nothing but thanks to offer for the care I received."
9. For class day the boys wear blue suits and white carnations in their buttonholes.
10. The most dangerous job besides the shock troops was the signal corps.
11. By conquering something, whether it be an opponent or a skill, gives one a feeling of pride.
12. The people in a modern democracy no longer consist of small cities as they did in the days of Greek democracy.
13. It surprised us to find that Napoleon is the person most frequently assumed by the mentally ill.
14. Tomorrow is my sister's engagement party.

15. With increasing tension in the world is another reason why we have trouble.

69. COMPARISONS

A special part of the logical clarity of a sentence has to do with comparisons.

69a. Compare only things of a similar nature.

Illogical: Unlike most seaside places, the food here is very poor. (*Food* is compared to *seaside places.*)

Improved: Unlike most seaside places, this one does not serve very good food.

Illogical: In the new school, the teachers were more friendly than my old school.

Improved: The teachers in the new school were more friendly than those in the old school.

Illogical: I like Kipling's poetry better than T. S. Eliot.

Improved: I like Kipling's poetry better than T. S. Eliot's.

69b. Use *other* or *else* to exclude the subject with which something is compared.

Wrong: Sanderson's *Animal Treasure* is better than any book I have read recently. (Since *Animal Treasure* is one of the books that I have read, I am saying that it is better than itself.)

Right: Sanderson's *Animal Treasure* is better than any *other* book that I have read recently.

69c. Use *all*, not *any*, with the superlative degree.

Wrong: Biology is the most enjoyable of *any* of my courses.

Right: Biology is the most enjoyable of *all* my courses.

69d. Complete the elements of one comparison before another is introduced.

Awkward: Colonel Benton is one of the finest, if not the finest, infantry officer in our army.

Improved: Colonel Benton is one of the finest infantry officers in our army, if not the finest.

Awkward: Ralph is as clever if not more clever than Stanley.

Improved: Ralph is as clever as Stanley, if not more clever.

69e. Be sure that every comparison is clear.

Vague: I missed her more than Florence. (More than I missed Florence or more than Florence missed her?)

Improved: I missed her more than Florence did.

or

I missed her more than I missed Florence.

EXERCISE 19

On your paper, rewrite these sentences, making the comparisons logical:

1. Salt Lake City is larger than any city in Utah.
2. Stanley Moore is one of the most successful, if not the most successful, lawyer in town.
3. Unlike most hotels, the radio reception is powerful.
4. Although the baseball team in Richmond cannot compare with New York, the people enjoy watching it.
5. Our posters are prettier than any posters in the con-test.
6. The number of hotel rooms that Boston could offer us for the convention was larger than any city.
7. Marianne learned to love her nurse better than her mother.
8. Flowers from Kirkwood are fresher than any florist in town.
9. Crop conditions in all parts of the country have been more favorable than last year.
10. I think that he is funnier than anybody I've ever seen.
11. I am happy to tell you that the Prisoners' Aid Association is about to enter a period of as great usefulness or greater than any in its history.
12. The food of our merchant seamen is as good as any marine group in the world, but our operating costs are higher than any country.

13. The early settler knew more about planting than the Indians.
14. Edith likes oranges better than any fruit.
15. I have no interest nor desire to learn to play golf.

EXERCISE 20

Many of the following sentences lack coherence as a result of violations of principles explained in Sections 64–69. Review these sections. Then on your paper, rewrite the sentences. If a sentence needs no correction, write C beside its number on your paper.

1. Walking down the hall, my eye was attracted by a beautiful painting.
2. The principal asked us were we interested in getting summer jobs.
3. Jim told me that one day last week he stayed in school until 5·30.
4. Walter Reed's work differed from other scientists because he used people instead of animals for his experiments.
5. Her antique furniture is more beautiful than any furniture in our community.
6. The best autobiography of all is Benjamin Franklin.
7. Choose the presents you bring into a hospital with care.
8. I only saw small fish swimming in a fish bowl at first glance.
9. Not being able to read, his only exposure to propaganda would be through the radio.
10. The woman took a sleeping tablet which made her relax completely, in hot milk.
11. Every week the boys would have races to see whose boat was the fastest in a nearby quarry.
12. The game being Friday night, we had to leave Friday noon.
13. In early England, the actors were the monks who performed in the church but later grew into private enterprise.
14. While living in the serene, hospitable atmosphere of New Haven, the minor arts and social graces were cultivated.

15. Preston Sproll is as good if not better than any electrical engineer in the city.

16. We asked Mrs. Hunter would she serve on the committee for the church supper.

17. Sally said, "Oh, Mother, I saw a squirrel coming home from school today."

18. Edmund Burke seems to me greater than any other English statesman of his day.

19. His experiences with the people in China were like all doctors who spend years among alien people.

20. The date has been set and the invitations for the wedding sent out.

21. Mr. Lansdale, as a result of studying for many years, was able to speak five languages.

22. A person who budgets his allowance toward the end of the month has money.

23. Recalled to office by an emergency situation, it was necessary for Mr. Hammond to rearrange all his affairs.

24. After 1666 there was no epidemic of plague in London, though a few cases appear in the records up to 1679, and finally disappeared in 1703.

25. You are so hazy that I can't understand anything very well that you say.

70. PARALLEL STRUCTURE

Sentences may be unified and clear and yet be ineffective. Some of the principles that make effective sentences are discussed in Sections 70–74. See also Section 53 on Wordiness.

Parallel structure means the use of "like construction for like ideas." Sentences do not always have to be arranged in an absolutely parallel structure, but such an arrangement often gives clarity and force.

70a. Use the same structure on both sides of a coördinating conjunction (*and, but, or*).

Ineffective:　The movie actress told the reporters that she likes *swimming* and *to drive*. (Here the conjunction *and* joins a gerund, *swimming*, and an infinitive, *to drive*.)

Improved:	The movie actress told the reporters that she likes *swimming* and *driving*. (Or *to swim* and *to drive*)
Ineffective:	I had the rugs taken up in order *to clean the floor* and *for coolness in summer*. (Infinitive phrase *and* prepositional phrase)
Improved:	I had the rugs taken up in order *to clean the floor* and *to make the house cool* for summer. (Infinitive phrase *and* infinitive phrase)
Ineffective:	We decided *to telephone you* and *that we could then tell you all the news*. (Infinitive phrase *and* subordinate clause)
Improved·	We decided *to telephone you* and *tell you all the news*. (Two infinitives)

70b. Be particularly careful not to join a relative clause and an independent clause by *and*, *but*, or. Do not use *and which*, *but which*, *and who*, *but who* unless there is a preceding "which" clause or "who" clause.

Ineffective:	Jessie is a person of strong will *and who always gets her own way*.
Improved·	Jessie has a strong will and always gets her own way.

or

Jessie has such a strong will that she always gets her own way.

or

Jessie is a person who has a strong will and who always gets her own way.

70c. Keep the members of a series in the same construction.

Ineffective:	She is tall, slender, *and a girl of great beauty*.
Improved:	She is tall, slender, and very beautiful.
Ineffective:	He took a job as clerk, salesman, *and mixing sodas*.
Improved:	He took a job as clerk, salesman, and soda mixer.

70d. Keep the members of a list in the same construction.

As a result of its study, the committee recommended the following:

1. To move the storage room to the first floor.
2. To employ an additional clerk for the filing department.
3. To arrange typists' desks in one room.
4. We should provide a rest room for women employees.

The fourth item in the preceding list is a sentence and is therefore not parallel with the infinitive phrases of the other three items. It should read:

4. To provide a rest room for women employees.

70e. Use the same structure on both sides of a correlative.

Faulty: He is either *lazy* or *he doesn't feel well.*
Improved: He is either *lazy* or *ill.*

EXERCISE 21

On your paper, rewrite the following sentences, using parallel structure to improve them:

1. Dolores has studied filing, bookkeeping, and how to type.
2. Harold is intelligent, honest, and a man of genuine ability.
3. The family decided to rent a cottage at the beach and that Sally and I could use it for a month.
4. I do not know anybody more capable than you or who I feel is better qualified for the job.
5. We suggest either selling the lamps at a lower price or that you return them to the factory.
6. Harris tried to decide whether he should go to college or to enter his father's business.
7. I shall always remember the good times you gave me, the rides, the swims, and especially that you taught me to handle a surfboard.
8. A successful salesman has the following qualities: pleasantness, be courteous, dress properly, be helpful.
9. We regret being unable to ship the order at once and that we must ask you to be patient.

10. I'm sorry that I haven't written to you for some time, but I have been very busy in school and doing my homework at night.

11. To want a new dress for the dance and not being able to get it can spoil a girl's week end.

12. The housewife is always busy, for she must do the dishes and buy the food as well as sweeping, dusting, and cooking.

13. In department stores there are jobs in buying departments, merchandising, stock management, adjustment managers, bookkeepers, and window dressers.

14. In Shakespeare's day people with well-known names and who had plenty of money would send servants to the theater to save seats for them.

15. Mexican opals are famous for their brilliancy and because they are durable.

16. The travelers had many thrilling experiences crossing desert territory and into unknown lands.

17. It is a question of either reducing our overhead, or we must find new outlets for our product.

18. Driver education teaches students to become better drivers by obeying traffic laws, never to exceed speed limits, and always to watch signals.

19. Use your horn to signal other cars that you are about to pass or as a courteous warning to pedestrians.

20. The two soldiers were ordered dishonorably discharged from the army and to forfeit all pay and allowances.

21. Jay's father spent fifteen days teaching him to park a car, the hand signals, and the fundamentals of driving.

22. Since Mr. Emory knows our merchandise very well, he will be able to discuss with you the materials handled by us and which will be usable in your business.

23. A Sunday song festival has been organized by the Mexican government and will be presented in Chapultepec Park as a treat for the strollers and to glorify the folk songs of the country.

24. The amateur radio operators are always ready to give their services in case of disaster and when normal communications fail.

25. Too many people go to college for football, to earn
money, to find a husband, or for the purpose of putting off the evil day when they must go to work.

71. POINT OF VIEW

A sentence loses its strength and confuses the reader
if there are within it shifts in construction. (See Section
16.)

71a. Avoid unnecessary shifts in tense.

Weak: Dick *ran* quickly to the end of the beach and
           jumps into the water. (*Ran* is past tense; *jumps*
           is present tense.)

Improved: Dick ran quickly to the end of the beach and
           jumped into the water.

71b. Avoid unnecessary shifts in subject.

Weak: The *garbage* is collected, and then the *city* con-
           verts it into fertilizer.

Improved: The city collects the garbage and converts it
           into fertilizer.

71c. Avoid careless shifts in voice.

Weak: I *learned* how to accommodate customers, and
           the stock *was kept* dusted and orderly. (*Learned*
           is active voice; *was kept* is passive.)

Improved: I *learned* how *to accommodate* customers and
           to keep the stock dusted and orderly.

71d. Avoid unnecessary shifts in mood.

Weak: *Make* your decision carefully, and then you
           ought to stick to it. (*Make* is imperative; *ought*
           is indicative.)

Improved: Make your decision carefully and then stick
           to it.

71e. Avoid shifts in person or number.

Weak: Each *boy* was told that *we* must replace labora-
           tory materials which we broke. (*Boy* is third
           person singular; *we* is first person plural.)

Improved: Each boy was told that *he* must replace laboratory materials which *he* broke.

EXERCISE 22

On your paper, rewrite the following sentences, correcting shifts in construction:

1. Elaine fell in love with Lancelot, but he finally tells
   her that he could not marry her.
2. In the junior high school, the students were treated
   like babies; but in the senior high school, we are expected to assume some responsibility.
3. First mix the ingredients carefully; then the pan should
   be greased.
4. Not only did I go to school in the day time, studied
   at night, and worked on week ends, but time was
   found for athletics.
5. She wore a little white tam on her blond curls, a white
   bag with a strap over her shoulder, and white shoes
   completed the costume.

EXERCISE 23

Some of the sentences in the following selection contain incorrect shifts in the tenses of verbs. On your paper,
rewrite such sentences correctly.

1. My first visit to the circus, ten years ago, was a thrilling
experience. 2. I loved the smell of roasting peanuts, the sight
of the delicious pink and orange lemonade, the crackling pop
corn, and the funny old clown. 3. I was so excited that I see
everything at once, the roaring lions, the clumsy elephants,
and the trained seals that acted as if they were almost human.
4. Then there is the fat lady, who must have weighed at least
five hundred, or the thin man, who looks as if one could push
him over with a little finger. 5. The freaks were really a pitiful
sight, but I gaze in admiration at the strong man, who was the
image of Atlas. 6. And now I want food, hot dogs, lemonade,
peanuts. 7. Somehow, at the circus they taste so much better
than when I bought them in the corner store. 8. To top off
that perfect afternoon is a ride on the ferris wheel. 9. Everyone was so gay that all troubles are forgotten the minute one

walks into the circus grounds. 10. The band keeps playing a cheery tune in order to keep everyone in a gay mood, but no band is necessary to keep my spirit gay when the circus tents are near.

72. COÖRDINATION AND SUBORDINATION

Inexperienced writers have a tendency to join all clauses with *and* or *but*. As a result, their writing is ineffective because it does not show the proper relationship between ideas. Ideas are presented as if they were all statements of equal value. Actually, in any thinking, some ideas are the cause of others; some are the result of others; some exist only *if* others exist. Showing this relationship of cause, result, or condition is called *subordination*. It is important to put in coördinate structure only those ideas which are really equal. Other ideas should be subordinated. Be sure to use the subordinate conjunction which expresses exactly the relationship between the ideas.

72a. Avoid too frequent use of coördinate conjunctions. (See Sections 61 and 62.)

Immature: George bought a new automobile, *and* it had free wheeling, *and* there was a radio.

Improved: George bought a new automobile which had free wheeling and a radio.

Immature: The meals in camp were dreadful, *and* how anybody ate them, I'll never know.

Improved: The meals in camp were so dreadful that I don't know how anybody ate them.

72b. Select the conjunction carefully.

Do not use *and* if a contrast is needed.

Weak: All the inhabitants except seven were rescued, *and* timberland valued at $30,000,000 was lost. (Here is a contrast between what was saved and what was lost. Use *but* as the connective.)

Weak: The Severn team was one of the best that we faced, *and* we lost by a score of 35–0. (Use *consequently* as the connective. Remember to use a semicolon when two independent clauses are joined by a conjunctive adverb.)

72c. Avoid inaccurate and false coördination.

Do not use a coördinate conjunction to join an independent clause and a dependent clause. (See Section 70b.)

Inaccurate: The nurse was a pleasant person and had had good training, but *who* was a failure.

Improved: The nurse was a pleasant person and had had good training, but she was a failure.

72d. Avoid too many subordinate clauses in one sentence.

Confused: We talked by phone with our representative in your town who told us that at the time of your recent snowstorm, he received so many inquiries concerning road conditions that since he was the only man in the office, they could not all be handled and information which the people wanted was given to members only.

Improved: Our representative in your town told us that the recent snowstorms brought to his office a great many inquiries about road conditions. Because he was the only man in the office, he was obliged to answer the inquiries of members only.

EXERCISE 24

On your paper, rewrite this paragraph. Make the sentences more effective by using coördination and subordination and by using conjunctions that show accurately the relationship between the ideas. Make any changes in wording that you think will help to express the ideas logically. If necessary, join sentences that are now separate.

1. Wolfgang Mozart was a great musician and has contributed much to the artistic life of today; but when he was a

small boy, his father was eager to have him succeed as a musician and took him on a tour of the capitals of Europe, and here he received great acclaim. 2. He started on this tour when he was only seven years old; so the court and intellectuals praised him highly. 3. Although he wrote his first opera when he was only twelve, he went to Italy when he was thirteen. 4. However, he was honored by the pope and packed the opera house in this country. 5. On most of these journeys, he was accompanied by his father and who was also a musician. 6. He returned to Salzburg and had trouble with the new archbishop, and no definite job was offered him although many places commissioned him to write music for them. 7. Wolfgang later fell in love with a girl who was the daughter of a musician; and his father, who did not want him to marry at this time, sent him to Paris in order to keep him away from the girl. 8. The young musician had many problems. 9. He composed matchless operas, symphonies, and chamber music.

73. EMPHASIS THROUGH POSITION AND ARRANGEMENT

Not all sentences are meant to be emphatic. A writer must learn to judge the tone of his work and emphasize what he wishes to have stand out in the mind of the reader. If he is dealing with material that should give a chatty, casual, or dreamy effect, emphasis is unimportant. For strength in writing, however, some attention to rules for emphasis is necessary.

73a. Place at the beginning or the end of a sentence words or ideas to be emphasized.

Unemphatic:	You are certainly not going skating in this weather.
Emphatic:	*Certainly* you are not going skating in this weather.
	In this weather you are certainly not going skating.
Unemphatic:	People drive on the left-hand side instead of on the right-hand side in England.
Better:	Instead of driving on the right-hand side, people in England *drive on the left*.

73b. Repeat words to be stressed.

Occasional repetition of words will emphasize their importance. Do not, however, make a habit of repetition. See Section 54.

> Give! *Give* money when people are hungry. *Give* sympathy when a man suffers. *Give* time to participate in the affairs of your community. *Give* your whole self to help the ideal of peace.

Repetition is frequently used in business writing.

> Do you want comfort? Buy at Oakleigh. Do you want refined neighbors? Buy at Oakleigh. Do you want beauty? Buy at Oakleigh. Oakleigh will satisfy every need of discriminating people.

73c. Use the active voice for emphasis.

Acceptable: Reservations *have been made* for Tuesday evening.

Stronger: We *have made* the reservations for Tuesday evening.

73d. Use periodic sentences occasionally.

A *periodic sentence* is one in which the meaning is not completed until the end. The type of sentence which could end at one or more places before the actual end of the sentence is called a *loose sentence*.

Periodic: Because city driving is very complicated, it is important to keep in the right line of traffic.

Loose: It is important to keep in the right line of traffic because city driving is very complicated.

Too frequent use of either type of sentence is not desirable. Frequent use of periodic sentences gives a formal tone to the writing.

EXERCISE 25

On your paper, rewrite the following loose sentences, making them periodic:

1. Florence Nightingale faced problems of official etiquette and red tape when she tried to improve conditions for the wounded soldiers at Scutari. 2. She was months completing jobs that should have been done in days if she had not been obliged to follow an elaborate set of rules. 3. Finally she took things into her own hands and ignored the time-consuming rules. 4. The wounded were made clean and comfortable only after great effort by this brave woman. 5. She is called the founder of the nursing profession because of the great work that she did in the Crimean War.

73e. Use balanced sentences occasionally.

A balanced sentence is one in which several parts are of similar length and structure. This type of sentence is particularly useful as a means of making contrast effective.

> Judith is fat; Marilyn is thin.
> Honesty recommends that I speak; self interest demands that I remain silent.
> Severity breeds fear, but roughness breeds hate.

EXERCISE 26

On your paper, write a balanced sentence based on the contrast in each of the following groups of words:

1. travel by automobile—travel by airplane
2. living in the city—living in the country
3. academic course—commercial or technical course
4. beauty of the sea—beauty of the mountains
5. flower garden—vegetable garden

73f. Arrange ideas in the order of their importance.

Building up to a climax is effective if the device is used only occasionally. It is especially valuable in dramatic speeches.

> I call upon you to give your money, your time, your lives for peace.
> That man has lost his money, ruined his home, destroyed his honor.

EXERCISE 27

On your paper, rewrite each of the following sentences in climactic order:

1. The organization is dishonest, incompetent, and out-of-date.
2. Florence Nightingale found that the wounded soldiers had little care, that the hospitals were filled with a dreadful stench, and that the floors were filthy.
3. She asked for cleanliness, medical care, and ventilation.
4. She appealed to the minister of war himself, to doctors, to nurses.
5. So great has been her accomplishment for humanity that the simple people have given her memory attention, adoration, honor.

74. VARIETY OF SENTENCE STRUCTURE

Sentences cannot be effective if they are monotonous in structure. A good writer varies the length, the word order, the form of his sentences according to the mood of the piece of writing.

74a. Vary the beginnings of sentences.

The easiest way to write is to begin each sentence with the subject, but a paragraph written entirely in this style would be very dull.

The following examples show different ways of beginning sentences. Notice that there are two sentences in each pair. The first sentence in each pair begins with the subject; the second begins with some other construction.

1. Begin some sentences with a subordinating conjunction.

Sentence beginning with subject: Florence Nightingale gave up an easy life of wealth and position when she decided to become a nurse.

Sentence beginning with subordinating conjunction: When she decided to become a nurse, Florence Nightingale gave up an easy life of wealth and position.

2. Begin some sentences with a prepositional phrase.

Sentence beginning with subject: Women in those days were expected to spend their time on simple household tasks.

Sentence beginning with prepositional phrase: In those days, women were expected to spend their time on simple household tasks.

3. Begin some sentences with a participial phrase.

Sentence beginning with subject: Miss Nightingale won her point only after struggling, working, and planning for years.

Sentence beginning with participial phrase: Struggling, working, and planning for years, Miss Nightingale won her point.

4. Begin some sentences with an infinitive:

Sentence beginning with subject: She found it difficult to fight her family and public opinion.

Sentence beginning with infinitive: To carry on her work, she had to fight her family and public opinion.

5. Begin some sentences with an adjective. This is a device popular with some magazines. Do not overwork it.

Sentence beginning with subject: Florence Nightingale, a vigorous woman, visited hospitals in many countries.

Sentence beginning with adjective: Vigorous and determined, she visited hospitals in many countries.

74b. Avoid frequent use of *there is, there are, it is.*

Monotonous: In some of the coastal towns, there are very primitive conditions. There are mud huts shaded only by a few sick-looking palms. When there is a breeze, clouds of dust blow through the unpaved streets.

Improved: In some of the coastal towns, very primitive conditions exist. Mud huts, shaded only by a few sick-looking palms, are covered with clouds of dust whenever a breeze blows.

74c. Use some relative clauses in the middle of sentences.

Simple sentences: Miss Sauers has just returned from a trip to Paris. She is a fashion expert from the T. S. Bentz Company.

Combined: Miss Sauers, *who is a fashion expert from the T. S. Bentz Company,* has just returned from Paris.

74d. Use an occasional noun clause. (See Section 7.)

That some of the costumes were overloaded with detail surprised her very much.

That she would be able to sell these costumes in the United States she doubted.

74e. Use an absolute phrase at the end of a sentence. (See Section 23n.)

All the men of the small South American town came to meet the boat, *their dogs and pigs following behind them.*

The natives dived from the little boats, *their brown bodies gleaming in the sun.*

74f. Vary the length and form of sentences.

Any type of sentence used too frequently causes a monotonous style. Use a variety of simple, compound, complex, compound-complex sentences. (See Section 8.) Use some loose, some periodic, some balanced sentences. (See Sections 73d, 73e.)

EXERCISE 28

On your paper, rewrite the following paragraph to make it effective. Vary the sentence structure, choosing the types of sentences that will suit the mood of the material. If it is necessary to add some connecting links, do so. The order of details may be rearranged.

There are primitive conditions in some of the coastal towns of Venezuela. They are unbelievable. These towns are not far from a sophisticated city like Caracas or a bustling commercial port like La Guaira. In some of these cities there is not a tree except the tall palm. It has only a few sick-looking fronds at the top. Dust blows in clouds whenever there is a breeze. There are one-room houses. They are made of mud. They are painted blue or pink or lavender. They have only dirt floors. Sometimes the dirt is not even leveled off. The walls have simply been thrown up over rough ground. There is little furniture. Every house has a hammock. A hammock is more comfortable than a bed. The heat is very great. Most houses have also a Singer sewing machine. The Singer men must be great salesmen. There are no tables, no chairs. The people wear few clothes. The Singer man still sells his sewing machine. Children are often naked until they are eight or nine years old. Their diets are poor. They run through the dusty streets. Scrawny dogs, pigs, and chickens play with the children. They all live together in the mud huts.

EXERCISE 29

Follow the directions in Exercise 28.

One of the most important writers of the eighteenth century was Samuel Johnson. He was the son of a bookseller. He read many of the books in his father's shop. He was desperately poor when he went to college. He was very proud. Once somebody felt sorry for Samuel and placed a new pair of shoes at the poor boy's door. Samuel spurned the gift. Many things that he did were strange, but he became practically a literary dictator of London. He is remembered today chiefly as the author of a dictionary and the founder of the famous Literary Club. Significant men in art, literature, politics, and economics were members of the club. They dined heartily and talked. The brilliance of Johnson's conversation is recorded in one of the greatest biographies in English. It is *The Life of Samuel Johnson* by James Boswell. Boswell was a member of the club. David Garrick, a great actor, Edmund Burke, a great statesman, Oliver Goldsmith, an important writer, were also members of the club. The literary influence of the club was great. All London speedily knew its opinion of a new book. All London respected its opinion. It is said that these men could cause a whole edition of a book to sell in one day. Their opinion could also ruin a book completely.

75. ACHIEVEMENT TESTS ON THE SENTENCE

The first test is easy and deals only with the most important principles discussed in the material on the sentence. Review very carefully Sections 57–74. Then take the test. If you do well, take the more difficult test that follows.

75a. Achievement Test I.

On your paper, rewrite any of the following sentences that need revision. Make the sentences correct, clear, and effective. After each sentence, tell briefly why you have corrected it. A sentence may need more than one correction. Some sentences may be right. If you find a sentence that seems to you correct, write the number of the sentence. Then write C beside the number. An example is given for you.

Example:

Sentence: 1. After receiving first aid, the camp officials rushed me to a hospital.

Correction: 1. After receiving first aid, I was rushed by the camp officials to a hospital. *Dangling modifier.*

1. The fat man made the commercial announcements then he introduced the master of ceremonies.
2. I could not believe that I was to have a coat with a real fur collar at the age of sixteen.
3. Do remind me to show you the picture that I took of the chief of the Indian village when you come to Boston.
4. According to this news article, in some mental hospitals there is very little furniture. So that the patients often have to sit on the floor.
5. Some students do not go to college for the purpose of learning or to prepare for a profession.

6. For the sake of simplifying the handling of our accounts and to keep our records up to date, we should appreciate prompt payment.

7. It was the general opinion that the new law permitted the appointment of influential people to the board who could not participate in its work actively.

8. My cousin's engagement party was better than any party I have gone to.

9. At seven o'clock work begins, and we start filling the molds with ice cream after two and a half hours of steady work, there is a fifteen-minute break.

10. I was the driver of a light tank. One of the ten that were sent immediately to the front.

11. I have learned by experience to try to avoid serious arguments with good friends. Because it is very easy to ruin a friendship by arguing.

12. Even though the old lady behaves in a peculiar way does not prove she is crazy.

13. We cleaned the house and hung the curtains, and in a little while the other tasks were completed.

14. Some people gave up their freedom to gain a degree of protection. To be free from the worry of making decisions.

15. Nothing hurt me except the night before the operation I had pains in my back.

16. After calling for help many times, some coast guards heard the cries and went to rescue the children.

17. During the holidays we entertained not only our relatives but also our friends.

18. The colors are wine, navy, blue, and red. Sizes nine through fourteen.

19. Besides studying bookkeeping, we learned business organization.

20. The light on the table is much brighter than the light on my desk.

21. Being embarrassed at such an unusual situation, her face became red.

22. The first rays of dawn were reflected in the still, calm lake and shone on the rolling, barren hills which supported only dry, burnt grass with occasional groves of pine or blackjack oak which, to-

gether with the weatherbeaten rocks, gave a strang
appearance.

23. Doris's house is larger than any place in the com
munity.

24. Edith, although she was terribly frightened, man
aged to run to the telephone.

25. In examining our correspondence carefully, there
no record of your letter.

75b. Achievement Test II.

Follow the directions for Test I.

1. The trip in the funicular railroad terrified me,
seemed to be flying in midair.

2. In my job I have learned to sell and work wit
many kinds of people.

3. I agreed to drive with Walter to Maine and the
that I should return alone by train.

4. Instead of campaigns, bazaars, tag days, and oth
energy-wasting drives which often did not produc
even minimum funds for welfare work.

5. While moving to the next group of cages, a lou
bark broke the quietness of the zoo.

6. We have written to you repeatedly asking for pay
ment, to come down and talk things over, and w
have even offered financial adjustment.

7. Being made of glued plywood, the life of a prefabr
cated house is less than a standard frame house.

8. Of the prisoners eligible for parole, sixty-three wer
not recommended because they were bad risks, n
jobs waiting for them, or there were not enoug
parole officers.

9. When approaching the pylon at night, the safet
zone was difficult to see.

10. Stanford's course in clear thinking will help him
evaluate what he reads and to make logical dec
sions.

11. Passing the stadium, the crowd reminds us of
football day.

12. The purpose of the club is to promote better unde
standing between the faculty and the students an
for improvement of the building and campus.

13. We are fortunate that in Winston Churchill we have a great man of genius and whose advice has often helped us.

14. His sources of income consist of the following: owner of a small vegetable market, and for the past four years he has been manager of a produce department.

15. Although it was a beautiful morning with the sun shining brightly, I left the house with a feeling of optimism.

16. The salesman told Mrs. Banks that the factory could not make the pair of shoes that she wanted and would she consider buying another type?

17. The principal asked me to secure for Dr. Brown and the State Department of Education the books on this list.

18. Mrs. Carter was once a great singer and applauded by the whole country.

19. I like Helen better than Eva.

20. Leon is the most popular of any boys in his class.

21. We approached the city with great interest, it was not a small city with narrow streets, as we had expected, but a large city with towering skyscrapers.

22. Although man has been able to invent such destructive forces as the atomic bomb, he has also found some new drugs which are very effective and some instruments that help greatly in wartime like the rheostat which can locate a bullet in a man which cannot be located in the usual way.

23. Recently I read where plastic surgery really got its start in the Franco-Russian War.

24. Carefully trained at a special school for dogs, we think that our Irish setter is the best behaved dog in the neighborhood.

25. The building program of the hospital calls for the remodeling of the operating suite, expanded kitchen and dining room services, and beds arranged with more space between them.

The Paragraph

A paragraph is a group of sentences developing either
single topic or a specific part of a larger topic. A series of
carefully constructed paragraphs adds clarity just a
punctuation marks do. The reader sees the group of sen
tences as a unit of thought and is consequently able t
follow with greater ease the ideas which the writer de
velops.

76. TOPIC SENTENCE

The *topic sentence* is a statement of the centra
thought of the paragraph. It helps the writer to stick t
the subject, and it helps the reader to know exactly th
point that the writer intends to communicate.

The following are examples of topic sentences from
students' papers:

> The spring mixer was a great success.
> A big family is fun.

76a. Use a topic sentence as an aid in gaining para
graph unity.

A paragraph is composed of a number of sentences, a
of which contribute to the development of a single idea
Any sentence which does not contribute to that idea de
stroys the unity, or oneness, of the paragraph and con
fuses the reader. A clear statement of the idea to be de
veloped will help the writer to keep his thinking straigh
and to be sure that every detail included in the para
graph really helps to develop the central idea.

318

It is wise for the inexperienced writer to practice writing with the topic sentence before him. As the writer gains experience, he may use other positions for the topic sentence. When he has gained real control of his thinking, he may sometimes keep the topic sentence in his mind and not express it at all.

76b. Vary the position of the topic sentence.

1. The topic sentence is often placed at the beginning of a paragraph, as in the following selection:

A fire warden has to work hard. He has an area to patrol, and he has to see that no one builds a fire within that area, except at State-designated camp grounds. You just can't go into the woods and camp anywhere, for obvious reasons of safety. Then if there is a lumbering operation going on, he has to manage to show up in the slashes, unheralded and ghost-like, often enough to deter the men from smoking in the woods. This involves a lot of walking in the course of a week, and lots of patrolling around the lakes in a kicker boat. If a forest fire starts in his territory, he has to organize the fighters, and if it's in someone else's territory, he has to go over there and help. He has to coöperate with the game warden in seeing that the game laws are observed, although naturally this is a reciprocal arrangement, and he can call on the game warden for help whenever he needs it. If someone gets lost, they both have to join the search, along with whatever talent they can scrape up around the countryside.
—From *We Took to the Woods,* by Louise Dickinson Rich

2. The topic sentence may be placed within the paragraph, as shown in the following paragraph:

On the outer platform I met Zurabeg, an Ossetian, who had been in the steerage, too. *But Zurabeg was no greenhorn coming for the first time.* Zurabeg was an American citizen with papers to prove it, and a friend of Gospadin Buffalo Bill besides. This Zurabeg came first to America twenty years before as a trick show rider, and later he was boss cook on the road with the Gospadin Buffalo Bill. Every

few years, Zurabeg, whenever he had saved enough money
went home to find a wife—but so far with no luck.

—From *Anything Can Happen*
by George and Helen Papashvili

3. The topic sentence may be used at the beginning
and at the end of a paragraph. Sometimes when a writer
wishes to make his point very strong, he uses a topic sentence to begin a paragraph and says the same thing in
stronger words at the end. The following selection is
from the *Sportsmanlike Driving Series,* published by the
American Automobile Association.

*How one uses any power which is placed in his hands dis-
closes just what kind of person he is and the degree to which
he has grown up.* Any power—whether of money, office, political prominence, or a fine car—makes a foolish man look
more foolish and a wise man look wiser. What we do as
pedestrians may be mild enough to deceive many people,
but when we get behind the wheel of a powerful car, every
personal quality we have, good or bad, becomes magnified
and easily observable. *Power in your hands shows up the
real You!*

4. The topic sentence may be implied. In the paragraph which follows, no topic sentence is stated, but it is
clear that the author means to show a special characteristic of Mary Todd. The reader is left to draw his own
conclusion from the example.

During her first year in Springfield both Abraham Lincoln
and Stephen A. Douglas took their turns at being entertained
by Mary Todd in the big parlor of the Edwards house, took
their turns at escorting her to parties and balls; she was asked
which of the two she intended to have for her husband, and
answered, "The one that has the best chance of being President."

—From *Abraham Lincoln,* by Carl Sandburg

EXERCISE 1

The following paragraphs written by students lack
unity. On your paper, write the topic sentence of each

paragraph. Then write any sentences which should not
be included because they destroy the unity. Sometimes
the ideas in a paragraph do not seem to be closely related because the writer has not shown the relationship.
A new topic sentence which would take in all of the details in the paragraph could make the paragraph unified.
If you can correct any of these paragraphs by writing a
new topic sentence, do so.

1. Knute Rockne was really a man builder, not just a football coach. Although he started his education in Chicago, he
went to high school in South Bend, Indiana. After he was
graduated from high school, he went to Notre Dame, where
his great career started. Always friendly toward his players,
he frequently arranged little gatherings at his home where
the men would discuss good sportsmanship and good football. He was always against smoking, drinking, and swearing
and taught his men to dislike these activities. One day while
flying to California, his plane crashed; and one of our great
Americans was lost.

2. A musician, even if he is famous, has little security.
Most of the musicians are uncertain today whether they will
have jobs tomorrow. Although most of them are well paid,
they can seldom save any money because they must travel
from town to town under heavy expense. The leader of an
orchestra makes much more than the players do, but he has
to work much harder for his money. He has a great many
responsibilities, but if his orchestra is a success his name will
become famous. In music, there is always a feeling of beauty
and a sense of making other people happy. The life of a
musician may be rough, but there are many compensations.

3. Some educators have said that the comics are good for
children. They point to the strips that teach history or one
of the classics in literature. For a time, I remember, *Silas
Marner* and *Idylls of the King* were both in comic strips, but
of course they were greatly simplified and the beauty of style
was lost completely. These educators speak also of the development of the imagination. Yet both the moving pictures
and a good book would be more valuable, for they are more
stirring, more exciting. When, finally, they talk of the good
habits that can be developed through the comics, I disagree

entirely. In most of the comics that I have seen, people are involved in crime or in some stupid, impossible adventure. I do not know one comic strip that has anything to do with good habits. Many children read these wild, ridiculous things because their parents read them. Then the parents are surprised if the children develop a taste for crime. There are similar arguments about the effect of television programs on children.

77. SUBSTANCE OF A PARAGRAPH

A paragraph may have details which stick rigidly to the topic sentence and yet be very dull. The details that make the substance of the paragraph should be carefully chosen.

77a. Try to avoid stating the obvious.

Your writing is an attempt to communicate some fact or idea to another person. If the fact or idea is already well known to your readers, there is no point in communicating it. A student recently wrote the following paragraph. He was discussing a newspaper which he read regularly.

> The newspaper has several kinds of headlines. Among them are the main headings and the subheads. The main headlines are found at the top of the page.

Such information is common knowledge. The student has added nothing to his readers' experience by what he has communicated.

77b. Choose interesting details.

Inexperienced writers think that they must state every detail involved in a story or in the discussion of an idea. Choose only the interesting or important details. Then develop them fully.

> Dull: When we entered the store, a salesgirl approached us. "May I help you?" she said. I told her that I wanted to buy a coat. Since she had nothing that I liked, we left the store and went to another one.

These details are not interesting, but by using his observation, the writer might have written an amusing or entertaining account of a shopping trip. Colorful details describing the store, the people, and the goods, and some details showing the writer's own state of mind would have been more interesting.

Dull: After a very exciting day, we set out for home. On the way we sang some songs, and Leo told a few jokes. Then we reached my house, and the bus driver let me off in front of my door.

These are dull details. How might the writer have improved on them?

77c. Develop ideas.

A paragraph is usually not simply a statement. It is a development. Neither hazy generalizations nor mere repetition of the central thought builds good paragraphs. After you have phrased the topic sentence, draw upon your own experience and the experience of others as revealed in newspapers, magazines, books, and conversation. Make use of your own imagination, observation, curiosity. Then *discuss* the idea stated in the topic sentence.

78. METHODS OF PARAGRAPH DEVELOPMENT

Paragraphs may be developed in a number of ways, depending upon the subject matter to be presented, the mood of the material, and the effect that the writer wishes to obtain. Using a variety of methods to develop a number of paragraphs is often desirable. Sometimes a whole paragraph will be developed by one method; at other times, the writer may use in one paragraph several methods. Some of the most common methods of developing an idea are explained in this Section.

78a. Develop a paragraph by details.

In the paragraph that follows, the topic sentence is the first sentence. After the writer has said that there was

considerable ceremony in the life-saving course, she pre
sents details to show of what that ceremony consisted.

There was quite a little ceremony connected with this par
of the course. Miss Folgil, and some lucky creature named
as timekeeper and armed with a stop watch, rowed the pro
spective victim out to deep water. The pupil, dressed in
high, laced tennis shoes, long stockings, heavy bloomers, and
a middy blouse, then stood poised at the end of the boat
When the timekeeper yelled "Go!" the future boon to man
kind dived into the water and, while holding her breath
under the surface, unlaced her shoes and stripped down to
her bathing suit. Miss Folgil never explained what connec
tion, if any, this curious rite had with saving human lives.
                    —From *My Sister Eileen,* by Ruth McKenney

78b. Develop a paragraph by definition.

The following paragraph is developed by definition
In the topic sentence, the writer states that there are two
kinds of snobbishness. The rest of the paragraph defines
these two kinds of snobbishness.

There are two kinds of snobbishness. That of the man who
has had a good many opportunities and looks down on those
who lack them is recognized by all. The other kind of snob
bishness is rarely understood, yet it is real. It is that of the
self-made man who glories in his success in overcoming diffi
culties and admires greatly people who have achieved the
things he considers of importance.
                    —From *This I Remember,* by Eleanor Roosevel

78c. Develop a paragraph by example or illustration.

In this paragraph, the writer is discussing integrity in
historians and scholars. As an example of what he means
he tells of an incident in the life of Sir Walter Raleigh.

Their pattern of delusion (believing rumor) is so brilliant
that even the most objective historians and scholars, attempt
ing to record the sum totals of their own investigations, fre
quently find themselves hypnotized by startling events which
never happened and revealing conclusions which were never

drawn. All too few have had the integrity of Sir Walter Raleigh, who, imprisoned in the Tower of London, was writing the second part of his *History of the World* when, one day, his work was interrupted by the noise of a fight in the courtyard below his cell. Through the barred windows, Raleigh carefully watched each detail of the incident. The following day he was visited by a friend who had been in the brawl. And, upon discussing the entire event, Raleigh discovered that his own version of the fight was incorrect throughout. Realizing that he was unable to present an accurate account of one little incident, Sir Walter Raleigh abandoned the writing of his *History of the World* and, in disgust, destroyed the manuscript.

—From *Affairs of Dame Rumor,* by David Jacobson

78d. Develop a paragraph by comparison or contrast.

The following paragraph is developed by contrasting the control of infection among the wounded in World War I with that in World War II.

During World War I, more than three-fourths of the men who sustained abdominal wounds died as a result of infection; but infection was almost completely absent following the Pearl Harbor attack. There were a few amputations required, where limbs had actually been hit by shell or bomb fragments, but none because of infections. Yet during 1914–1918 at one hospital 47 percent of the amputations were caused by infections of gas gangrene alone. In December, 1941, wounds healed quickly and cleanly. Even though their injuries would undoubtedly have been fatal in an earlier period, the men recovered rapidly and were soon anxious and able to join the fight once more.

—From *Science Remakes Our World,* by James Stokley

78e. Develop a paragraph by several methods combined.

In the following paragraph, two methods of development have been used: example and details. The second sentence introduces an example to explain what has been stated in the topic sentence. Another example follows. The last two sentences in the paragraph contain details.

Another advantage of fluorescent light is that, when necessary, it can be kept at low intensity, and since the ultra violet that excites it is invisible, the total amount of light is also very low. For instance, in a motion picture theater, you may want to have a sign giving, possibly, emergency instructions. If the sign is printed in the usual way, the whole card must be illuminated, and a great deal of light is reflected from the background. But the Continental Lithographic Corporation, in Cleveland, has introduced a line of fluorescent inks. A sign thus painted can be flooded with enough ultra violet so that the letters shine with sufficient brightness to be read; but no other light is seen. Such a method is useful for blackouts, as has been demonstrated in England. Road signs, too, or even a guide line down the middle of the road, might be painted with phosphorus.

—From *Science Remakes Our World,* by James Stokley

EXERCISE 2

In his book, *Mirror for Man,* Professor Clyde Kluckhorn discusses the American character. Some of his topic sentences follow. Using three of these topic sentences, write three unified paragraphs. Develop each one by a different method or combination of methods. In the margin of your paper, indicate which method or methods you have used in each paragraph.

Topic Sentences

1. All Europeans are struck by American attitudes toward women.
2. Even the most bitter critics of the United States have conceded us material generosity.
3. Americans have been shy about expressing their deepest convictions.
4. Countless European observers have been impressed by enthusiasm as a typically American quality.
5. Griping is a characteristic American trait.
6. Americans are devoted to the underdog.
7. Americans are interested in devices or gadgets.
8. American friends tend to be casual and transitory.

9. In America, having a good time is an important part of life.
10. Americans love bigness.

79. ORDER OF DETAILS

When the writer has selected his details, excluding those that will destroy unity, and has decided on his method of development, his next problem is the arrangement of those details in some acceptable order. Such an arrangement will aid the coherence of the paragraph. What the arrangement should be depends upon the material itself and the effect which the writer wishes to produce. There is no standard rule. However, there is one essential of order: it requires progress, a forward movement of some sort.

Notice the disorder in the paragraph which follows:

1. A hot rod can also be called a custom-made car. 2. By this we mean that it has a custom-made engine and a special body. 3. Most hot rods are built around stock parts from standard model cars. 4. They can do ninety to one hundred miles an hour and get twenty or more miles on a gallon of gasoline. 5. Most of the parts from which they are made are as old as fifteen or twenty years. 6. The car which holds the speed record can go 189 miles an hour. 7. "Souping up" the engine for high speed is the most important step in making a hot rod. 8. The motor is torn down, and the block is adjusted for an easier flow of fuel to the combustion chamber. 9. Ideas which may appear on future automobiles are now being developed by hot rodders. 10. If the car is to be used for ordinary driving, the motor is adjusted to get 140 miles an hour; but if the car is used for racing, the original horsepower is almost doubled. 11. The latter cars do not work well at low speeds, burn gas at a high rate, and wear out in one-tenth of the mileage expected of a stock engine.

EXERCISE 3

The student who wrote the preceding paragraph did not arrange his ideas in logical order. The paragraph deals with three points: 1. details of building hot rods (sentences 1, 2, 3, 5, 7, 8); 2. speed (sentences 4, 6, 10, 11); 3. outlook for the future (sentence 9). On your paper, rewrite the paragraph, putting related statements together in a logical sequence. It will probably be necessary to change the wording in some sentences.

EXERCISE 4

As you did in Exercise 3, group together related ideas in the following paragraph written by a student. If any sentence seems to destroy the unity, omit it.

1. Some people consider jazz the one original contribution that America has made to modern music. 2. Jazz is said to have originated in New Orleans. 3. Some musicians would come together and improvise counter melodies on a clarinet while a pianist or a cornetist played the tune. 4. Europeans never quite caught the secret of playing jazz. 5. The early jazz players performed on river boats, at private parties, and in taverns. 6. To most people, Louis Armstrong is the true king of jazz. 7. He formed a band which he called "Louis Armstrong and his hot five." 8. Although many people tried to imitate him, there was only one Louis Armstrong. 9. In the early days of jazz, people thought of it only as a product of the Mississippi delta region. 10. Soon it attracted the attention of serious musicians. 11. When it was taken to Europe, it was frequently looked down upon, but people liked to dance to its fascinating rhythm.

EXERCISE 5

Follow the directions in Exercise 4.

1. One of the most interesting features of eighteenth-century London was the coffee houses. 2. The places were really clubs for men only. 3. Men drank their coffee and talked. 4. If a man was interested in talking about politics, he could find a Tory coffee house or a Whig coffee house; if he preferred conversations on literature, fashions, society gossip, he could easily find the appropriate group of people interested in similar topics. 5. Some of the women objected to the coffee house because their husbands were so often away from home. 6. Out of these coffee houses grew an interest in clever con-

versation. 7. Soon society and literature were affected by this development. 8. In the coffee house, a man could read, write, or paint to amuse himself. 9. Some coffee houses even had their own glee clubs. 10. The women disliked the coffee house because women could not go out alone and their husbands were too well entertained in the coffee house to take them out. 11. A few of the coffee houses had gambling and auction rooms. 12. The alehouse keepers disliked the coffee house. 13. They now found that they were losing business. 14. It is said that through this eighteenth-century place of amusement, England developed essays, novels, and poetry.

EXERCISE 6

Follow the directions in Exercise 4.

1. New housing projects are making an effort to correct the dreadful conditions of houses in the slums. 2. In a country like the United States, where standards of living are supposed to be very high, we should be ashamed of the buildings in which some people live. 3. Packed together like herds of cattle on their way to a slaughter house, five or six families live in a building with one bathroom or no bathroom. 4. The filth is unbelievable. 5. A few weeks ago when we visited a slum district, we were all shocked at the debris piled in the back yards, perfect nests for rats. 6. In most cases, the buildings themselves were dilapidated wrecks in which no human being should be allowed to live. 7. Children's dirty clothes lay on the floor, unwashed dishes filled the sinks, where there were sinks, and sick people slept all day in the kitchen. 8. Because the buildings are old, unpainted wooden structures, fires are frequent. 9. The people are then homeless. 10. The sanitary facilities were completely inadequate. 11. Providing new homes for the people is not the whole answer to the problem. 12. The people will have to be taught cleanliness, or the new home will soon be as dirty as the old one.

80. TRANSITIONAL DEVICES

An orderly arrangement of details will help to make the paragraph clear. Another method of obtaining clarity is the use of transitional, or connective, expressions. Our own processes of thought are so familiar to us that we are likely to forget that our readers do not understand the relationship between our ideas unless we show them what that relationship is.

80a. Use transitional expressions within the sentence, between sentences, and between paragraphs. Be careful to use the appropriate expressions.

To add some ideas:	in addition, moreover, another way, a second method, besides, also
To contrast ideas:	but, yet, nevertheless, however, still, in contrast, otherwise, on the other hand
To compare ideas:	like, similar
To show purpose:	in order to, for this reason
To show result:	therefore, as a result, consequently, thus
To show time:	then, a little later, immediately, meantime, afterwards, in those days, earlier

Notice the use of transitional expressions in the following sentences:

> There are today, *for instance,* 12,000 more steel fabricators—predominantly small—than there were at the eve of the first world war.
>
> —Peter Drucker

> Progress, *however,* is only another word for civilization.
>
> —*Saturday Review of Literature*

80b. Repeat key words.

Notice the repetition of key words, which have been italicized, in the following sentences:

> We Americans are victims of the pernicious notion that good books are beyond the comprehension of the average *mind.* But millions of average *minds* have comprehended them in ages past.
>
> —Milton Mayer

80c. Use demonstrative adjectives *this* and *that,* and pronouns *he, she, they, it,* to refer to nouns in preceding sentences.

Demonstrative adjectives and pronouns used to make transitions have been italicized in the following examples:

A farmer should have a thorough knowledge of crop rotation. *This* knowledge will save him money on many occasions.

Unfortunately, our forefathers were destructive of natural resources. *They* moved through a wealthy land and left it ruined to seek still other fields.

Notice the transitional expressions in the following paragraph:

Hot rods are useful in many ways. *First,* they give pleasure to their owners because of their fine performance. *This pleasure* is experienced most keenly in the stock car races in which *hot rod* owners often participate. *Then, too,* they are valuable to police, for their greater power and speed make catching a criminal an easier job. *But speed and power are not their only advantages.* Some West Coast taxi companies use *them* for economy, and a few commercial vehicle operators have found that the cars can move heavier loads on steep grades. *Undoubtedly,* they have contributed something to the efficiency of automobiles.

Notice the italicized sentence in the middle of the preceding paragraph. Here the whole sentence is used as a means of moving from one idea to another.

80d. Transitional expressions are especially important between paragraphs. Without these expressions, each paragraph seems a separate unit instead of part of a whole.

Notice the transitional expressions (*italicized here*) in these topic sentences from five successive paragraphs from William Beebe's *High Jungle.*

1. One of the unexpected aspects of the wild life of Rancho Grande was the scarcity of ants.
2. *Nevertheless,* we soon learned that when we wanted ants, whether singly or in tens of thousands, it was a simple matter to find *them.*
3. The leaf cutters (*ants*) or attas are vegetarians.
4. The army *ants,* or ecitons, are nomads.
5. The two types of *ants* correspond to similar human aggregations or groups.

EXERCISE 7

Reread one of the revised paragraphs that you wrote in Exercises 4, 5, and 6. Have you used transitional expressions to show the relation of details? Add transitional expressions if they will improve the paragraph. Do not, however, use too many such expressions. The result should be natural, not forced.

EXERCISE 8

Select from these topics three which appeal to you. Write two unified, coherent paragraphs for some phase of each of the three topics. Use transitional expressions when they are needed.

1. Family Reunions
2. Blind Dates
3. A New Plastic
4. My Favorite Beach
5. Billboards on Highways
6. A Great Actor
7. Congressional Investigation
8. Jitterbugging
9. Our Athletic Prospects
10. False Advertising
11. Highway Races
12. One Advantage of the Diesel Engine over the Steam Locomotive

81. PROPORTION AND LENGTH

There is no general rule for the length of a paragraph. In a well-written article designed to give information, the paragraph is the development of a unit of thought, and its length may vary from 100 to 200 words. If the development seems to run to more than two hundred words, the paragraph will be a bit heavy; and it might be wise to divide it. There must, however, be no arbitrary slicing in half. The division should come at the end of an idea.

81a. Adjust the length of a paragraph to the idea and the purpose.

A series of long paragraphs makes heavy reading. Short, choppy paragraphs, on the other hand, give the reader the feeling that the ideas are not developed.

Writers for newspapers and magazines often use very short paragraphs to make the ideas stand out. However, such writers are often simply stating facts, not developing ideas. Businessmen also are likely to use short paragraphs in business letters.

81b. Adjust the length of the paragraph in proportion to its importance in the whole article.

Do not deal at length with unimportant ideas or treat lightly important thoughts. In a five-hundred-word theme, for example, do not write a long paragraph that is merely introductory. See Section 84 for further discussion of the division of material into paragraphs.

82. MECHANICS OF THE PARAGRAPH

Neatness and order are important in every paper.

82a. Indent the first line of every paragraph.

The first line of every paragraph is indented except in business letters that are written in block form. The paragraph then begins at the left margin.

82b. Do not leave part of a line blank unless a new paragraph is to begin on the next line.

Keep the margins to left and right as symmetrical as possible.

82c. In writing dialogue, use a new paragraph for each new speaker.

Notice the paragraphing in the following dialogue:

For hours we drove through the beautiful country until finally our chauffeur pointed out the object of the trip.

"That," he said, "is the Great Pitch Lake. When even large quantities are taken out, the holes close right up again."

"Now that solves a problem that has puzzled me all my life," said Jane. "This is just like the streets of Baltimore when the temperature has been 98° for several days. I always wondered why the city government chose that stuff for paving. Now it's clear. If a hole comes in the street, it closes right up again."

"Oh no, miss," the guide said seriously. "I don't think that will happen on a street."

The Whole Theme

Before you attempt to write a theme, you should master the technique of writing a paragraph; for a theme is simply a number of paragraphs carefully joined to present a unified whole. All of the principles of unity and coherence discussed in the section on the paragraph are important for the theme. First, of course, you must choose an interesting topic.

83. CHOICE OF TOPIC

Students frequently complain that they do not know what to write about. Usually their lack of ideas is a result of the fact that they are not observant. Life is filled with interesting things about which a student could write if he would keep all his senses alert. Every day you see something amusing or exciting or alarming. Every day you hear people express opinions with which you do not agree. Then out of your own experiences, you develop an attitude toward life. All of these experiences may be interesting subjects for writing. The subject that you choose should be one about which you really want to write. For that reason, the topics presented here are only suggestive. Some of them are too broad for a short theme. They have purposely been expressed in broad, general terms so that you may choose any phase of the subject which seems interesting to you.

83a. Use your own thought and experience.

In everybody's life there is material enough for a novel.

Here are some general topics which may suggest to you specific experiences or thoughts of your own:

1. Moving to a New Neighborhood
2. An Embarrassing Moment
3. Fighting a Bully
4. I Learn to Read
5. A Travel Experience
6. My Ideas of Friendship
7. My Family
8. An Unusual Neighbor
9. Observance of Yom Kippur or Christmas
10. The Young People's Group at Church

83b. Use the thought and experience of others.

Talk with your parents and friends about experiences that they have had. Your father will enjoy telling you of his youth or of his war experiences. Classroom discussions are also an excellent source of material. The following topics may suggest subjects for you to write about:

1. Travel in My Father's Youth
2. My Mother's Girlhood in Poland
3. An Old Seaman
4. Our Family Doctor
5. My Aunt's Education in Sweden
6. Love at First Sight

83c. Use current problems.

Read your newspaper and write your reactions to an item of news such as one of these:

1. Price Controls
2. A Candidate for Public Office
3. Hoarders
4. Parity Prices
5. Voting as a Duty
6. Censorship of a Moving Picture

83d. Use a moving picture, a play, a book, or a magazine article that has interested you. Discuss the ideas presented and give your reaction.

The following topics may suggest ways of using your reading or theater-going as a source of subject matter for your themes:

1. Underprivileged
   Children
2. New Housing
3. Social Injustice

4. Safe Automobile Driving
5. Figures Can Lie
6. New Art Exhibit

83e. Choose a topic which can be handled adequately.

It is impossible to write an effective 300-word theme on a subject which would require 3000 words. It is possible, however, to discuss in a short theme one phase of a vital topic or to give one's own reaction to this one phase. A thorough discussion of the topic "Social Injustice," for example, would require a book or several books; but your reaction to social injustice as you see it in your neighborhood could be handled in a short theme. The American Automobile Association has discussed *Safe Driving* in a series of five pamphlets, but you can write a short theme about *Errors in Driving Made by Teen Agers* or *Points for Drivers to Remember* or *Good Sportsmanship at the Wheel.*

EXERCISE 1

Be alert to interesting things that happen in the next few days. Talk to other people about things in which they are interested. Read books, newspapers, and magazines. Then write five titles which you think could be used for themes of two or three hundred words, based on your observation, your reading, and your conversation.

84. OUTLINES

No theme can be a success without a plan. We all think haphazardly when we are trying to gather materials for a piece of written work. Related ideas do not necessarily come to our minds in order.

84a. Analyze your material.

The first step in making a plan is to examine the material to see which points go together and what method of development would be best. In order to remember all of the ideas that come to your mind, use a worksheet. As you think through the topic, jot down your ideas. If you are planning to write on the topic "Good Sportsmanship at the Wheel," these ideas might come to your mind:

1. Disobeying traffic regulations
2. Consideration of others
3. Careful use of horn
4. Recklessness
5. Knowing the power of a car
6. Tolerance of others
7. Driving when intoxicated or sick
8. Taking chances
9. Showing off
10. Self-control

84b. Arrange related ideas under appropriate headings.[1]

An examination of the ideas listed in Section 84a shows that they fall naturally under three topics:

    I. Fouls in driving (topics 1, 4, 7, 8, 9)
   II. Courtesy in driving (topics 2, 3, 6, 10)
  III. Knowledge of the power of a car (topic 5)

84c. Use subtopics under main headings to develop ideas.

    I. Fouls in driving
      A. Infractions of traffic regulations
        1. Passing on hill
        2. Going through stop lights

84d. Write the outline.

The following outline is written in topics. It could also be written in sentences. The writer should be careful, however, not to mix the topic and sentence methods.

    I. Fouls in driving
      A. Infractions of traffic regulations
        1. Passing on hill
        2. Going through stop lights

[1] The material for the outline is based on Chapter IV of the pamphlet *Driver and Pedestrian Responsibilities*, published by the American Automobile Association.

      3. Turning corners without signal
      4. Taking right of way
   B. Bad behavior on road
      1. Being reckless
      2. Showing off
   C. Driving in unfit condition
   D. Driving in unfit car
II. Courtesy in driving
   A. Consideration of other people
      1. Drivers
      2. Pedestrians
   B. Tolerance of others
      1. Poor drivers
      2. Beginners
      3. Show-offs
   C. Careful use of horn
   D. Self-control
III. Knowledge of the power of a car
   A. Knowing relationship of speed to force of impact
   B. Knowing relationship of speed to stopping distances

84e. Decide on the method of development.

The best development for some topics may be humorous; for others, ironic. Topic I of your outline in Section 84d could be developed by details, or the fouls in driving might be compared with the fouls in playing a game. Consult Section 78 for methods of development.

EXERCISE 2

Write an outline for three of the topics you listed in Exercise 1.

EXERCISE 3

Write an outline for some phase of one topic from Section 83a, 83b, 83c, or 83d or for a topic of your own choice.

84f. Notice the form of a good outline.

1. Write the first word of each topic with a capital letter.

2. Indent headings so that those of parallel rank are under each other. See example of form in 84d.

3. Use some consistent scheme, like the following, to show which ideas are to be used to develop other ideas.

I.
   A.
      1.
      2.
        a.
        b.
   B.
      1.
      2.
        a.
        b.
          (1)
          (2)

In this form 1, 2 will explain A; a, b, will explain 1 or 2; (1) will explain a or b under B.

4. As far as possible, keep topics of equal rank in parallel form.

Weak: A. Consideration of other people
           B. To tolerate others
Improved: A. Consideration of other people
           B. Tolerance of others

5. Do not permit one topic to overlap another.

Weak: I. History of jazz
           II. The Original Dixieland Jazz Band
Improved: I. Origin of jazz
           II. The Original Dixieland Jazz Band

6. Avoid the following topics:
           I. Introduction
           II. Body
           III. Conclusion

An outline containing specific topics provides a more useful plan than does an outline with these three general heads.

85. BEGINNINGS AND ENDINGS OF THEMES

The beginning of a theme should attract attention, make it interesting enough for the reader to want to continue the reading. Sometimes a little anecdote or a bit of striking conversation will help. Effective endings summarize the composition.

Beginning: Mark Twain once said, "Always do right. This will gratify some people and astonish the rest."

Ending: After all my efforts, I could only hope that more of my friends were gratified than astonished.

EXERCISE 4

Write the opening and closing sentences for the theme that you outlined in Exercise 3.

86. MANUSCRIPT FORM

Your teacher may give you special directions for preparing a manuscript. Neatness will always be required. The following suggestions may help you:

1. Word the title so that it will arouse interest. Write the title in the center of the top line of page 1 of your theme. Capitalize all important words. Do not capitalize prepositions, conjunctions, or articles unless they are at the beginning of a title or consist of five or more letters.

2. Write in ink or use a typewriter. No instructor should be asked to read a paper written in pencil.

3. Number and arrange the pages in correct order.

4. Unless you are given other instructions, fold the paper lengthwise and write on the outside your name, your class, the date, and the title of the composition.

5. Leave a margin of at least an inch on the left side of each page.

6. Do not use brackets or parentheses to cancel a word. Erase the word.

87. REVISION AND PROOFREADING

No paper should ever be submitted until it has been carefully revised and proofread.

1. Check spelling.
2. Check punctuation.
3. Check grammar.
4. Check unity, coherence, emphasis.
5. Check effectiveness.

EXERCISE 5

Write a theme based on one of the outlines which you made for Exercise 2 or 3. When your teacher has indicated the errors, write a second theme, proofreading carefully in order to avoid the errors which you made in the first one. Remember that the outline is the plan and the theme should follow it. After making the outline, be sure to follow it when you write your theme.

The Research Paper

The research paper is sometimes called also a *term paper*. It is usually from two to six thousand words long and requires reading source material, taking careful notes, and organizing these notes in writing a unified whole. The problems of the actual writing are the same when you write a short theme or a research paper, but the preparation for the writing of the latter requires a different and more involved procedure. Skill in the use of the library and in careful note taking are necessary. This skill will be valuable, too, when you must make a report for your club or a business report. Before you begin the work on a long paper, learn to find material in the library.

88. USING THE LIBRARY

In some libraries, most of the books are on open shelves easily accessible to the students. In large libraries, however, it is necessary to store some of the books in stacks away from the main reading room. Usually only the librarian or some advanced students who have had special permission go to these stacks, but the librarian will get books for you if you identify them properly.

88a. Use of card catalogue.

In most libraries, every book has a number that tells the student or the librarian on which shelf the book can be found. These numbers are on library cards (3″ x 5″) [1]

[1] Heavy paper cards, three inches wide and five inches long, are commonly known as "index cards" or "library cards."

in small drawers which have labels in alphabetical arrangement. The cards are filed alphabetically. Many books are listed on three cards: one with the author's name at the top, one with the name of the book at the top, and one with a subject classification at the top. If, then, you want to find books by a certain author, you look for his name in the card catalogue. All of his books will be together in alphabetical arrangement. If you know the name of a book, you can find a card for it. If you have simply a subject on which you would like to find information, you look in the appropriate drawer for the subject. Subject cards often contain references to related subjects.

Notice the following examples of the three types of library cards. These three cards are for the same book. In the card catalogue, they will, of course, be the same size.

Subject Card

PE 2808
.M54   AMERICANISMS
1923

Title Card

PE 2808
.M54   The American Language.
1923

In the upper left corner of each card is the call number. Before you go to the card catalogue, secure some call slips. If you do not see any, ask the librarian to give you some. Write the name of the book, the author, and the call number on a call slip (a separate slip for each book). It can then be used to locate the book.

Libraries classify their books according to the Dewey Decimal System or the Library of Congress System.

Books classified by either system are arranged according to the subjects they treat.

Author Card

PE 2808
.M54
1923

MENCKEN, HENRY LOUIS, 1880–

    The American Language; an inquiry into the development of English in the United States, by H. L. Mencken, 3d ed., rev. and enl. New York, A. A. Knopf, 1923.

    ix, 489 p.   24½^{cm}

    "Proper names in America": p. 329–368

    1. English language. 2. Americanisms. 3. Names-
       U.S. 4. Names, Personal-U.S.   1. Title
    Library of Congress   23–8337
    ————— ————— Copy 2.   PE2808.M54   1923
    Copyright A 704457   (35p2)

If the library is small, you will notice headings on the shelves. There will probably be a science section with numbers 500–599, a literature section with numbers 800–899, a history section with numbers 900–999. It is not likely that you will learn all the numbers, but you will soon learn the sections in which are found the types of books that you use most frequently. Do not hesitate to ask the librarian to explain the system of the library and the rules by which it operates.

If the library is large, there will be special rooms for books of each type. Ask to see the chart of the library so that you can locate the room that you need.

Read these books for detailed information on how to use a library.

    Broening, Angela, and others, *How to Use the Library*, Noble and Noble, 1936.
    Hutchins, Margaret, and others, *Guide to the Use of the Library*, H. W. Wilson Co., 1936.

EXERCISE 1

Your teacher may divide your class into four groups each of which will be responsible for one of the fou assignments that follow.

1. (a) Find out what books by Mark Twain are in you library. On a separate index card, write the title of each o these books, with the author's name and the call number o identification used by your library. (b) Find out what book on baseball your library has, and list each on a separate card as in (a). (c) List on index cards the titles, authors' names and call numbers of five French or Spanish books in your li brary.

2. (a) Copy on index cards the titles, names of authors and call numbers of five books on history in your library (b) List as in (a) the books that your library has on conser vation. (c) Examine some of the books in the fiction sectior and list as in (a) three which seem particularly interesting.

3. (a) On index cards, list the titles, names of authors and call numbers of all books on banking that you can finc in the card catalogue in your library. (b) List as in (a) fiv books on biology in your library. (c) List as in (a) all the books by Sinclair Lewis in your library.

4. (a) What books has your library on airplanes? On sepa rate index cards list their titles, names of authors, and cal numbers. (b) List as in (a) five library biographies thai you think would be interesting to read. (c) Here are the titles of two books that boys enjoy very much; if your library has them, list them on cards as in (a): *Conquest of Space, Un der the Red Sea Sun.* If these books are not in your library, find two books on travel or science that would interest youi group and list the books as in (a).

88b. General reference books.

Reference books such as encyclopedias and atlases are useful for a summary of information. They are kept together in a special section of the library and, unlike other books, may not be taken out of the library. Among the best reference books are the *Encyclopedia Britannica,* the *Encyclopedia Americana,* and the *New Inter-*

national Encyclopedia. A full list of reference books may be found in *Guide to Reference Books* by I. G. Mudge. Since a reference book cannot be published every year, the encyclopedias are kept up to date by yearbooks which can usually be found on the shelf near the books which they supplement.

It is always important to know the publication date of any reference book because in a field that is developing, old information must be supplemented or replaced by more recent details. Outstanding events, changes, and progress in the fields of industry, government, literature, and education should be sought in the yearbooks for the period. The *Statesman's Yearbook,* for an example, gives data regarding the government, population, and industries of many nations. Current volumes of both the *Statesman's Yearbook* and the *World Almanac* are valuable for up-to-date information.

EXERCISE 2

Make a list of the encyclopedias and yearbooks in your library. Consult one of them for information on one of the topics that follow. Write the name of the reference book which you use, and the date of its publication. In topic form, list the main points made in the article.

Advertising	Chemical warfare	Heredity
Agricultural machinery	Chess	Homer
	Chinese painting	Horse racing
Alexander the Great	Diving apparatus	Naples
Amatitlan	Dresden	New Mexico
Andrea del Sarto	Drowning and life-saving	Numismatics
Artillery		Tibet
Francis Bacon	Fingerprints	Tolstoy
Bavaria	Football	Trade Unions
Daniel Boone	Henry Ford	Treason
Caveat emptor	Benjamin Franklin	

EXERCISE 3

Refer to the *World Almanac* in order to be able to answer the following questions:

1. Who won the British Open Golf Championships in 1946?
2. Name five outstanding motion pictures of last year. Who were the stars?
3. How many homes in the United States have radios?
4. What is the population of Rome, Rio de Janeiro, Moscow?
5. What is the capital of the Republic of Israel?

88c. Reference books on special subjects.

Because general reference books must cover such a broad field, they can give only very limited information. A reference book in a special field will give many more details on the subject. The following list suggests some helpful special reference books.

1. Biography:

> *American Biographies*
> *Authors Today and Yesterday*
> *Dictionary of American Biography*
> *Dictionary of National Biography* (English)
> *Living Authors*
> *Who's Who* (Principally English)
> *Who's Who in America*
> *Current Biography*

2. History:

> *Dictionary of American History*, New York, Charles Scribner's Sons, 1941, 5 vols.

3. Literature—Special Indexes:

> *A. L. A. Index . . . to General Literature*
> Firkins' *Index of Plays, 1800–1926*
> Granger's *Index to Poetry and Recitations*

4. Literature—General Reference Books, Quotation Books, and Guides:

> Baker's *Guide to the Best Fiction*
> Baker's *Guide to Historical Fiction*
> Bartlett's *Familiar Quotations*

Book Review Digest
Cambridge History of American Literature
Cambridge History of English Literature
Oxford Companion to American Literature
Oxford Companion to English Literature
Sonnenschein's *Best Books*
Stevenson's *Home Book of Quotations*
U.S. *Catalog*, with *Cumulative Book Index*

5. Music:

Grove's *Dictionary of Music and Musicians*

6. Business:

United States Statistical Abstract

88d. Indexes to magazine and newspaper articles.

The most recent information on some subjects may appear in newspapers and magazine articles. There are a number of indexes which make it possible for you to find current information on any subject that has appeared in periodicals. The *Readers' Guide to Periodical Literature* is one of the most useful. When you use an index, it is always important to read the first few pages, which will explain how to use the book and what abreviations are used.

The *Readers' Guide* is published every two weeks. At the end of the year, all the material for the year is gathered in one volume. If you wish to see whether the last month has produced anything on your special subject, you use the most recent index of the *Readers' Guide;* but if you want to see what last year offered, you consult the volume for the whole year. There are also volumes for periods longer than a year.

Other useful indexes are the following:

1. *The New York Times Index,* 1913—This is a guide to events of national importance by reference to date, page, and column.
2. *Agricultural Index,* 1916—This is a cumulative sub-

ject index to a selected list of agricultural bulleti
and periodicals.

3. *Engineering Index,* 1884—Since 1928 this index h
been an author-subject index to periodicals in all eng
neering fields.

4. *Industrial Arts Index,* 1913—This is a subject inde
to a selected list of engineering, trade, and busine
periodicals, books, and pamphlets.

5. *Public Affairs Information Service*—This is an inde
of books, pamphlets, government documents, and p
riodicals in the fields of sociology, political scienc
economics, and finance.

All these indexes refer to articles by subject and au
thor, not by title. For example, if you wish to investigat
the topic of conservation of natural resources, you woul
look in the *Readers' Guide* for the topic "Conservation.
You might find an entry similar to the following:

Conservation of resources
America faces challenge to live within own mean
Science N L 55: 9 Ja 1 49.
Country that can feed the world? F. Osborn Atlai
181: 71–6 Ap '48.

If you consult the list of magazines in the front of th
book, you will find that *Science N L* means *Science Neu
Letter.* The article appears in Volume 55, page 9, fc
January 1, 1949.

The second article was written by F. Osborn. It is o
pages 71–76 in Volume 181 of the *Atlantic Monthly.* I
was in the April, 1948, issue of this magazine.

EXERCISE 4

Use the *Readers' Guide to Periodical Literature* to fin
the topics listed below. Copy the entries which seem us
able. Then ask the librarian to give you the volumes c
the magazines which you need. Since libraries do nc
have bound copies of all magazines, you may need t
limit your choice of articles. Read one of the article

and write in topic form the main points presented on your subject.

Juvenile delinquency	Government regulation of industry
Propaganda	
Orchestras	Electronics
Airports	Conscription
Iran	Uranium

89. CHOOSING THE TOPIC OF A RESEARCH PAPER

89a. Choose a topic that interests you.

You have probably discovered that you write better when you are interested in what you are investigating. Since you, like most other students, are likely to be interested in a vocation, you might find a suitable theme topic related to the work you expect to do in the future. You might like to investigate the opportunities in your chosen field, the preparation required, or the salary to be expected. Or perhaps one of these topics for research would interest you.

1. Television
2. Trick Photography
3. Commercialized Athletics
4. Modern Dancing
5. Present-Day American Indians
6. Is America's Freedom in Danger?
7. Eighteenth-Century Coffee Houses
8. Homes of the Future
9. Propaganda Techniques
10. Our National Parks
11. Conservation of Soil
12. Radio Advertising
13. The Theater in the Round

89b. Choose a topic that requires research.

A topic may be very interesting to you but be too narrow or too personal to require an investigation. Which of these topics would require research?

1. Winning a Photography Contest
2. Making a Farm Pay
3. What Do I Inherit?
4. New Techniques in Medicine

5. Is My Family Unusual?   8. My Favorite Moving-Pic-
6. A Trip to Washington   ture Actress
7. A Mountain Hike

89c. Limit the topic. (See Section 83e.)

Choose a topic which can be handled adequately in the number of words to be used.

EXERCISE 5

On your paper, write for each of these broad fields several topics which might be handled in 2,000 words:

Science	Modern Art
Farming	Plastics
Conservation	American Education
Ballet	Costume Design

89d. Choose a topic on which your library has adequate information.

Keep in mind the resources of the library which you will have to use. Before you decide finally on a topic for a research paper, use the *Readers' Guide to Periodical Literature* (see Section 88d) and the card catalogue (88a) in your library to see what material is available. Remember that your research paper should be based upon material from different sources: reference books, magazines, books, newspapers, and pamphlets. Unless you have consulted at least five or six sources, you cannot write a satisfactory research paper.

EXERCISE 6

From the lists given in Section 89 or from your own interests, choose a topic which you would like to investigate. Read in an encyclopedia a summary of the topic and bring to class for discussion five or six subtopics which you think might be examined in other sources and used in your paper.

90. TAKING NOTES

After you have read in an encyclopedia a summary of your topic, you will be ready to select the books and magazine articles that will give you the information for your paper. Then you will take notes from these materials. Much of the success of your paper will depend upon your ability to take notes that are really helpful. If you follow a systematic procedure, you will save yourself much time and write a better paper. Use the card catalogue (see Section 88a) and the appropriate periodical index (Section 88d) and choose the books and magazines that you will use.

90a. Materials for note taking.

Many people have found that the most efficient note taking for a long paper is done on index cards (3" x 5"), or on larger cards. Some people, however, prefer sheets of paper or notebooks. The important thing is to use a different card or piece of paper for each fact recorded. You can then move the cards or papers into position so that all notes on one subject are together. Such a procedure will simplify the organization of your paper.

90b. Method of note taking.

The first notes to be taken are notes for the bibliography. (See Section 94.)

1. Use the index and the table of contents of a book to see on which pages you will find material that can be used.

2. Skim the material to find the leading points.

3. Before any notes are taken, copy on the card the name of the author, the name of book or magazine article, and the page from which the note is taken. These details are important for your footnotes and also for any further examination of the source. In the right-hand corner of the card, write the heading that will show where this material will fit into the outline:

> Jacobson, David　　　　　　　　　　　　　Rumor
> Affairs of Dame Rumor p. 7

4. Condense your notes. They should be full enough to keep the meaning clear, but not so long that every detail is included. Notes are often taken in topic or phrase form so that the main idea is retained, but modifiers and articles are omitted. Sections 95 and 96 will give you additional information on note taking.

If your main subject is *Propaganda Devices*, you might want to show how rumors or whispering campaigns can be used. Here is a passage on which you might take some notes. The notes taken on it are on the sample card that follows the passage.

"Perhaps the most potent pipe-dream rumors are those which satisfy the yen for financial gain. These morsels, whispered everywhere in the strictest confidence, to be sure, have sent the stock markets and financial exchanges throughout the world soaring and diving. They have set mass migrations in motion. They have sent men crawling about the bottoms of the oceans, searching in the deserts, and scouring the lands for wealth which was to be found only in the imaginative stories."

> Rumor
>
> Jacobson, David
> Affairs of Dame Rumor, p. 7
> Most powerful rumors those which suggest ways of making money. Result of these: stock markets rising and falling, mass migrations, searches in oceans and deserts for wealth that probably did not exist.

5. Try to use your own words in taking notes. If you find a striking statement that you wish to quote, copy it *exactly* with quotation marks around it. Be very sure to note the source and the page on which the statement is found.

6. Be careful to distinguish in your reading and in your note taking between facts and the author's opinion. The value of opinions depends on who says them and on the information upon which they are based; therefore, a good paper should tell the reader whose ideas are being presented.

91. PREPARING THE OUTLINE

Before you begin to write your research paper, you will prepare an outline for it. (See Section 84.) Because the long paper will include many more details than the short paper, the outline for the research paper is even more important than an outline for a shorter paper. In making the outline, show clearly the relationship of facts and ideas.

91a. Organize the notes.

The topic in the right-hand corner of each card will show which cards carry related material. Put together all cards on the same topic.

91b. Choose a central idea for presentation.

From the material that has been collected, choose an idea or a point of view toward which everything can be directed. Discard whatever does not fit in with this large idea.

91c. Select the main divisions of the central idea.

From the topics in the right-hand corner of the cards, select the ones to be used as large divisions designated by Roman numerals. (See Section 84a–c.)

91d. Subordinate ideas in a logical fashion.

Following Section 84c–d, develop in topics the main ideas selected, and write the outline.

92. WRITING THE PAPER

All of the directions for writing a theme are again applicable. (See Sections 83–87.) In the long theme, however, it is important to give more careful attention to transitional expressions that will lead from one paragraph to another and keep the whole closely tied together.

Do not use the exact words of the reference unless you place them in quotation marks and state exactly where you obtained them. A paper that contains a large number of quotations shows lack of careful thinking on the part of the writer.

92a. Use of an introductory paragraph.

You have seen that in a short paper, a whole paragraph devoted to an introduction may destroy the proportion. In a long paper, however, an introductory paragraph to give a view of the whole topic may be desirable.

92b. Revision.

Be sure to revise your research paper after you have written the first draft. (See Section 87.) If you type the paper, read the final copy for typographical errors.

93. MAKING FOOTNOTES

The writer of a research paper must read what a number of people have said about a topic and present their ideas, together with some thinking of his own based on his reading. It is not honest to offer the thinking or words of other people as if they were his own. Consequently, he must learn to separate his thinking from the ideas of others and to acknowledge his indebtedness to anybody whose ideas he uses. The footnote is one method of making this acknowledgment. It is possible also to acknowledge the author in the body of the writing.

93a. Use a footnote to give the source of information.

The following sentences are not a product of a student's thinking. They contain information which must have been obtained in his reading. The small number (called a superior figure) follows the statements and refers to the same number at the bottom of the page. Following the number at the bottom of the page is the footnote, which tells where the writer of the paper obtained the information.

Because politicians have not been interested in the arts, the theater in America has received no state endowment. Its artistic development, however, has been aided by people like Otto Kahn, who helped the Theater Guild over its initial difficulties, and Irene and Alice Lewisohn, who endowed the Neighborhood Playhouse.[1]

[1] Sheldon Cheney, *The Theatre.* Tudor Publishing Company, New York, 1939, p. 505.

93b. Adopt a standard form of footnote and be consistent in its use.

There are various forms for footnotes. Choose *one* and use it throughout the paper.

1. Footnotes for books:

Book by one author:
Cheney, Sheldon, *The Theatre* (New York: Tudor Publishing Company, 1939) p. 505.
Sheldon Cheney, *The Theatre,* Tudor Publishing Company, New York, 1939, p. 505.
Henry Louis Mencken, *The American Language* (4th ed.; New York: Alfred A. Knopf, Inc., 1936), p. 168.
Book by two or more authors:
John Tasker Howard and Arthur Mendel, *Our American Composers* (New York: Thomas Y. Crowell Company, 1941), p. 82.
Book of two or more volumes:
Douglas S. Freeman, *George Washington* (New York: Charles Scribner's Sons, 1948), II, 142.
Book cited under editor:
Richard Aldington, ed., *Great French Romances* (New York: Duell, Sloan, and Pearce, 1946), p. 17.
Letters from W. H. Hudson, ed. by Edward Garnett (New York: E. P. Dutton & Co., 1923), p. 62.

A translation:
Homer, *The Odyssey,* tr. by George Herbert Palmer (Boston: Houghton Mifflin Company, 1891), p. 46.

2. Footnotes for articles, essays, stories:

From a magazine:
Walter D. Edmonds, "Arrival of the Lily Dean," *The Saturday Evening Post,* CCX (May 7, 1938), 5.
"Personality Tests," *Life,* XXI (October 7, 1946), 55.
From a collection:
Katherine Mansfield, "Bliss," *A Study of the Short Story,* ed. by Henry S. Canby and Alfred Dashiell (New York: Henry Holt and Company, Inc., 1935), p. 303.

93c. Use a shorter form for subsequent footnotes on the same source.

1. *Ibid.* If a footnote refers to the same source as the one referred to in the footnote *immediately* preceding, the abbreviation *ibid* (from the Latin *ibidem* meaning "in the same place") may be used.

First entry:
Cheney, Sheldon, *The Theatre,* Tudor Publishing Company, New York, 1939, p. 505.
Second entry:
Ibid., p. 508.

2. *op. cit.* After the first full reference to a given work, provided that no other work by the same author is mentioned in the paper, succeeding references may be indicated by the author's last name followed by *op. cit.* (from Latin *opere citato* meaning "in the work cited") and the page or pages to which reference is made.

Cheney, op. cit., p. 508.

3. *Short title.* Many writers now use a short title for footnote references other than the first. The following examples illustrate this form:

First entry:
Sir Arthur Quiller-Couch, *On the Art of Writing* (New York: Putnam, 1930), p. 84.

Subsequent entry for the same book:
Quiller-Couch, *Art of Writing*, p. 92.
First entry:
Clifton Fadiman, "Herman Melville," *The Atlantic Monthly*, CLXXII (October, 1943), p. 88.
Subsequent entry for the same article:
Fadiman, "Melville," p. 90.

93d. Numbering of superior figures and footnotes.

Unless your teacher gives you other directions, use consecutive numbers, beginning with 1 on each page, for the superior figures and footnotes in your research paper.

94. MAKING A BIBLIOGRAPHY

A bibliography is an alphabetical list of books, magazines, pamphlets on a given subject. Such a list is placed at the end of a research paper. While you are doing research for your paper, make a separate bibliographical card for each source that you consult. On this card, put the complete information that you will need when you make the bibliography. This information is shown in the model bibliography that follows. At the end of your research, arrange these cards in alphabetical order. They are then ready for typing. Be sure that each card contains name of author, book, and publisher, date and place of publication. The following is a short specimen bibliography:

BIBLIOGRAPHY

A. Books
Allen, Hervey, *Israfel, the Life and Times of Edgar Allan Poe*, New York, Farrar & Rinehart, Inc., 1934.
Boyd, Ernest Augustus, *Literary Blasphemies*, New York, Harper & Brothers, 1927, pp. 163–185.
Campbell, Killis, *The Mind of Poe and Other Studies*, Cambridge, Mass., Harvard University Press, 1933.
Encyclopedia Britannica, The (14th Edition, 1929), XVIII, 104–105.
Krutch, Joseph Wood, *Edgar Allan Poe: a Study in Genius*, New York, Alfred A. Knopf, Inc., 1926.

Woodberry, George Edward, *Life of Edgar Allan Poe, Personal and Literary, with His Chief Correspondence with Men of Letters,* Boston, Houghton Mifflin Company, 1909, 2 vols.

B. Magazine Articles

Cooke, A. L., "Edgar Allan Poe—Critic," *Cornhill Magazine,* LXXII, November, 1934, 588–597.

Huxley, Aldous Leonard, "Vulgarity in Literature," *Saturday Review of Literature,* VII, September 27, 1930, 158–159.

Macpherson, Harriet Dorothea. "Dumas and Poe Again," *Saturday Review of Literature,* VI, February 22, 1930, 760.

Wilson, James Southall, "Devil Was in It," *American Mercury,* XXIV, October, 1931, 215–220.

Notice that it is necessary to include in your bibliography the volume and issue number of magazines that you have consulted.

The Précis and the Paraphrase

95. THE PRÉCIS

A précis is a summary. Skill in using it is important in note taking of any kind. Business or professional people often ask their secretaries to keep a file of summaries of articles or reports on new developments in their special fields. When an executive has not the time to read the whole report of a committee that has investigated some important project, he may ask an employee to write a precise summary.

95a. Read the material carefully.

The précis must include *all* of the important ideas. List these as you read. It must not include your own opinions or reactions.

95b. Use your own words.

Reduce the important ideas to their bare essentials, making every word count. A word can often be substituted for a clause. The précis should usually be not more than one-third as long as the original.

95c. Retain the plan of the original.

Altering the order in which details are presented may distort the meaning of the article.

95d. Write the précis in exact English.

The condensation must not be a jumble of disconnected words; it must be written in sentences, in precise English. Be especially careful to join the ideas by means

of transition expressions that show exactly the relationship between the ideas.

EXERCISE 1

Write a précis of this selection from William Beebe's
High Jungle:

It is occasionally advisable and often necessary for an attacked nation temporarily to sacrifice some unimportant portion of its land for better concentrated defense. This temporary national self-mutilation is reflected in jungle warfare by
certain long-tailed lizards. Headlong they flee before the on-
slaught of a swooping hawk. Their race for sanctuary may be
a fractional second too slow, and the clutching talons seize
the long tail just before it would have vanished to safety. But
nature balances delicately her scales of life and death, and for
just such a crisis as this have been developed the short,
loosely interlaced, proximal tail muscles. Momentarily there
ensues a crucial tug of war between lizard legs and hawk
talons. The muscles give away, the reptile hurtles to safety
down the hole, and the hawk finds meager pickings on the
captured tail. The lizard has this advantage over the human
nation, in that within a few weeks, a brand-new tail will
sprout out from the old stump.

EXERCISE 2

Write a précis of this passage from Louis R. Reid's
American Movies Today:

Unchallenged is Hollywood's technical supremacy. In such
details as photography, sound recording, set and costume de-
signing, the California producers lead the world. Their artistic
progress is still hampered by the seemingly inescapable necessity of making their dominant appeal to childish intelligence.
Of secondary importance is that production be based upon a
maturity of story and treatment. Upon those occasions when
progressive and imaginative directors break away from trite
and childish formulae to make pictures of mature intelligence,
the result, in many instances, has been astonishingly profit-
able. Such films have been received with rejoicing among that
portion of the public to whom movie-going means something
more than a time-passing habit or an escape from realities.

So responsive are the West Coast artisans to this acclaim that they have fallen into the grievous error of copying their newly found formulae to tiresome lengths. Thus has come a succession of films, built upon the themes which had proved refreshingly adult. So impressed is Hollywood by what seems sure-fire that variety and change of pace, the mainstays of all genuinely successful amusement, are neglected.

EXERCISE 3

Write a précis of this selection from Carl Glick's *Three Times I Bow:*

Even when it comes to marriage, the younger generation of Chinese women are, in their own way, breaking tradition. The old custom demanded philosophical detachment and an implicit obedience to one's parents. For it was the elders who selected the future husband or wife, and it was all done by a hired matchmaker who consulted the stars, blended personalities according to an ancient law, and collected a fat fee. It worked out nicely, too, for divorce is rare among the Chinese. And even though many a bridal couple did not actually see each other until the day of the wedding, they remained married a lifetime and passed on the good old custom to their children.

And while these pre-arranged marriages, with the parents doing the selecting still take place in Chinatown, many of the present generation object and do their own choosing in their own way. For with their new-found freedom came also the opportunity for women to take a discreet look at the yearly crop of marriageable males and make some decisions of their own. Not that they descend to the catch-as-catch-can method of their often more aggressive and predatory "foreign sisters." But what the eye has seen, the heart has coveted—and then the rest (preserving the proper respect for their elders) is left to the parents, who arrange the wedding in the good old manner.

96. THE PARAPHRASE

A paraphrase is a restatement in different words. It is most useful in handling difficult poetry or prose passages that contain involved thoughts or technical language.

96a. Read the passage carefully.

Use reference books to determine the meanings of obscure words and allusions.

96b. Use your own words to present the essential ideas in clear, simple English.

EXERCISE 4

Write a paraphrase of a selection from a literature textbook that you are reading.

Letters

Do you want to keep in touch with a new friend who lives in another town? Do you need a job? Have you made an unsatisfactory purchase? All of these occasions call for skill in letter writing.

97. BUSINESS LETTERS

Styles in business letters have changed a great deal in recent years. The pompous tone of old-fashioned business letters is no more appropriate for today than the clothes of thirty years ago. The tone now is one of casual friendliness.

97a. Form.

Because the appearance of the letter makes the first impression, spacing is important. Leave a good margin on all sides of the paper. If the letter is short, consider carefully the space that it will take and plan the margins accordingly.

97b. Heading.

The heading includes the writer's complete mailing address and the date. These items are placed in the upper right-hand corner of the sheet at least an inch and a half from the top. The longest line ends at the right margin. On stationery with a letterhead, the writer places the date at least two line-spaces below the letterhead in the center of the page or at the right, extending to the right-hand margin. The lines of the heading may be in block form or indented form. Business firms now usually prefer no punctuation at the ends of the lines in the heading.

Block Form	*Indented Form*
R. N. Penrose Company	R. N. Penrose Company
714 Ensor Avenue	714 Ensor Avenue
Rochester 6, New York	Rochester 6, New York
March 12, 1950	March 12, 1950

97c. Inside address.

The inside address is the address of the person to whom you are writing. It usually extends from the left-hand margin, at least two line-spaces below the date, but it may appear at the end of the letter in the lower left-hand corner. It should follow the form (block or indented) used in the heading.

White Garment Company
8639 West Street
New York 17, New York

97d. Salutation.

The salutation should extend from the left margin, two line-spaces below the inside address. It is followed by a colon.

Dear Sir:	My dear Sir:
Dear Madam:	Dear Mr. Brown:
Gentlemen:	My dear Mr. Tweedy:
Mesdames:	Dear Doctor Bard:

NOTE: Do not abbreviate *Professor* or *Reverend*. Do not use the title *Reverend* or *Honorable* with the last name only.

Correct: The Reverend Howard C. Lane
The Honorable Charles H. McLaughlin

97e. Body of the letter.

The body of the letter should have the following characteristics: clearness, correctness, conciseness, courtesy, and character. Avoid hackneyed expressions like the following:

according to our records	party
acknowledging your letter	per
are in receipt of	prox.
attached hereto	pursuant to our conversation
beg to advise	referring to
beg to inform	state (for say)
by return mail	take pleasure
contents noted	take this opportunity
enclosed please find	thanking you in advance
in reply wish to state	this is to inform you
in re	under separate cover
kindly inform	wish to say
our Mr. Edmonds	you claim
our records show	yours of recent date

97f. Complimentary close.

Place the complimentary close slightly to the right of the middle of the page, two line-spaces below the last line of the body of the letter. Only the first word is capitalized. A comma usually follows the complimentary close, but some firms are now omitting the comma if no punctuation has been used for the ends of lines in the heading.

Yours truly,	Sincerely yours
Very truly yours,	Cordially yours

NOTE: Avoid participial phrases like *Hoping for an early reply, Thanking you in advance.*

97g. Signature.

Sign your name in ink. A married woman signs her own name followed by her married name.

Janet Louise Black
(Mrs. Henry R. Black)

Miss, Mr. or *Mrs.* is never used as part of a signature.

Academic degrees and professional titles should not be used with a signature.

Incorrect: Dr. Samuel White
                 Sue Jenkins, Ph.D.

NOTE: For a full discussion of all the various types of letters used in the transaction of business, see *Effective Letters in Business,* by Robert L. Shurter, published by the McGraw-Hill Book Company.

97h. Letter of application.

The object of this letter is to state clearly your qualifications for holding a specific position. Do not try to get the job by creating sympathy for yourself. The employer is interested in the kind of work that you will do and the attitude that you have toward your work.

> 814 Tenth Street, N.W.
> Washington 16, D.C.
> May 20, 1950

Mr. Alfred Preston, Personnel Manager
Benton, Ward and Company
410 Sixteenth Street, N.W.
Washington 4, D.C.

Dear Mr. Preston:

Your advertisement in the Washington *Post* for a secretary interested me very much. I should like to apply for the position.

In a few weeks I shall be graduated from Central High School, where I have had four years of commercial training. In my senior year I earned an award for typing at the rate of 60 words a minute and made the Honor Roll for receiving a grade of 80 or more in all my subjects.

For the past two years I have been a member of the Business Service Club at school. This is an organization that does typing, mimeographing, and ditto work for the various departments of the school. Since I worked for the club during two study periods each week, I have had some experience in many kinds of office jobs and have learned to work with neatness and accuracy. Last summer I used this experience to obtain a position as relief typist at Denton's Department Store. Here I took dictation, typed, and did some filing.

Information concerning my work and my character may be obtained from the following:

> Mr. Theodore Smart, Denton's Department Store,
> 31 H Street, S.W., Washington, D.C.

> Miss Hilda Newman, Adviser, Business Service Club,
> Central High School

> Miss Sarah Burton, Counselor, Central High School

I should be glad to come for an interview at any time convenient to you. My telephone number is CO-4679.

> Yours truly,
> Mary Henderson

97i. Order letter.

Notice the form of the following order letter:

> 311 Patuxent Street
> Crisfield, Maryland
> October 20, 1950

Harmon Brothers
Connecticut Avenue and F Street
Washington, D.C.

Dear Sirs:

Please send me by parcel post the following items advertised in the *Crisfield Mentor*.

2 Colonial style silver candlesticks,		
@ 7.95		$15.90
1 Colonial style silver platter		5.95
Sales tax		.43
		$22.28

A money order and the checked advertisement are enclosed.

> Yours truly,
> Jane Holmes
> (Mrs. H. R. Holmes)

97j. Request for adjustment.

Notice the form of the following request for adjustment connected with a purchase:

311 Patuxent Street
Crisfield, Maryland
October 31, 1950

Harmon Brothers
Connecticut Avenue and F Street
Washington, D.C.

Dear Sirs:

On October 20, I ordered from you two Colonial style silver candlesticks. When they arrived yesterday, I found that one of them has a decided scratch on the base. Consequently, I am returning it. Please send me a perfect candlestick of the same style.

Yours truly,
Jane Holmes
(Mrs. H. R. Holmes)

EXERCISE 1

Select an advertisement from the *Help Wanted* section in your newspaper. Write an application for the position.

EXERCISE 2

Order from Hinson, Warner Co., 48 Main Street, Montgomery, Alabama, the following materials. Be sure to specify size, color, catalogue number, material, style. In an order letter, always tell how payment will be made. Order: 1 sweater, 2 pairs hose, 1 dozen handkerchiefs.

EXERCISE 3

Write a letter to a theater in New York, ordering tickets for the current play.

EXERCISE 4

Write a letter ordering a subscription to a news magazine to be sent to a friend as a Christmas present.

EXERCISE 5

You have received as a present a subscription to a magazine. For three months the copies of the magazine arrived promptly. For the last two months no copy has arrived. Write a letter to the publisher, explaining the situation and asking for adjustment.

EXERCISE 6

A store with which you have a charge account has sent you a bill listing an item which you did not purchase. Write a courteous note asking for adjustment of the bill.

98. FORMAL INVITATIONS AND REPLIES

Formal invitations are usually printed or engraved. The answer is written in ink. Never typewrite an answer to a formal invitation. This type of letter and its reply are always written in the third person. Since they permit no expression of individuality or originality, the wording in the models given here may be copied. Dates and hours are written in full, and no abbreviations except Mr., Mrs., Dr. are permitted. The message should be centered upon white paper. The letters R. S. V. P. mean that an answer is expected.

Formal Invitation
Mr. and Mrs. Frederick Harris
request the pleasure of your company
at a dance to be held in honor
of their daughter Elizabeth
Saturday, February the tenth
at nine o'clock
The Condado Hotel
R. S. V. P.

Invitations should be answered as soon as possible.

Acceptance
Miss Catherine Harding accepts with pleasure
the kind invitation of Mr. and Mrs. Frederick

Harris to the dance to be held in honor of
their daughter Elizabeth on Saturday, February
the tenth, at nine o'clock at the Condado Hotel.

918 Warwick Road
February the first

Regret

Miss Catherine Harding regrets that because
of illness she is unable to accept the kind
invitation of Mr. and Mrs. Frederick Harris
to the dance to be held in honor of their
daughter Elizabeth on Saturday, February the
tenth, at nine o'clock.

918 Warwick Road
February the first

EXERCISE 7

Write a formal invitation to a dance and a reply to the
invitation.

99. INFORMAL NOTES

All personal notes should be handwritten in ink. Since
these notes are an expression of you, the language should
be the simple, courteous language that you would use in
conversation. For an example, don't say, "You are cor-
dially invited to attend a dance to be given at my house,"
or "I should like to take this opportunity to thank you."
These sentences are stiff. They lack personality. The
letter that follows is better form.

99a. Informal invitation.

University of Delaware
Newark, Delaware
December 13, 1950

Dear Jack,

Elsa Baklor is going to spend the Christmas holidays with
me, and I want to have a little party for her on Tuesday,
December 27. We shall probably dance to some new records

that I have bought recently. I should like very much to have you join us at nine o'clock. Will you?

> Sincerely yours,
> Gertrude Holtz

99b. Informal acceptance.

> Madison Apartments
> Orange, New Jersey
> December 16, 1950

Dear Gertrude,

Nothing could make me miss one of your parties! It will be fun to see Elsa again and to hear her version of college life in California. Thank you for including me. I shall be very glad to join you at nine o'clock on Tuesday, December 27.

> Sincerely yours,
> Jack Leonhardt

99c. Informal regret.

If you must refuse an invitation, courtesy requires that you give some legitimate excuse.

> Madison Apartments
> Orange, New Jersey
> December 16, 1950

Dear Gertrude,

Your party for Elsa on December 27 sounds like great fun. I wish I could be with you. Unfortunately, I shall be in Washington visiting relatives for the holidays. It will be disappointing not to see you and Elsa. I do hope that we can get together when you come back to Orange for another visit.

> Sincerely yours,
> Jack Leonhardt

99d. Thank-you note.

Carelessness in acknowledging a kindness is inexcusable. Whenever you receive a present or someone does a special favor for you, a telephone call or a note to express your appreciation is necessary. Brides are sometimes criticized for not expressing thanks for the presents sent them at the time of the wedding. Boys and girls graduating from high school sometimes forget to thank people who are kind to them. For every present there must be some expression of gratitude, even if you do not like the gift. A note of thanks should mention the present, express appreciation of any special quality that it possesses, and tell how happy you are to have the gift.

McWhorter Apartments
Des Moines 14, Iowa
June 25, 1950

Dear Aunt Jane,

When I came home yesterday and found awaiting me the lovely string of pearls that you sent me for my graduation, I was so excited that I had to try them on at once with my graduation dress. The dress is soft white net, and the pearls are perfect with it. Thank you for helping to make my graduation day a very happy one.

Sincerely yours,
Adele

99e. Bread-and-butter letter.

The bread-and-butter letter is written to a host or hostess who has entertained you away from your home town. If a friend invites you to spend a week end at her summer place on the beach or to visit her family during a college vacation period, a bread-and-butter letter should be written immediately upon your return to your home or college. Young people usually write a note to the mother of their friend as well as to the friend herself.

August 10, 1950

Dear Saundra,

There is nothing like a beach party at Ocean City. What fun we had! I enjoyed swimming in the ocean, the long hours on the beach with your gay and charming friends, and the dances at night. You couldn't have planned a better week end for all of us. I know that you will not want to leave Ocean City very soon, but I look forward to seeing you in town and hope that you will have dinner with me when you return.

Thank you again for a perfect visit.

> Sincerely yours,
> Alan

99f. Note of sympathy.

The letter of sympathy is one of the most difficult to write and is often badly done. It should be simple and sincere. Avoid flowery expressions and Biblical quotations.

Dear Barbara,

The news of the death of your mother came as a great shock to me. Although I have not seen her for several years, I have always remembered her kindness to all of us when we were children. Her cookie jar made many of us happy.

Nothing that I can say will lessen your grief, but I want you to know that my heart too is heavy with a sense of personal loss.

> With sincere sympathy,
> Alice Carvel

Hamilton Hall
Lake College
October 28, 1951

EXERCISE 8

Write an invitation to a Christmas party. Then write a reply accepting the invitation and one expressing regret at being unable to accept it.

EXERCISE 9

Write a thank-you note for a present.

EXERCISE 10

Write a bread-and-butter letter to a friend who has entertained you for a week end. Write a letter of thanks to her mother.

EXERCISE 11

Write a letter of sympathy.

100. FRIENDLY LETTERS

In these days of easy travel by automobile, people make friends in many places distant from their homes. Good letters help to keep these friends, but a good letter requires careful planning and writing; it cannot be merely "dashed off." Letters can be improved if the following suggestions are practiced.

100a. Choose interesting material.

The daily routine of your existence is seldom interesting. Consider the interests of the friend to whom you are writing. One friend may be interested in model airplanes; another, in good moving pictures; a third, in music, art, books, football games. Choose from your experiences those things which will meet the interests of each person to whom you write. Your health or the weather is seldom interesting unless there is something unusual to say about it.

100b. Give details.

A full, clear discussion of a football game or a dance is likely to prove far more interesting than a series of choppy notes on a dozen topics. Try to write letters made up of unified details, not random notes which really are only topic sentences needing expansion.

100c. Take your time.

If a friendship is worth developing, it deserves the courtesy of time and consideration. "I am sorry that this letter will be brief, for I am in a great rush" is as rude as "Hastily yours."

100d. Do not waste time on a statement of the obvious or the trite.

Avoid expressions such as "I received your letter" or "We are all well and hope you are also." Begin the letter, instead, with a reference to something that your friend said in his last letter. Answer some questions that he asked or comment on some idea that he presented. Do not close the letter with statements such as "I must close now" or "That's all for now."

100e. Avoid participial phrases at the close.

The interesting letter will not close with comonplace expressions such as "Hoping to hear from you soon" or "Wishing you all the success in the world" or "Hoping that this finds you well." These expressions are not complete sentences. They are, in addition, exceedingly trite.

100f. Give attention to the appearance of the letter.

Write in ink in a neat, legible handwriting. Use letter paper of good quality. White, cream, or pale gray paper is preferable to that of other colors. Never use lined paper or paper pulled from a note pad. Leave a margin of approximately one and one-half inches at the top of the paper and one-half inch at the left. Use the pages in book order. Do not make your friends spend time looking for the next page.

EXERCISE 12

Examine these beginnings and endings of letters. Come to class prepared to discuss which ones are good and which ones are poor. Explain why.

Beginnings:

1. I received your letter yesterday and was glad to hear from you.
2. Now that the holidays are over, I have time to write to you.
3. Here's the best news of the season. We beat Polytechnic on Friday.
4. Time really flies. It has certainly been a long time since we saw each other.

Endings:

1. Hoping that this finds all of you well and happy.
2. I must close now and do my lessons.

3. Looking forward to seeing you.
4. Be sure to let me know how you get along with your model airplane.
5. Don't forget to give me the news of the convention.

EXERCISE 13

Write five good opening sentences and five good closing sentences for friendly letters.

EXERCISE 14

Write an interesting friendly letter.

Index

The figures in this index refer to pages.

Index of Exercises

The figures in this index refer to pages.

Grammar

Usage

Capitalization

Punctuation

The Word